n-Publication Data

s for construction / Hal Johnston, G.L. Mansfield.—

on the earlier ed.

. Building—Estimates. I. Mansfield, G. L. (G. Leo) II. Title.

00-047900

hen Helba
Ed Francis
: Christine M. Buckendahl
or: Robin G. Chukes
Jeff Vanik
ernational Stock
ager: Matt Ottenweller
ager: Jamie Van Voorhis

s set in Times by Carlisle Communications, Ltd., and was printed and bound by Courier Kendallville, Inc.
as printed by Phoenix Color Corp.

MW00861649

10 9 8 7 6 5 4 3 2 1
ISBN: 0-13-082197-7

Prentice
Hall

BIDDING ESTIMATIN PROCEDURE CONSTRUCTI

SECOND EDITION

HAL JOHNSTON
California Polytechnic University

G. L. MANSFIELD

Prentice Hall

Upper Saddle River, New Jersey
Columbus, Ohio

In loving memory of Alexandra Marie Swan

G. L. Mansfield

To my wife, Joy Lynn Johnston, for her help and support on this book and the many other things she makes possible.

Hal Johnston

PREFACE

This book reviews procedures and methods that would assist an estimator to prepare an estimate in a professional manner. Examples of quantity takeoff and pricing are limited to those trades traditionally performed by general contractors with their own labor force (although many of these are now subcontracted to specialty contractors): excavation and general earthwork operations, concrete and formwork, masonry, and rough and finished carpentry work.

This is not an estimating reference book that an estimator can flip through to find unit costs of plastering, or painting, or plumbing or heating installations, or other specialty trade work. There are many excellent books available that cover those and similar items.

For whom, then, has this book been written? The person we visualized when we started writing was a young person presently taking, or having recently completed, a two-year construction technology course at a university or polytechnic institute. This course would emphasize quantity surveying and estimating techniques. We hope this book might prove a useful source of reference or add further dimension or perspective to what had been taught and studied, or be equally useful to someone starting a career in the construction industry, particularly as a junior or trainee estimator.

Who else might find it useful? A construction company manager might dip into these pages for some background on estimating and bidding functions. Also, someone starting a new construction company—an ex-superintendent or engineer perhaps—might learn a few pointers about organizing an estimating division. Even a few veteran estimators (our peers, in fact) might gain a certain satisfaction from seeing some of their own methods endorsed or might feel even more satisfied with their own methods where they differ from those recommended in these pages.

The quantity takeoff examples are provided to demonstrate some of the fundamental quantity surveying techniques, although I fully agree that time limitations would restrict the indulgence in such meticulous recording and side-noting of the dimensions. However, it is beneficial to all of us, trainees and experienced estimators alike, to be occasionally reminded about the basic rules of good quantity surveying practices.

The quantities and examples of priced estimates evolve around a university or college building to be used as a research center. The drawings of this building in the text show only the pertinent details necessary for a demonstration of quantity takeoff. In some instances, items appear on the quantity sheets or in the estimate summaries for which no drawings or details are provided in the text.

A brief work should be said about the metric or SI (Système international) units noted on the Schedules of Items and Measurements in later chapters. These units are intended to show the recommended units of measurement for work measured in the metric system; they do not represent the exact equivalent in metric for an American unit of measurement. For example, the recommended unit of measurement for an item stated in American as a "square foot" is usually stated in metric as a square meter of m^2, even though a square meter (10.764 sft) is closer in actual size dimensions to a square yard. Also the metric dimensions shown on the drawings are hard metric conversions, indicating what these dimensions would be if the project were designed in metric.

ACKNOWLEDGMENTS

As with a construction project, it takes many individuals, organizations, and disciplines to build a book. Our book owes many different people thanks for its completion. In the Preface to the first edition, special thanks were given to Stan Dean, who meticulously read and offered valuable suggestions on early drafts. His contributions are still acknowledged as being major ones. Other first edition debts were owed to Peter Mansfield and to Hilary Oosterhof.

Thanks also to the reviewers of this edition for their helpful suggestions and comments: Richard Harrington, State University of New York at Delhi; Ward Holderness, University of Southern Colorado; and Randy Rapp, Milwaukee School of Engineering.

We also wish to acknowledge and express our appreciation to the following organizations:

- American Society of Professional Estimators (ASPE)
- Construction Specifications Canada
- Construction Specification Institute
- Microsoft® Corporation
- The Canadian Institute of Quantity Surveyors
- The Canadian Construction Association of Documents Committee.
- The American Institute of Architects
- The Clay Brick Association of Canada
- The Corps of Engineers (United States Army)
- WinEstimator, Inc.

We also wish to express our deepest and loving thanks to our wives. First, Bee Mansfield, who spent many hours of personal support checking through the initial manuscript, produced a solid piece of work to build on. Second, Joy Johnston, who gave her time and effort on this second edition of *Bidding and Estimating Procedures for Construction*. Without either of these individuals, our lives would not be complete, nor would this book.

Many other people formed a voluntary backup team and contributed assistance in numerous and varying ways for both of us. To these people, you are not forgotten; our deep and sincere thanks goes to each and every one of you.

Hal Johnston
G. L. Mansfield

BRIEF CONTENTS

CONTENTS

1

INTRODUCTION TO ESTIMATING AND THE BID PROCESS

1.1 GENERAL INTRODUCTION

As the title implies, this is a book on the subject of estimating construction costs, but one written with a particular emphasis on the preparation of a stipulated sum bid by a general contractor. The aims of the book are

- To review all the normal bid-preparation activities that take place in a contractor's estimating section. This covers the areas of selection and strategy, the initial receipt of the drawings and specifications, the final hour of bid submission to the building owner, and then a review of the bid itself after it has been turned in.
- To recommend and outline practices and methods to test handle these functions.

Included among these activities would be the recording of the bid documents; organizing and planning the estimate format; reading the specifications; formulating quantity takeoffs; analyzing subcontractors' quotes; assessing the cost of onsite overhead; and adjusting and closing the bid. These operations are not confined solely to a general contracting organization. Trade contractors, who usually become subcontractors to the prime contractors, also employ estimators and quantity surveyors who undertake similar responsibilities and provide the same expertise.

"What's so special about a stipulated sum contract?" someone will ask. "Surely, quantity surveying and estimating skills are equally essential to other types of construction contracts—construction management, for example, or a unit price contract, or a guaranteed maximum price contract. Also, what about cost feasibility studies for owners and architects? Surely these functions demand as much construction costing expertise as a stipulated sum bid?"

Agreed. However, it is the opinion of the authors, an opinion no doubt influenced by the many years we have worked in general contractors' offices, that the preparation of an estimate for a firm or fixed price type of contract is always a challenging exercise for a construction estimator. Contractors are usually allowed only a short period of time in which to establish a monetary agreement to which they will be committed for a very long while—many months or years. During that short, usually hectic, bid-preparation period much planning and organization are needed, and expertise and experience are of the essence. Everything must be done quickly and done right, or as right as is humanly possible. It also should be done methodically.

The estimator in a contracting organization, general contractor, or single-trade contractor has a professional obligation to his or her employer to provide with proper care and judgment a realistic estimate of cost. He or she must ensure that the estimate faithfully represents all the information provided in the bid documents—the drawings and specifications, and addenda thereto. Nothing should be intentionally ignored or distorted for the sake of satisfying the contractor with a low bid. I am not inferring with this last statement that an estimator or quantity surveyor should be uninterested in his or her company's performance. Everyone likes to be successful and be on a winning team, but company loyalty should never sway an estimator from examining and assessing the facts as they appear in the documents. Speculation, strategy, probability factors, market assessment—all these are as common to the construction industry as to other business enterprises, but they should always be recognized as forming part of the bidding function rather than the estimating function.

1.2   ESTIMATING AND BIDDING

Estimating and bidding are often defined as processes. A process is a group of different individual events (bids or bid submissions), subprocesses, and/or items linked together to produce a final product. Processes generally have a start and an outcome, or final result. The estimating process takes on different forms depending on the final outcome one is pursuing, e.g., buying material, bidding a project, costing a value engineering proposal, or evaluating a change order. The numbers of levels, the detail, and the complexity of the problem can change the method or estimating process to be used.

Estimating is a process of generating, analyzing, and summarizing projected costs by combining the experience and judgment of a team of construction professionals. The professionals review the requirements of contract documents so as to project the methods, materials, and the costs that will be needed to construct the project. This approach to estimating is methodical and systematic. Decisions are made with judgment based on the best experience of the professionals involved. Risk and return are key elements in the choices made at the beginning, in the middle, and at the end of the process.

Estimating can further be categorized as factual or conceptual when discussing how it relates to business development (procurement of work). Additional construction work is gained through the bid process or the negotiated process. Construction work can be performed as public, private, or public/private partnerships. The estimating process is further defined or modified by the type of contract being proposed, such as stipulated sum, guaranteed maximum price, cost plus, unit price, or target contracts. All of these contracts can have different modifiers; for instance, fixed fees, bid fees, share of saving, how a contractor will be paid (profit), the payment for the

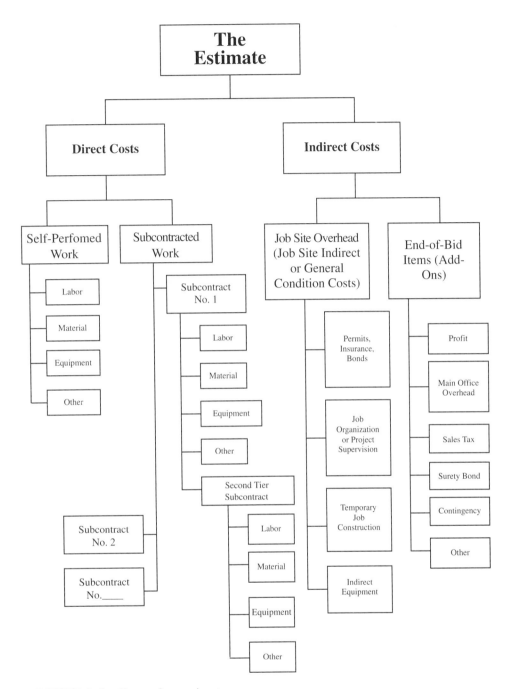

FIGURE 1–1 Parts of an estimate.

cost of doing business (main office overhead), and the cost of the project (job site direct and indirect costs). Figure 1–1 shows a breakdown of an estimate as it relates to these factors.

The estimating process brings specific information on costs and methods together. How this information is accumulated and retrieved for the estimate will be further discussed. Profit, risk, and competition also play large roles in the estimate and bid process.

Two considerations determine the quality of an estimate process and the estimate itself: one, how complete the estimate is, and two, how accurate the items are within the estimate. Complete and accurate are not the same. A complete estimate could be defined as an estimate that is whole in its entirety or has no parts missing. An accurate estimate, on the other hand, shows a level of exactness or precision, and is correct or free from faults.

The answers to the following questions will determine how sound or complete an estimate is:

- Has the estimator determined who is responsible for which items, and is everything included that should be? Are the work and materials described by the specifications and drawings all covered?

- Have all items that are shown been taken off the drawings?

- Are the labor productivity rates in the estimate based on sound historic information, and has a thorough analysis of the work, the job, and the conditions been done?

- Have there been a sufficient number of subcontract and vendor quotations to provide coverage and analysis? Is everything covered, and are all exclusions incorporated into the estimate if they are part of the project?

- Is the company using a system and a set of standards to put the estimate together? Does the system allow for cross-checking of items and mathematics? Can one estimator understand and read the other estimators' work?

- Does the estimate include all the end-of-bid factors, and does it provide adequate markup (profit and main office overhead)? Has the risk of the project been thoroughly analyzed and the costs reflected in the work items and the profit of the project?

- Does the estimate reflect the methods and techniques that will be used, the accountable conditions, the costs that will be incurred, and the job site management that will be used during the project?

The level of accuracy of an estimate depends on a different set of questions and guidelines:

- Before the estimate is started, has the company's data base of costs been updated to reflect any increases in prices?

- Is the estimator using the most recent labor costs from accounting? (Have there been any new labor contracts?)

- Are the costs and productivity rates being used reflective of the marketplace? Is skilled labor available?

- How accurate are the quantities?

- Is the estimator pricing and analyzing the installation of the right type of permanent materials, those that the specification calls for?

- Is the estimator analyzing subcontractor quotes with due care?

- Are the phone quotations taken from subcontractors accurate and complete as to what the subcontractor is proposing?

- To minimize math errors, estimators should check math as they go, back-checking from the drawing immediately.

- At the completion of the estimate, check every item over again.
- The estimator should have someone else recheck extensions, carryovers, and additions.
- All sheets should be read and reread.
- Check that the bond costs have been updated and are current.
- Main office overhead should be recalculated on a quarterly basis.
- Permit costs should reflect the actual costs that will be paid for permits.

The final test of an estimate's completeness and accuracy is in a way determined only after a project is built. On so many projects the field personnel remarks concerning the estimate that their performance was being measured by have been similar. If the project made money, it was only through the effort of the field personnel in how they ran the work and picked the methods to accomplish the work. If the project lost money, the loss occurred because the estimate had left out items or underpriced other items and did not reflect the true conditions of the project. Estimators always believe just the opposite. If a project makes money it is because the field followed the estimator's vision, and when a project loses money, it has to be the result of poor field management or noncompliance with the estimate. Neither position is entirely true or false. Profits in construction can only be made on a project through a complete and accurate estimate and subsequent performance by a field team that is experienced and efficient in the task of building. Projects need to be thoroughly analyzed through an estimate and professionally managed in the field.

It has been said that companies fail because of poor judgment and poor management. Not many construction companies go bankrupt simply from lack of technical competency, lack of business, bad luck, or inefficient operations. These do contribute to failure; however, estimating problems often are the most easily identified reason for companies going out of business. To allow estimating errors to occur and not be corrected, to have inadequate markups, and to make poor decisions when forecasting labor productivity are definite contributors to large company failures.

The bid or bidding process is always a challenging exercise for a construction estimator. Contractors are usually allowed only a short period of time in which to establish a monetary amount for the cost of a job. The contractor will be committed to that monetary amount for a long period of time, many months or years. During that short, usually hectic, bid-preparation period, a great deal of planning and organization is needed. Expertise and experience are put to the test; everything must be done quickly and done right, or as right as is humanly possible. When one experiences this exercise for the first time, the question is always "Why is the process done in such a compressed time, and how is it possible to come up with accurate numbers?" The process of formulating the bid adds an element of risk to the estimate. Figure 1–2 outlines from start to finish the bid process and will be referred to throughout the book. Thoroughly examine the actual flow of the work and note that at the central core of bidding is another process, the process of estimating.

The bid process begins with the company's interest and decision to bring the plans and specifications of a potential job into the office for review. A job to bid can be advertised through contractors' trade journals, flyers, or by word of mouth, or it can be a project that has a negotiated contract. The major difference between a bid project and a negotiated project is the ability to eliminate competition at an earlier stage. An invitation to participate in negotiating a contract or selection to bid or submit proposals along with a select group of contractors always seems like a better piece of fruit to

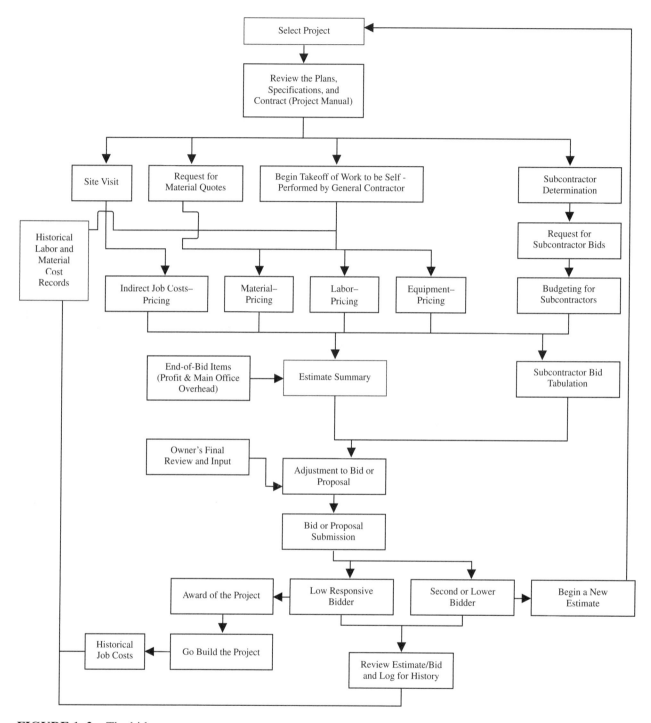

FIGURE 1–2 The bid process.

pick than does a competitive open bid project. Generally this is true, but not always. Often those select bidder groups are being asked to bid or provide proposals on the project just to keep one of the bidders honest. This provides the owner with a dollar amount for a preselected contractor. When being selected for any select bidders' list, a firm must weigh the possibility of actually winning the contract and check to see if the cost of bidding the work is worth the time spent. During the bid process the type of estimating used may differ due to the completeness of the drawings and specifications. When bidding in the public sector, contractors generally are bidding on what is assumed to be one hundred percent complete plans and specifications. On a negotiated project, the contractor may be providing a mix of preconstruction services, all linked to the estimate with little or no plans at the earliest stages. Some of the concepts applicable to the early stages of design will include value engineering, value analysis, conceptual budgeting and estimating, and help with the actual budget and design issues and later construction. The idea of using an estimate as a marketing tool has taken on new meaning today; moreover, the estimator can play a key role in the negotiated market besides the traditional role in the bid process.

A number of different considerations argue the wisdom of taking part in the negotiated process of obtaining work, besides profit or loss. Remember,

- Marketing is a long-term, proactive, and broad-range function of a company's efforts.
- Long-term relationships are often the key to obtaining work.
- Companies build on positive relationships from past projects.
- Adversarial relationships with designers and owners are discouraged.
- A company is selling preconstruction services along with construction services.
- Plans are often not as complete when early budgets are developed.
- Contractors may have input to some design decisions.

The primary goal of an estimate is to cover all costs that will probably be incurred during the project. The estimate must reflect or mirror reasonably well the company's actual ability to perform and manage the work. The company's ability to buy materials at the cost projected in the estimate, procure subcontractors that can perform their portion of the work, and lastly complete the project under the actual job conditions imposed by the contract, drawings, and specifications will ensure a job well done. The goal is not only to cover all direct job costs, but also to have enough at the end of the year to pay for the main office overhead costs and provide a return of investment in the form of profits.

One should conclude that the construction industry is a high risk business, projecting costs of projects never before built on new sites with a number of unknowns and a lack of complete control over influences on most projects. Beyond these elements of uncertainty mentioned, an estimator must also deal with the market situation, as well as how competitors perceive the business. A number of firms will attempt to bid every project they feel they can financially support, often not realizing the limited resources available in their estimating groups, thus putting extreme pressures on the estimating staff and causing potential errors. Other firms become so desperate to obtain work that they continue to lower margins, cut overhead, and underprice work until they obtain a contract, often to their detriment. Such questions lead to discussions on bid strategy, the decision to bid, bid selection, bonding, and other topics in the next chapter.

2 BONDING, BID STRATEGY, BID SELECTION, AND DECISION TO BID

An estimator selecting projects for the company to bid or submit proposals on must be discriminating in what projects are chosen. The time it takes to put together a bid is neither a trivial matter nor an unlimited resource. The chief estimator is looking to maximize the number of profitable projects the company can be awarded. The estimator is also looking to maximize the potential profit from each of these projects. A project that is negotiated or one on which bidding is less competitive will yield a better return on the time spent because it may be easier to win the project. Also, a less competitive project may allow a higher profit margin to be applied to it. Some negotiated projects may allow high markups and, in addition, may allow mechanics to lower risk. This can be done with contract language changes such as cost plus or guaranteed max proposal (GMP) type contracts, and/or bid qualifications.

When selecting projects, estimators must understand the nature and culture of the company employing them. The estimator must understand the direction that the owners or principals have set and the goals and objectives associated with the strategic plan. The company's business plan is a critical document for the estimator to follow. If the business plan is not adhered to, possible loss of money and waste of valuable time spent on selecting and obtaining competitive and sellable jobs may occur. Generally speaking, the construction firm's primary goal is to achieve profits for its owners or shareholders.

Depending on the market or market mix set for a company, sales growth, reputation for quality workmanship and quality project management (under budget/under time), a good safety record, or other tangible objectives may become good secondary goals or marketing tools to be used to gain other work. Successful contractors use profit as their main goal, to which the selection process contributes. Contractors say they would rather get a smaller project at a larger profit than a larger project with a smaller profit. One should not take this statement at face value because some smaller projects will not support a larger firm's overhead. When analyzing which projects to bid or what RFP (request for proposals) to respond to, the estimator must also have a firm grip on the company's financial condition. If the project requires performance and payment bonds, the estimator must understand the bonding capacity of the firm and bonding in general.

2.1   BONDING

Bonding is a key element in the construction industry for firms working in the public sector. It is less critical in the private segment of the construction industry. There is a growing trend among some private owners, however, to use bonding as an added monetary protection during the job and as a method for preselecting and prequalifying construction companies they are unfamiliar with or have not used in the past.

Bonding is the general term used by the industry to describe more than one type of bond. As bonds and their relationship to estimating are discussed, the need is to examine the relationship between the contractor and the surety providing the bond. This role of the surety is a cross between "big brother" and "partner". The surety guarantees to the owner that the project will be completed and that the project will be free of encumbrances caused by debt or default of its contractor. On the other hand, the surety wants the contractor to succeed, grow, and be profitable. Through a close relationship the surety balances growth (size of projects and work in progress) of its contractors with the contractor's ability, financial strength, management, experience, and reputation. Often the terms *capital, character,* and *capacity* are used in describing a company's level of bonding.

The basic bonds that estimators are initially interested in are the bid bond, payment bond, and performance bond. The bid bond is closely related to the performance and payment bonds because when one obtains a bid bond from a surety, the surety is also in essence saying that the contractor can obtain a performance and payment bond on this project. The bid bond is a promise by the bidding contractor (guaranteed by the surety) that it will enter into the contract required by the bid documents if awarded the project. This requirement is usually connected to a specific time frame and is not an open ended or unlimited time period. Figure 2–1 illustrates a bid bond. It should be noted that the penalty amount does not exceed the bid bond amount. If the difference between the low bidder and the next bidder is less than that of the bond value, the smaller amount would be considered the amount of damages the owner could receive. Bid bond values vary from 5 percent to as high as 20 percent in the case of federal work. Other than federal projects, most public projects generally have specified 5 percent to 10 percent as the value of the bid bond required. Generally speaking, contractors bid work to obtain the work. They are not bidding work that they would not take if they were low responsive bidders. In most cases (by law) when major errors occur in the bid, the contractor will be excused without any penalty, thus reducing the risk to the surety that a bid bond will be called in or can be called in. Because of the low risk in supplying the bid bond, most sureties do so as a service to their contractors at no cost.

One generally hears payment and performance bonds spoken of together as one bond, and they are usually asked for together. In reality they are two different bonds with different purposes. Under the performance bond, the surety guarantees the fulfillment of the contract obligations for the bonded principal. Also, the surety is responsi-

(See instruction on reverse)	DATE BOND EXECUTED *(Must not be later than bid opening date)*	OMB NO.:

Public reporting burden for this collection of information is estimated to average 25 minutes per response, including the time for reviewing instructions, searching existing data sources, gathering and maintaining the data needed, and completing and reviewing the collection of information. Send comments regarding this burden estimate or any other aspect of this collection of information, including suggestions for reducing this burden, to the FAR Secretariat (MVR), Federal Acquisition Policy Division, GSA, Washington, DC 20405.

PRINCIPAL *(Legal name and business address)*	TYPE OF ORGANIZATION *("X" one)*
	☐ INDIVIDUAL ☐ PARTNERSHIP
	☐ JOINT VENTURE ☐ CORPORATION
	STATE OF INCORPORATION

SURETY(IES) *(Name and business address)*

PENAL SUM OF BOND					BID IDENTIFICATION	
PERCENT OF BID PRICE	AMOUNT NOT TO EXCEED				BID DATE	INVITATION NO.
	MILLION(S)	THOUSAND(S)	HUNDRED(S)	CENTS		
					FOR *(Construction, Supplies, or Services)*	

OBLIGATION:

We, the Principal and Surety(ies) are firmly bound to the United States of America (hereinafter called the Government) in the above penal sum. For payment of the penal sum, we bind ourselves, our heirs, executors, administrators, and successors, jointly and severally. However, where the Sureties are corporations acting as co-sureties, we, the Sureties, bind ourselves in such sum "jointly and severally" as well as "severally" only for the purpose of allowing a joint action or actions against any or all of us. For all other purposes, each Surety binds itself, jointly and severally with the Principal, for the payment of the sum shown opposite the name of the Surety. If no limit of liability is indicated, the limit of liability is the full amount of the penal sum.

CONDITIONS:

The Principal has submitted the bid identified above.

THEREFORE:

The above obligation is void if the Principal - (a) upon acceptance by the Government of the bid identified above, within the period specified therein for acceptance (sixty (60) days if no period is specified), executes the further contractual documents and gives the bond(s) required by the terms of the bid as accepted within the time specified (ten (10) days if no period is specified) after receipt of the forms by the principal; or (b) in the event of failure to execute such further contractual documents and give such bonds, pays the Government for any cost of procuring the work which exceeds the amount of the bid.

Each Surety executing this instrument agrees that its obligation is not impaired by any extension(s) of the time for acceptance of the bid that the Principal may grant to the Government. Notice to the surety(ies) of extension(s) are waived. However, waiver of the notice applies only to extensions aggregating not more than sixty (60) calendar days in addition to the period originally allowed for acceptance of the bid.

WITNESS:

The Principal and Surety(ies) executed this bid bond and affixed their seals on the above date.

	1.	2.	3.	
SIGNATURE(S)	*(Seal)*	*(Seal)*	*(Seal)*	Corporate Seal
NAME(S) & TITLE(S) *(Typed)*	1.	2.	3.	

	1.	2.	
SIGNATURE(S)	*(Seal)*	*(Seal)*	
NAME(S) *(Typed)*	1.	2.	

NAME & ADDRESS		STATE OF INC.	LIABILITY LIMIT ($)	
SIGNATURE(S)	1.	2.		Corporate Seal
NAME(S) & TITLE(S) *(Typed)*	1.	2.		

AUTHORIZED FOR LOCAL REPRODUCTION
Previous edition is usable

(REV. 10-98)
Prescribed by GSA - FAR (48 CFR) 53.228(a)

FIGURE 2–1   A bid bond.

ble for the timely and proper completion of the project requirements included in the signed contract and project manual. With the addition of the payment bond, the surety is also obligated to pay all outstanding legitimate claims, bills, and subcontracts that have been brought about by a defaulting contractor. This leaves the owner with a title clear from any potential liens and lawsuits that would occur from nonpayment by the defaulting contractor. These bonds, unlike the bid bond, have a much larger risk to the surety. The cost of the performance and payment bonds is only incurred when one is awarded a project and it is executed. The cost of these bonds thus becomes a project cost and more specifically, an indirect job cost. As discussed in later chapters, bond costs are generally an end-of-bid item (add-on). The cost of these bonds varies based on a contractor's strength. The definition of "contractor's strength" has changed over time to be based more on his or her financial strength even though the complete company is analyzed. The cost to the project is between one percent and four percent. The amount will vary from company to company and surety to surety.

Availability of bonding varies somewhat with the economy, but even in upswings of the economy the small contractor may have trouble obtaining a bond for the first time. Generally, small contractors' difficulties arise in presenting their financial situation to the sureties. As stated before, capital, capacity and character have historically been the areas sureties based their evaluations on. Today, the contractor's financial conditions and resources will override a company's experience in the type of work it is looking to bid on, the reputation of the firm and principals of that firm, and experience in a specific geographic area. When addressing a financial statement, a company must use percentage of completion accounting methods, have complete financial disclosures and footnotes, and lastly (but not always) an audited statement. The following red flag checklist for sureties to judge construction companies was developed by Singer, Lewak, Greenbaum & Goldstein, Certified Public Accountants & Management Consultants, Los Angeles, California:

- Lost jobs and a history of declining profit on jobs.
- A declining or inadequate amount of construction volume to cover overhead. This may create an impetus to bid lower-margin jobs to get work.
- Rapid expansion and too much volume, which spreads management and supervisory personnel too thin. This causes a loss of job control and strains financial resources.
- The percentage of overhead being too high for the work performed.
- A poor collection record on receivables. This leads to excessive bad debts.
- Overinvestment in fixed assets such as construction equipment or real estate. Investment in nonproductive fixed assets such as company cars.
- Ventures that spread resources too thin, such as real estate development or other start-up companies.
- New types of construction work not previously performed by the company.
- Financial problems such as inadequate working capital and equity for volume of work performed.
- No unsecured lines of credit to cover short-term working capital shortages.
- Extensive litigation on jobs. Claims that take a long time to resolve or that are resolved unfavorably.
- Using an accountant with little or no contractor or construction industry experience.
- Poor job profit history. Profit spreads from the beginning to the end of the jobs greater than 10 percent.
- A list of uncompleted jobs that drag on and can't get final release from the owners.
- Complaints from owners and subcontractors about job performance or payment practices.
- A widespread territory of operations.

2.2 BID STRATEGY

Many of the problems just listed develop from poor business plans and/or poor implementation of those business plans. A company beginning to develop its bid strategy usually sets as its main business objective the ability to achieve a responsible profit based on the investment of the company's shareholders and the risk the company will be assuming. An article by Hugh L. Rice titled "Profit Is Not a Dirty Word" discusses risk and reward and the idea that construction capacity is greater than demand for such services, thus driving down profits. If this premise is true (and the authors believe it is), a company's strategy for managing risk and providing an adequate return is of the utmost importance. Estimating and the procurement of work should be the foundations of such an overall strategy. The article further talks about the mentality of "volume at any cost" and how destructive this is to a company and to the construction industry. To combat other companies in the struggle for growth, a company has to have a strategy based on some surer foundation. A strategy based on matching a company's own strength against the competition's weakness, or one based on attempting to meet uncertain competition under favorable terms can be one direction in which a company may turn to increase its profit and productivity. Construction companies do this by looking broadly at the economy as a whole and at their segment of the economy, and where their companies fit within the industry. Construction companies typically do not look long term enough to enjoy moving from one part of the industry to another. Timing is a key element in implementing long-term strategy that may include expanding or contracting in one segment of the industry, satisfying developing specifications within the industry, or moving into a new area of the marketplace.

In setting any bid strategy, a company should first start with past estimating performance. How and where has this company been successful? In what area has the company not been as competitive as it may have wished? Projects that have been bid must be continually recorded as to the type of project it was, the number of bidders and who the bidders were, distribution of the bids (what was the spread?), and then information on the projects won. What profit was anticipated? Did the project follow the estimate, what were the number of changes and their amounts, and did the actual profit mirror the projected profit? There is no mathematical or statistical approach that can be used that will ensure being low bidder or tell how to bid against other companies. The analysis proposed below will help in a company's decision to bid and further enhance its bid strategy. During the analysis of the bid some patterns will become apparent, helping the estimator put in perspective other influences that may arise.

It is important that the estimator understand where to look for bid calls. No one source can provide all the variety of bids on the market, or the number of different owners looking for contractors to complete their work. As mentioned in Chapter 1, distributing a company's work between public and private projects generally means that a company has decided to obtain a mix of bid work and negotiated work. As the economy moves toward tighter money, the private sector tends to slow faster than the public sector. Government also likes to use the public sector to "prime the pump" during slow economies. The negotiated market is a market of relationships, not one of lowest costs. Working relationships generally end when the contractor trips up, not on a whim of the owner. This book is more focused on the bid market and less on the negotiated market. A comprehensive look at estimating should include some discussion on the role of estimating as a marketing element. A complete text could be written on conceptual estimating, preconstruction services as they relate to estimating, value engineering, feasibility estimating, and other uses of estimating during a negotiated process. It should be noted that the final estimate of any process looks very much like a detail estimate that will be described and used throughout this book.

2.3 BID SELECTION

After a strategy is defined, the selection process or the final decision to bid must also be based on further expanded criteria. Estimators and company executives will analyze potential projects and pick projects to bid based on desirable and undesirable characteristics. Be aware that an undesirable characteristic for one firm may be a desirable characteristic for another firm under certain circumstances. But generally speaking, the following warning signs should reduce the desirability on a project for most firms:

- The specifications and drawings on a project are too brief; this requires the estimator to make too many assumptions. In a negotiated contract situation, where lowest cost is not the defining factor, this is not necessarily a negative because a company can make a conservative assumption, covering the owner and contractor for the cost risk. In a bid situation, though, one contractor's cost assumptions may not be the same as the next contractor's, putting them at different risk. One risks not getting the job, while the other risks not having enough money to complete the project.

- The estimators and field personnel lack experience in this type of work, generally unusual or technical in nature. This could be less than desirable for a firm. If the estimator lacks experience, the estimate could be flawed; if the field personnel do not have the expertise, the project could have cost overruns resulting from "learning by doing" by the field people.

- Project time frames are not based on realistic expectations, or liquidated damages are placed too high for the rewards (profits) that the project will generate. If the time frame risk is clearly described and the estimator expects all bidders to adequately plan for overtime, weekend work, schedule overrun, and the other requirement needs of inadequate contract time, then the bidding of the project could make some sense. In the less sophisticated marketplace, one contractor always appears who believes that he can ignore the contract time without any consequence and so does not adequately plan for it in the estimate.

- In some instances, projects require a task that can only be performed by one subcontractor, or a material that can come from only one supplier or manufacturer or fabricator. This is not a value that will define a project as an undesirable project. However, if we add the reality that not all subcontractors, suppliers, manufacturers, or fabricators are equal and the project specifies something that must be performed by a group whose ability to perform is questionable, the estimator may wish to pass on the project or attempt to mediate the potential problem. Bonding of subcontractors is one method of reducing this kind of risk.

- In the heavy construction arena, more than the residential area, not all contractors have the same equipment or at times their required equipment is busy. If a project requires a specific type of equipment and only the competition has that equipment, it may be a waste of your estimating time if the competitor's equipment can be shown to be more productive, thus reducing their estimate. This can also be true of skills required to perform certain work by your craftspeople. If a company does not have the specific craft skills, its productivity and workmanship may not let it be competitive. This is a very specific topic that needs to be discussed when developing a bid strategy. Part of a strategy may be to look for and hire specially trained employees, or to buy certain equipment during the year.

■ Lastly in this general list, time is a finite item for the estimating group. The estimator must make choices between projects when bid times conflict. When choosing between bids, the estimator and owner should look at potential changes in bid dates, the time it takes to bid, potential returns on the project, company resources that will be needed to accomplish the project if successful, and other project specifics.

2.4 ░ DECISION TO BID

Some companies have shaped these general rules into very specific questions in deciding whether or not to bid. As mentioned previously in this chapter, once a company has defined its primary field or type of work, based on what the company does best, a project can be quickly eliminated by being out of the company's range set forth by its business plan and stated strategy.

The main categories of construction are:

■ Residential
■ Commercial
■ Industrial
■ Heavy/civil/highway
■ Specialty

Generally each of these categories can be further defined as either new work or falling in the alterations/remodels/renovations/tenant-improvement subcategories. This is not a definitive list, and many other estimators might change this list in one fashion or another. The important question to ask is, "Is the project to bid the kind of work our company has been successful at completing to the owner's satisfaction, and will our company make a reasonable profit for that work?"

The project size is often stated in an engineer's, architect's or owner's estimate. This has more significance than just to advise the community of the relative dollar size. If it is a bonded project, each company interested in the project must make initial judgments as to the project's size compared to its own bonding capacity. In analyzing past performance, some companies have determined that project size can play a part in profits. Larger companies may determine that to repeatedly work with the same project size creates too many competitors, or not enough profits to justify the resources required for the work proposed. Other companies may determine that they are not effective at managing large projects. The key is looking at all the factors that project size brings to the table. If a company is determined to "grow into" a larger project, a reevaluation of main office support and personnel should be conducted along with a rethinking of job site overhead.

Remember from the list of red flags from surety companies, they are concerned about wide-spread operations. Company estimators must also use location as selection criteria. Can the firm manage the project once it has it, in the location in which it is to be built? A construction company may have just the right employee to build the project, but if he is not willing to move to the project location, the company may have to select another person. Another alternative is to employ a new person at the location who has no loyalty to the company or, worse, lacks the skills to build the project. Also consider the local competition. Are they looking for work at any price? Will the local economy create a very competitive situation? This lack of understanding of the local construction environment is what bothers sureties. In a future discussion of subcontractor quotes, the concept of "playing on a home field," or "home field advantage" or just plain preferential treatment or advantage given to local general contractors by local subcontractors will be covered. Local subcontractors might not know an incoming general construction firm, but they know that they must live with the local general contractor, for whom they have already worked. This same idea can also be said of the local architect and owner. They may fear a new company coming into an area. At bid time this may have no effect, but during the construction phase, trust may be a missing component.

All estimators when reviewing a project look at the owner and designer. Construction companies find some agencies better to work for and thus more profitable. Anytime a company finds people it can "work with," it generally indicates a successful project for both parties. Construction companies will often have lists of owners and designers on whose projects they will not bid.

Many times owners do not have the resources to complete their projects if changes occur. The quality and reputation of the owner as to fairness during the process and knowledge of the construction process should determine whom one should bid to. More than one estimator has remarked, "Remember that in the case of disputes, the owner with a larger construction budget will normally be easier and quicker to resolve money issues than one on a tight budget." Some owners are always on a tight budget, while others have adequate initial budgets and realistic views on changes. In the list of undesirable traits, poor specifications and drawings were mentioned. This should never be underestimated when picking a project to bid. It may not be a proven fact, but no designer sets out to produce a bad set of documents or wishes to have the owner think less of him or her for doing so. Unfortunately, a project that appears to create conflicts because of poor drawings will be making such a statement to the owner, a statement that will be greatly contested by the designer. Project conflicts often result in an unsuccessful project for both the contractor and owner.

This chapter has covered the concepts useful for the estimator in developing guidelines concerning the decision to bid. Because of the large impact bonding places on the public-sector bid arena, and trends toward bonding in the private sector, any discussion of project selection, bid strategy, and the decision to bid must also include the topic of bonding. A company's business and marketing plan must be based on a solid understanding of the role of estimating in the marketing process. Without a solid bid strategy it is impossible to make a profitable decision when selecting a project to bid. One expert has said that the first step to a successful and profitable company is a business plan that has as its foundation methods of selecting a project that a company can be successful in acquiring through sound estimating practices. In other terms, the use of a bid strategy that matches a company's position and strength to other companies in weaker positions is a must. The decision to bid is not a trivial decision within a construction company, and a poor selection can result in a mismatch between the field operations, the estimator, and the company's profit margin.

Once a decision to bid had been made, certain preliminary procedures are followed to ensure a positive transition to a completed estimate and a delivered bid. That is the subject of the next chapter.

3 PRELIMINARY PROCEDURES

3.1 THE BID CALL

The methods by which a general contractor is informed about a potential bid will generally depend on whether it is an open bid or a closed bid. In an open bid, work is to be financed wholly or partially by public funds, and will therefore be called by some branch of government (federal, state, or municipal) or a public authority such as a school or hospital board. A closed bid is called by private individuals, companies, or organizations.

Public bids are usually advertised in national or regional newspapers or trade journals, although it is not unusual for such public announcements to be supplemented by printed "flyers" mailed to general contractors. With growing technology, web sites have recently been added as another area in which a contractor can obtain knowledge of upcoming bids. It is also not uncommon for architectural offices to delegate someone to telephone all known contractors in a given area or locality and draw their attention to the publicized bid call.

Figure 3–1 illustrates a typical advertisement for a public bid. Please note that this particular example announces that the bids will be opened publicly. It is the rule that bids for publicly funded projects be opened and the results read out publicly, which is not always (or need be) stated in the bid call advertisement. Estimators should check early in the bidding period with the architects if there are any doubts about this.

Invitations to bid on nonpublic work are sometimes mailed in individual letter form to a number of selected contractors. However, a common practice is for the initial contact to be made by telephone to ascertain the contractor's interest and intention, and then to confirm the invitation (and the contractor's acquiescence) by letter. Figure 3–2 shows an example of such a letter.

PORT CRAGFIELD,
Ontario

Sealed stipulated sum bids clearly marked "Bids for Johnson Heights High School" will be received until 3:00 p.m. local time,

TUESDAY, AUGUST 12, 1998

At the offices of the Port Cragfield Board of Education, at which time and place the bids will be opened publicly. General contractors may obtain drawings and specifications from the office of the architects, Peck and Hugg Partnership, 1 East Street, Port Cragfield on the deposit of a certified check in the amount of $100.00, refundable when the documents are returned in good condition.

Bids must be accompanied by a bid bond equal to 10% of the bid amount.

Lowest or any bid not necessarily accepted.

Peck and Hugg Partnership

FIGURE 3–1   Typical advertisement for a public bid.

DODGSON AND CARROLL, ARCHITECTS

August 12, 1998

Gellem Construction Company
23 North St. W.
Centreville, Ontario

Attention: Mr. S. Gellem

Dear Sirs:

Re: New Research Wing,

Jackson University

Further to our telephone discussion of this date, wherein you expressed interest in submitting a bid for the above-noted project, we are pleased to confirm the inclusion of your firm's name on the list of selected bidders.

The drawings will be available at our offices April 24, 1998.

There will be two (2) sets of drawings and specifications available to you. A deposit of $ 100.00 per set in the form of a certified check made payable to Dodgson and Carroll is requested. This amount will be refunded upon the return of the bid documents.

The bid closing date is May 27, 1998.

Yours truly,

L. Carroll

FIGURE 3–2   Example of a confirmation of a bid letter.

The selection of contractors to be invited to bid on certain projects is often made by the process of prequalification. Printed forms are made available to general contractors, and a date and time announced (usually advertised in a trade journal or paper) for the completion and return of their forms to the architect's office. The information requested usually pertains to a contractor's financial background, previous experience in similar projects, and details of the designated supervisory staff. The American Institute of Architects (AIA) publishes a standard prequalification document, which requires only the most pertinent information about the contractor's organization and experience. Some owners and/or architects prepare their own prequalification documents with similar requirements, but occasionally contractors are confronted with menacing fact-finding dossiers that attempt to extract every morsel of confidential information about their companies.

The wording of bid calls (public and private) is usually restricted to the following information: the name of the project, the date and time of the bid closing, the monetary deposit required for the bid documents, the type and amount of the bid security (certified check or bid bond), and where the documents can be examined. Also, a statement might be included regarding the period the bid must remain open before actual award of a contract. When the documents are received, they should be checked to ensure that any repeated information agrees with the bid call. For example, the bid call might state the bid would remain open for a period up to thirty days before a contract is awarded, whereas the specifications might state sixty days. Such a discrepancy should be queried immediately with architects.

The phrase "the lowest or any bid not necessarily accepted" is common to all bid invitations, whether public or private.

3.2   RECORDING THE BID DOCUMENTS

Contractors are usually allowed two sets of drawings and specifications for bidding purposes, for which they are normally required to provide some form of monetary deposit, usually a certified check. However, some architectural firms only permit the issuance of one set of documents for the deposit and require the contractor to pay the cost of printing of any additional sets required. A deposit will still be required on this extra set, redeemable upon return of the documents to the architect's office. (Architects request that these extra drawings be returned as a protection of design copyright.)

It is important to properly record the receipt of the bid documents as soon as they are received in the contractor's office. A separate record for each project being bid is recommended rather than keeping a general office register that lists all drawings received in the estimating department. This record for a specific project will not only be used for the initial receipt of the documents, but it will also be used to keep track of the distribution to subcontractors during the bidding period.

Contractors' estimators are accustomed to being perpetually trapped in the "squeeze" between the utilization of the drawings and specifications for their own bid preparation work (quantity surveys, specification reading, scheduling, and so on) and the pressures from the many subtrade contractors who also require these documents to prepare their own estimates. When two sets of documents are made available to the contractor, it is quite often the practice to make one set constantly available for inspection by subcontractors or suppliers. Many trade contractors, particularly those whose trades are major ones in a specific project and therefore demand a considerable amount of takeoff, will often request the loan of the drawings and the specifications—for an evening, a weekend, or a longer period. This results in an unavoidable amount of juggling of the documents trying to satisfy everyone's needs. There is constant movement of the bid documents in and out of the contractor's office, plus the inevitable issuance of addenda and revised drawings that make it essential to keep an accurate record of all these events.

Apart from the obvious need to maintain an efficient and organized system, it should be recognized that these documents are the basis of a (possible) future contract; they are, in fact, potential contract documents. If the bid is successful, these documents assume a distinct status. They are the documents upon which the bid was based. It is not unusual for postbid revisions to be made to both the drawings and the specifications prior to the signing of the contract, and there will almost certainly be a number of such revised documents issued after that event. These documents are therefore the best and truest record of the information available to the contractor at the time of bidding.

On the less positive side, if the bid is unsuccessful, the documents will have to be collected and returned to the architect's office. Either situation demands that the process of locating and putting together all the bid documents be as smooth and painless as possible. Few activities in a general contractor's office present such a dismal picture of frustration as that of young estimators poking fruitlessly into dark corners of the office when looking for missing drawings and specifications. ("Jack says he gave the structural drawings to someone but can't remember who." "Volt Electric Co. say they returned the 'specs,' but no one's seen them.")

Figure 3–3 illustrates an example of a recommended type of record for a specific project. It is divided into two divisions: Receipt and Distribution. To record the

Bid Documents: Receipt **Estimate No. : 27/98** **Project: New Research Wing, Jackson University**				Bid Documents:Distribution							
Date	Dwg.	Description	No. of Sets	Date:		Dwg. No.	Description		Firm's Name	Initials	Date Ret'd to Arch.
				Out	In						
4/24/98	A1-A9	Architectural	2	4/26/98	4/30/98	S1-S6	Structural	(1 Set of Specs.)	Bar-Rod Reinf. Co.	B.W.	
	S1-S6	Structural	2	5/2/98	5/7/98	A1-A9	Architectural	(1 Set of Specs.)	Centreville Drywall Co.	A.J.B.	
	M1-M8	Mechanical	2	5/5/98	5/26/98	M1-M8	Mechanical	(1 Set of Mech. Specs.)	B.T.U. Plumbing & Heating	D.H.	
	E1-E5	Electrical	2	5/7/98	5/14/98	A1-A9	Architectural	(1 Set of Specs.)	Monarch Precast Co.	S.F.	
		Specifications: Architectural & Structural	2	5/7/98	5/26/98	E1-E5	Electrical	(1 Set of Elec. Specs.)	Volt Electric Co.	P.N.	
		Mechanical	2	5/23/98	5/25/98	-	A3, A6 (Revised) Addenda Nos. 1 & 2		Centreville Drywall Co.	A.J.B.	
		Electrical	2								
5/19/98		Addenda Nos. 1 & 2	2								
5/23/98	A3, A6	Revised Architectural	2								
		Revised Mechanical									
									All Documents		5/30/98

FIGURE 3–3   Example of a recommended type of record receipt and distribution form.

receipt of the documents requires such basic information as the date, the number of sets received, and the drawing identification numbers, and also information regarding the specifications accompanying the drawings. If for example, the divisions for architectural, structural, mechanical, and electrical work are issued in separate volumes, this should be noted.

This record will also be used if and when addenda and revised drawings are issued. (Note: It is a good idea to immediately insert a revised drawing into the set, locating it before the drawing being replaced, and note on the original the word "Superseded." This facilitates any necessary checking to ascertain the changes made to the original drawing.)

Under Distribution of the record, the pertinent information is again the date, the details of the documents that are being loaned out, the name of the company borrowing them, and the date they were returned to the contractor's office. Including the person's initials receiving the plans is also recommended.

The final column in the sample record is used to write the date on which the documents were returned to the architect's office. This is, of course, the sad announcement that the bid was unsuccessful; those words "plans and specifications returned to the architect's office on such-and-such a date" form the epitaph to many bids prepared in a general contractor's office.

The discipline of maintaining this type of record during the bid-preparation period may become sloppy, especially when the bid closing date is near and a certain "Oh, well, it doesn't matter now" attitude may develop. Estimators are exposed to considerable work pressures at this time. The temptation to rely on memory or on hastily written notes on scraps of paper (all done with every good intention of writing up the record at a later time) is very natural, but nobody's memory is foolproof. Unfortunately, those little notes have a habit of disappearing into jacket pockets and not re-emerging until the jacket goes to the cleaners.

3.3   CHECKING THE BID DOCUMENTS

Apart from recording the receipt of the documents, it is also important (imperative in fact) to ensure that all the documents have been received. The drawing numbers should be checked against those written on a transmittal sheet or an index provided either in the specifications or on one of the drawings. Failing the provision of such an index or transmittal sheet, the drawing numbers will need to be checked for sequence and a query put to the architect's office regarding the number of drawings included in a set. It is not sufficient to know that architectural drawings numbered A1 to A9 have been received unless it has been ascertained that the set is limited to nine drawings.

Checking that all the pages have been included in the set (or sets) of specifications is, admittedly, a somewhat awesome chore calculated to provoke teeth-gnashing and eye-rolling on the part of a junior estimator to whom this task will almost certainly be delegated. Frequently, the meticulous page-by-page check will be evaded, and some shortcuts advised. Reliance will be placed on the improbability of the same page (or pages) being accidentally excluded from two sets of specifications. Confidence will be expressed in the certainty of missing pages surely becoming obvious to someone reading the specifications during the bid period. With so many demands on an estimator's time during the preparation of the bid, the decision to avoid a proper, but time-consuming, check can be appreciated. Nevertheless, estimators should always be aware of the harsh truth of a building owner's unsympathetic response to a plea that a contingency sum of $300,000 was omitted from the bid amount because "that page was missing from our set of documents." That is a very extreme and exaggerated event and quite unlikely to happen, but it is always possible.

3.4   CHECKLIST OF TRADES

Construction company estimators become conditioned to the reality of the clock ticking away the minutes to the bid-closing hour while the drawings are still being unrolled in the office. It is imperative that all available time be used as constructively as possible. Idly thumbing through these documents, getting absorbed in some challenging detail on the drawings, attempting to decipher an obscure specification clause picked at random, muttering phrases like "How the hell do you build that?" or "I can't figure out what's holding that beam up"—all such diversions are natural to construction personnel. Indulging in them will not assist in the effective organization of an estimate or provide an early all-round comprehension of the project.

One way to start is to compile a checklist of all the trade divisions noted in the specifications. This list can be used to establish those trades where quantity takeoffs will be necessary (usually for that work to be performed by the contractor's own work force), the trades for which quotations from subcontractors will need to be solicited, and the trades falling into both these categories, that is, those trades upon which subcontractors will quote on a "supply only'" basis.

Figure 3–4 shows a suggested format for such a checklist. It will be noted in this example that some trades have been further subdivided into additional sections that might have appeared in the actual specification. For example, Item 03200 "Reinforcing Steel" has been subdivided into three categories:

- Supply, fabricate, and detail
- Placing
- Wire mesh reinforcement

The reason for these subdivisions is the estimator's anticipation (from experience) of the various options open to subcontractors quoting on this trade. Some may quote on the basis of both supplying and placing the reinforcing bars and others on the basis of "supplying only." Another subcontractor who specializes in the placing of reinforcing bars will quote on that part of the work, or the estimator may decide to prepare an estimate for this work to be performed directly by the contractor. The wire mesh reinforcement will usually be purchased and installed by the general contractor.

Note also a similar situation with "Precast Concrete" being split into two sections: (a) precast concrete wall panels, and (b) precast concrete paving slabs. Here again the estimator is prepared for the likelihood that one or other of the precast concrete companies bidding will either not include for subdivision (b) or will quote for the "supply only" of material. A requirement for quantities is therefore noted in order to estimate the cost of installation.

This checklist of trade divisions can also be used to establish some sort of bid-organization schedule by the use of columns showing "target" dates for the start and finish of the various quantity surveys required. In a large contracting company employing a considerable number of estimators, this would be supplemented with the initials of the personnel to whom the various sections of the work have been delegated. All this will be subject to revisions during the course of the bid period. Some

Spec. Section	Division	Take -off	Subtrade Quote	Take-Off		Estimator
				Start	Complete	
02200	Earthwork	x	x	4/28/98	5/5/98	B.E.W.
02480	Landscaping		x			
02500	Paving and Surfacing		x			
03100	Formwork	x		4/28/98	5/12/98	J.D.
03200	Reinf. Steel: Supply/detail		x			
	Placing		x			
	Wire Mesh	x		4/28/98	5/12/98	J.D.
03300	Cast-in-Place Concrete	x		4/28/98	5/12/98	J.D.
	Concrete Floor Finishing	x	x	4/28/98	5/12/98	J.D.
03400	Precast Concrete: Wall		x			
	Panels		x			
	Paving	x	x	5/14/98	5/16/98	J.D.
04200	Unit Masonry	x	x	5/7/98	5/15/98	B.E.W
05300	Metal Decking		x			
05500	Metal Fabrications	x	x	5/19/98	5/22/98	J.D.
06100	Rough Carpentry	x		5/16/98	5/20/98	B.E.W.
06200	Finish Carpentry	x	x	5/21/98	5/23/98	B.E.W.
07100	Waterproofing		x			
07500	Membrane Roofing		x			
07900	Sealants		x			
08100	Metal Doors and Frames	x	x	5/22/98	5/23/98	J.D.
08200	Wood and Plastic Doors	x	x	5/22/98	5/23/98	J.D.
08500	Metal Windows		x			
08800	Glazing		x			
09250	Gypsum Wallboard		x			
09300	Tile		x			
09500	Acoustical Treatment		x			
09650			x			
09680	Carpeting		x			
09900	Painting		x			
10000	Specialties	x	x	5/23/98	5/26/98	B.E.W.
14200	Elevators		x			
15000	Mechanical		x			
16000	Electrical		x			

FIGURE 3–4 Suggested format of a trade checklist.

takeoffs will prove to be more demanding than initially considered; other trades that appeared to contain complexities will turn out to be quite straightforward and will not require the scheduled time. Also, some estimators will have to double-up on trades because of the work load urgencies of other bids in the office.

3.5 BID-INFO REPORTS

Following the preparation of the list containing trade sections (or preceding it, according to the estimator's preference) a further perusal of the documents should be made for the purpose of identifying and recording those items and details that will quickly produce a clear outline of the project. The information provided on these capsule reports will be in the nature of answers to the many questions that estimators and other personnel in a construction office ask when new drawings are being reviewed: How big is it? What is the gross floor area? What kind of a structure is it? Any feature immediately identifiable as being unusual or unique should be noted.

Bid-Info Report

Re: Estimate No: 27/98

Project Title and Location:	New Research Wing, Jackson University, Centreville, Ontario
Architect:	Dodgson and Carroll
Building Owner(s):	Board of Governors, Jackson University
Bid Closing Time and Date:	3:00 p.m., May 27, 1998
Gross Floor Area:	31,485 sft (2,925 m²)
Estimated Value:	$ 1,754,000
Description:	Three-story building, Partial basement area approx. 13 ft (3.3 m) below grade. Reinforced concrete foundation and superstructure, metal roof deck at small single-story portion. S. and E. elevations–face brick. N. and W. elevations–precast concrete panels, concrete block backup, aluminum strip windows. Concrete block partitions. Interior finishes: drywall to walls (painted), acoustic ceilings, resilient flooring, ceramic tile to washrooms. Carpet in offices.
Bid Security:	Bid bond: 10% of bid amount.
Bonds:	50% performance bond 50% material and labor payment bond
Misc. Information:	30 days to award contract Completion date: October 31, 1999 Liquidated damages: $ 200.00 / calendar day Include all sales taxes

---

FIGURE 3–5   Suggested format for a report of information on a project.

Most specifications include a section entitled "Instructions to Bidders." This section usually includes certain data pertinent to the bidding procedures that should be included in information bulletins such as we are discussing. Figure 3–5 presents a suggested format for this type of brief report. The title and the location of the project along with the names of the owner and the architects are obvious requirements, as are the closing date and time of the bid.

The general description of the project should be concise and emphasize the major elements. The elements can be defined as the structure (reinforced concrete, structural steel, precast concrete, etc.); any noted requirements for perimeter shoring and/or underpinning; the materials of the exterior cladding ("skin"); a brief catalog of the most prominent interior finishes; plus any special equipment requirements, such as laboratory furniture, hospital or kitchen equipment, exotic wood finishes, or extensive landscaping. Information regarding mechanical and electrical systems is also useful.

Information concerning bid deposits (bid bonds or certified checks), performance and other bonds, and sales tax exemption (usual in bids for public or institutional works) should also be stated.

The gross floor area (GFA) not only indicates the magnitude of the project; it is also necessary in establishing a preliminary valuation of the total cost. This area given in square feet (square meters) should be computed in accordance with the recommendations made in *Measurement of Buildings by Area and Volume,* as prepared and published by the Canadian Institute of Quantity Surveyors.

This gross floor area will be multiplied by a unit cost applicable to the building's function (school, hospital, office complex, etc.) and based on the cost of similar buildings within the estimator's experience. A good source for this information will be a company bid analysis format. In the example shown, a new research wing to a local university has a gross floor area of 31,485 square feet (2925 m^2). The estimator will have checked through previous estimates and identified one for a building comparable in size and design and with a similar function or use. The cost per square foot for that building was $50.63/sft ($544.98/m^2), and this unit has been adjusted to $55.70/sft ($599.55/m^2) to allow for labor and material increases that have occurred since that other bid was prepared. This unit multiplied by the GFA produces an amount of $1,754,000.00, which is noted as being the estimated value of the project.

In some cases the owner may have had a preliminary budget prepared and this amount stated to the contractor at the time of the bid invitation; however, an experienced estimator would still check this amount by making a gross floor area cost comparison with previous estimates for similar projects. If, for example, the owner's budget amount for the research wing divided by the gross floor area had produced a unit of say $48.00/sft ($516.67/m^2), then the estimator would be justified in reporting an anticipated higher estimate of (probable) cost based on the historical data.

When a mandatory completion date for the project is stated in the specifications, it should be noted in this report, and also any clause regarding "liquidated damages" for not completing on that date.

It must be emphasized again that these bid-info reports should be restricted to those pertinent details that can be readily observed in the bid documents. At this time, only the broad outline and shape of the tree is necessary; the minute details about the leaves and branches can follow later. The intent is to present brief but relevant information on a single sheet of paper.

In large contracting organizations, these reports could be routed to other personnel or departments, senior management, accountants, contract departments, and so on. They would be of assistance to managerial decision making when debating the pros and cons of bidding a particular project. (A list of other known bidders would also be useful on this info report. The question "Who else is bidding the job?" will invariably be asked by someone.)

3.6 ▌ SOLICITING BIDS FROM SUBCONTRACTORS

Potential subcontractors and material suppliers should be contacted for quotations as soon as possible after the checklist of pertinent trades has been prepared. Several years ago it was not uncommon for many contractors to have something akin to an entourage of faithful subcontractors for the various trades, and these would probably be the only companies the contractors would approach for quotations. "We only use Smith and Co. or Jones and Sons for plumbing and heating work," a contractor would proclaim. "We know them and they know us and we've always used one or the other on our jobs, never anyone else."

In present times, and particularly in those areas where competition is fierce, every contractor bidding a project wants to receive the lowest price available for any given trade. In every city or region there exists a large body of subcontractors with established reputations for good workmanship and reliable performance who are known to most of the general contractors in that area; these will be the companies from whom probably all the contractors will solicit quotations. This statement must not be construed to imply that contractors might not experience smoother or more comfortable working relationships with some subcontractors than with others; nor, let it be hastily added, that the reverse situation of subcontractors' preferences for certain contractors no longer exists. However, the deciding factor in selecting a subcontractor is usually the lowest bid received for a particular trade.

It is recommended that general contractors make direct requests for quotations from the trade contractors. It should be observed, though, that when a certain bid call has been advertised or announced in trade journals, or the documents have been registered at a local construction association office, it will most often be the subcontractors themselves who will decide to prepare and submit their quotations to all the general contractors listed as bidding the project.

Most estimating offices compile a directory of local or regional subcontractors. Some directories may contain the names of all known subcontractors in a particular area with the names arranged in alphabetical order and the appropriate trade noted against the name. For example,

> Gibson and Son (address)—plaster, drywall, acoustics
>
> Goldwater Construction—excavation contractor
>
> And so on

The problem here is that only someone with an excellent memory and familiarity with the local construction scene can speedily run through this directory picking out the drywall and excavation contractors. As specifications are prepared in the format of trade sections, it makes sense for the contractor's directory of subcontractors to follow the same pattern:

> **Plaster and Drywall**
>
> Acorn and Beech Drywall, Inc.
>
> Supreme Plaster Enterprises
>
> And so on

This type of directory should preferably be patterned on a standard specification format (e.g., Masterformat).

The most common method used by general contractors to request quotations is to mail standard printed cards (or letters) to the selected subcontractors. Figure 3–6 shows an example of such a card. The details to be added to the printed wording will be the project title, the architect's name, and the bid closing time and date. On the reverse side of this card (not shown) will be printed or typed the name and address of the subcontractor.

This information can, of course, be typed onto the cards; but as the quantity of cards to be mailed out will often be considerable, this could become a very time-consuming and uneconomical operation. Most contractors use some patented system to speed up the processing of these cards or letters, say, a mail-merge function in a database system. Most of these systems will be coordinated with the subtrade directory previously discussed, and estimators will adopt the method and system most suitable to their own organizations. One factor to be considered when setting up and organizing any system is the inevitable implementation of address changes, company name revisions (Brown and Son, Ltd. to Brown Construction Innovations, Inc.), deletions (out of business), and additions (new companies). The system that permits these changes to be made quickly, cheaply, and easily should be given full

---

REQUEST FOR QUOTATION

We would be pleased to receive a quotation for the following:

PROJECT: New Research Wing, Jackson University, Centreville, Ontario

ARCHITECT: Dodgson and Carroll

BID CLOSES: 3:00 P.M., May 27, 1982

Bid documents are available for inspection at the address below, or at the architects' office, or at the offices of the local construction association.

GELLEM CONSTRUCTION COMPANY
23 North Street West
Centreville, Ontario.

FIGURE 3–6   Request for quotation.

NORTH YORK ONTARIO

BIDS FOR SUB TRADES

BIDS will be received by the undersigned until 2:00 p.m.

FRIDAY, MARCH 23, 1998

For all sub-trade and material prices required in the construction of additions and alterations to St. John's Convalescent Hospital.

Architects, Mathers and Haldendy, 10 St. Mary Street, Toronto, Ont.

Lowest or any bid not necessarily accepted.

V.K. MASON CONSTRUCTION, INC.
181 Eglinton Avenue East,
Toronto, Ont. M4PJ9

FIGURE 3–7   Advertisement—solicitation for bids.

---

consideration. Allowing backlogs of such revisions to accumulate will result not only in many communication problems with subcontractors, but also time-consuming administrative work in updating a lapsed system that could aggravate the normal bid-preparation operations of the Estimating Department.

Contractors usually supplement their direct solicitations for quotations by placing advertisements in trade journals for two or three days prior to the bid-closing deadline. Figure 3–7 shows an example of such an advertisement.

Neither the direct approach to subcontractors by mail nor the indirect approach of advertising will guarantee that contractors will receive quotes. The only known facts are the actual mailing of the cards or the physical appearance of the ad in the paper. The inclusion of a polite RSVP on the printed cards would provoke a very limited response. Apart from the knowledge of certain subcontractors who visited the office to examine or borrow the drawings and would therefore be classed as "definitely quoting," the estimator has no real assurance of the intention of other subcontractors. Therefore, at some time during the bidding period, the method of telephone communication will need to be exercised, at least to the subcontractors for the most difficult or specialized trades in the project.

Probably the combination of all three methods of bid solicitation will be the most effective in yielding the maximum response from subcontractors and suppliers:

1. Printed cards to those particular companies with whom the contractor has a past history of cordial relations. (This is a business courtesy gesture, indicating that the contractor is preparing a bid, that the subcontractor's particular trade is included in the project, and that a quotation would be welcome.)

2. A trade journal advertisement (to appear in one or more issues) to catch the attention of those other subcontractors who will also be bidding, who are equally competent to do the work, and with whom the contractor is prepared to do business.

3. "Zeroing-in" by telephone to the subcontractors for the most pertinent trades.

3.7   RECAP

Although a tremendous amount of work lies ahead for the estimators, the following groundwork for the bid preparation has been accomplished:

1. A system has been set up to record the receipt and distribution of the documents.

2. The trades applicable to the project have been identified and listed.

3. A schedule for the preparation of the quantity surveys is established.

4. The main details about the project are made known on capsule information reports.

5. The subcontractors have been alerted and their quotations requested.

The activities most essential to the bid preparation—quantity surveys, scheduling, and pricing—can now be started. The next chapter will deal with an aspect of bid preparation that is not always recognized as being a significant factor in the production of a realistic estimate: communication. It exists in the form of a "background'" series of activities continuing right through the bidding period and merits some discussion.

4 PREBID COMMUNICATION

4.1 INITIAL COMMUNICATION

The last chapter discussed some recommended procedures for recording the receipt of the bid documents when they are received at the outset of the bidding period. The rolls of drawings with accompanying volumes of the project manual received in an estimating office are the instruments of communication used by the building owner's appointed design team—architects, engineers, and other consultants—to convey all the pertinent information necessary for general contractors to:

1. Establish within a defined period of time an estimate of the cost of the building.
2. Properly construct the building.

The first event is naturally the one of primary concern to the estimator. The second event is the obvious objective of the first event and will only be carried out by the general contractor who submits the most competitive and successful bid. (Note: "Successful" in the context of winning a contract, not necessarily a guarantee of a profit-yielding project.)

There are many factors contributing to the preparation of an accurate estimate of cost, not the least of which is the ability to assimilate and correctly interpret everything contained in this communication package from the building designers. The duration of time between the receipt of the bid documents and the deadline date for the completion and submission of the bid is all too often very short. Even the most experienced estimator will flinch at the prospect of studying, reading, absorbing, and thoroughly understanding within this short time period everything shown in a roll of drawings about twelve inches in diameter and described in an eight inch thick volume (or volumes) of the project manual that will probably contain more words than the Bible and *War and Peace* combined (and probably be just as controversial).

This book is mainly concerned with the preparation of a bid or tender for a stipulated price (lump-sum) contract, and general contractors should be conditioned to accept two hard, inescapable facts common to all bids for this type of contract:

Fact 1

The unavoidable date and time set for the bid submission, that is, the ominous deadline that warns of the hour when the sands will run out and everything, rightly or wrongly, must be finished.

Fact 2

The binding nature of the documents, as expressed in statements contained (with varying phraseology) in almost all Forms of Agreement, General Conditions, or other similar documents. The American Institute of Architects Document A201 words it this way:

1.2.3 The intent of the Contract Documents is to include all items necessary for the proper execution and completion of the Work by the Contractor. The Contract Documents are complementary, and what is required by one shall be as binding as if required by all; performance by the Contractor shall be required only to the extent consistent with the Contract Documents and reasonably inferable from them as being necessary to produce the intended results. *

*AIA copyrighted material has been reproduced with the permission of The American Institute of Architects under permission number 82408. Further reproduction is prohibited.

Fact 1 stresses the time limitations for the preparation of the estimate. Fact 2 is a solemn reminder that the completed bid must include the estimated costs of everything required by the drawings, the specifications, and any other documents pertinent to the bid.

Estimators in a general contractor's office must not only be satisfied that they themselves understand the intent of the bid documents; they must also be satisfied that potential subcontractors and suppliers have equal comprehension as it applies to their specific trades. A quotation from a subcontractor that demonstrates a misinterpretation of something in the documents and is accepted by the contractor without challenge for inclusion in the bid, becomes in effect an error for which the general contractor will ultimately bear the responsibility. This leads to all kinds of subsequent conflicts and disputes. The estimator must be continually alert to the possibility of these situations happening and take all precautions to avoid them. For example, a technical specification for Section 07200—Insulation might state that: "Rigid insulation to be 2 inches (50 mm) thick, or as noted on the drawings." The drawings might include special details for certain areas in the building to require 2-inch (62-mm) or 3-inch (75-mm) thick insulation. If an insulation subcontractor provided a low quotation that included the statement "All rigid insulation to be 2 inches as specified," the contractor would find it difficult at a later date to make this subcontractor provide material of any greater thickness than was stipulated in the quotation. It is true the subcontractor misinterpreted the specification clause, but the contractor should have become aware of the misunderstanding at the time of the bid.

Apart from the obvious requirement that information be presented clearly and concisely, effective communication also requires that the people to whom it is addressed properly understand the information. Certainly, the chances of misunderstanding will always be greater when the given communication is vague or confusing, but even the most carefully considered phraseology or the most excellent draftsmanship can still be, and probably will be, misinterpreted by someone. Worse still, this misinterpretation might be passed along to a third person and accepted as a valid statement. A clear directive like "All interior wood doors are to be painted with black paint" will pop out of some branch of the communication pipeline network as a negative statement that they must not be painted white.

4.2   DRAWINGS

The drawings, being a graphic or visual mode of communication, are often less subject to misinterpretation than the technical specifications or other written documents. "Draw me a picture" is a common enough expression often heard where there is difficulty in understanding an oral or written description of something.

However, bad or sloppy draftsmanship can impede the process of understanding a drawing. A lack of explanatory wall sections, a bewildering cluster of notations and dimensions, absence of any dimensions, or indistinct lettering—all these things can be frustrating to someone stoically endeavoring to decipher a somewhat complex detail. Nevertheless, it is difficult to imagine how an elevation of a wall noted on the drawings as being constructed of brick could be misinterpreted as being something other than a brick wall.

The length and height of this wall can also be ascertained on the drawing; the thickness of the wall might also be noted. The drawing can communicate this information quite clearly; however, to properly estimate the cost of this wall, the estimator seeks more information. This information would include:

Brick sizes, types, special brand names, color, and so on

Mortar materials and mixes

Type of bond

Type and thickness of mortar joints

Masonry anchorage and reinforcement materials

Laying the brick, the workmanship expected

Cleaning and pointing

Winter heat and protection requirements

Other similar items

This information will, or at least should, be provided in the technical specification.

4.3   READING THE SPECIFICATIONS

The technical specification could be defined as the document that expresses in words those things that cannot be properly demonstrated graphically. It is also often described as the document that supplements the drawings. Many project manuals state that "technical specifications shall govern over drawings," and many other similar documents confirm the status of the technical specification in relation to the drawings, particularly with reference to conflict between these documents.

Specification writing is a profession with its own standards of methodology and performance. Effective reading of project manuals also requires an expertise that estimators should learn to develop.

If the technical specification is well arranged in appropriate trade sections (as Masterformat or similar) and uses clear language, with sentences short and concise, then the intended meaning should not be difficult to understand. But if a path to the exact meaning and intent has to be beaten and hacked through an undergrowth of ambiguities and lengthy and involved paragraphs, some of which trail into further obscurities, then the estimator must determinedly strip this verbiage down to a more concise and comprehensive format. The technical specification has to be streamlined into something brief but still explicit, reducing lengthy technical data to a few short statements that highlight the most pertinent items.

It is recommended that the technical specification be considered in terms of the following three groups, when reading and making notes, each group differing as to the amount of in-depth study required on the part of the contractor's estimator:

1. General conditions: This colloquialism encompasses a number of technical specification sections with titles such as General Instructions, Temporary Facilities, General Work, and so on, according to the differing practices in the design offices. (Masterformat Division 0, Bidding and Contract Requirements, and Division 1, General Requirements, provide a comprehensive list of applicable items.)

2. General contractor's work: These are sections devoted to the trades that the general contractor would consider carrying out with its own labor force, and for which detailed quantities and cost estimates will be prepared. These sections would probably include Excavation, Shoring, Underpinning, Concrete and Formwork, Masonry, and Carpentry Work.

3. Subtrade sections: These apply to the trades that the general contractor intends or is prepared to subcontract in whole or in part. These trades could include those just mentioned in group 2.

The technical specification sections falling under the categories of groups 1 and 2 must be read thoroughly and in their entirety, with the most important items effectively noted and recorded. Utilizing one of the following methods can help do this:

1. Underlining the items with a colored pencil.
2. Using a special marking pen to highlight the items.
3. Making brief notes on a separate sheet of paper.

It is recommended that method 3 be followed because this makes it possible to reproduce all the necessary information on one or two sheets of paper, expressed briefly in simple and comprehensive terms, thus simplifying the task of checking that all items are covered. The other two methods will necessitate thumbing through several pages of a large, probably unwieldy, volume of technical specification to locate and recheck the noted items, with the accompanying irritant of the book's refusal to remain flat and open at the appropriate place. Figure 4–1 shows a page from a technical specification, in this instance an extract from a section for Concrete Work. Note that the pertinent items have been underlined, as required in method 1. Figure 4–2 shows an example of method 3 with the same information repeated in the format of a few notes on a separate sheet of paper.

Division 003300-Concrete   Page 5 of 10

4. Slabs on Fill
    a. Place one layer of polyethylene vapor barrier over granular fill. Place in continuous length, lap joints a minimum of 6". Keep joints to minimum.
    b. Slab on fill to be 4" thick of 30,000 p.s.i. concrete. Maximum slump to be 2". Mix design to be subject to the Architect's approval.
    c. Slab to be reinforced with 6 x 6 – 6/6 wire mesh reinforcement, placed in flat sheets, lapped 6". Reinforcement to be extended within 2" of construction joints and slab edges, and placed 1" from top of slab.
    d. Provide screeds for leveling of concrete slab. Engineer's level to be used for setting.
    e. Concrete slab to be placed in continuous strips, with construction joints to be provided between the strips. Width of strips to be kept at a minimum to achieve fast placing without creating cold joints. Construction joints to be located on column lines.
    f. Provide control joints as soon as possible during concrete curing. Saw cut slab to panels of approximately 20' by 20'. Saw cuts to be 1" deep and should be made on column lines wherever possible. Saw cut joints to be filled with an epoxy resin material.

5. Column Base Plates
    a. Base plates to be provided by Structural Steel.
    b. Contractor to grout base after steel frame has been plumbed and leveled. Grout to be a premixed nonshrink material.

FIGURE 4–1   Page from a specification on concrete.

Estimate No. 3-81

Notes Re: 03300 Concrete

Polyethylene vapor barrier under slab, 6" laps (Query: gauge?).
4" thick slab on earth; 3000 p.s.i. concrete.
6" x 6" – 6/6 wire mesh reinforcement (6" laps)
Provide screeds set to engineer's level
Place in continuous strips, construction joints between strips (refer Typical Detail Drawing.)
1" deep sawcuts, rectangular 20'0" x 20'0" panels, filled with epoxy resin, column lines.
Premixed nonshrink grout to column baseplates.

FIGURE 4–2   Notes taken on specification.

The following shows how a complete section for Concrete Work, which might run anywhere from twenty to thirty pages in the original technical specification format, might be reduced to a series of brief notes representing nearly all the information needed by the estimator (supplemented, of course, by the drawings) to prepare an estimate for this trade:

Estimate No. 3-81

Concrete mixes:

- Skim slabs, 2000 pounds per square inch (p.s.i.)
- Footings pile caps, slabs on earth, 3000 p.s.i.

- Suspended slabs, shear walls, beams, columns 4000 p.s.i.
- Fill to metal deck, lightweight concrete.
- Toppings. ⅜ inches aggregate.

Grout base plates, nonshrink grout. (Base plates supplied by structural steel subcontractor.)

Water reducing admixture to concrete in slabs.

Clean and slurry coat slabs for toppings.

Sawcuts in slabs, panels 20 feet 0 inches × 20 feet 0 inches.

Slab on grade to be placed checkerboard fashion.

6 inches × 6 inches − 6/6 wire mesh to slab on grade.

Chamfers to beams and columns.

Rub exposed concrete.

Inspection and testing by owner.

Construction joints:

- Vertical, keyed to walls.
- Horizontal, keyed to wall slabs (run re-steel through joint).
- 6″ polyvinyl waterstop in all construction joints below grade (welded at joints).
- Install waterstop between walls and slab on grade.

Curing:

- Keep exposed surfaces continuously wet 7 days.
- Membrane curing to finished surfaces of slabs.
- Protect cured floors (tarps or plywood).

Forms:

- Reshore floor and roof slabs after stripping (maximum spacing 8 feet 0 inches each way).
- Dovetail anchor slots for masonry.
- Asphalt-impregnated expansion joints.

The estimator should supplement these notes with further information shown on the structural and architectural drawings. He or she will then have, in effect, a complete checklist of concrete items and work to be measured and included in the estimate:

Footings, pile caps, foundation walls, grade beams.

Slabs on grade.

Skin slab (under footings).

Suspended slabs, beams, drop slabs.

Columns: rectangular and circular.

Fill to roof deck.

Miscellaneous curbs and bases (interior and exterior).

Floor toppings, etc.

With all this gathered and listed information, the estimator can proceed to measure quantities, summarize the items, solicit material quotations and equipment rental rates, and price the labor, all with a minimum of checking and rechecking back through the pages in the project manual. It is also much easier to run through these notes and check off all the items to ensure their inclusion in the estimate.

4.4 TECHNICAL SPECIFICATION SECTIONS RELATING TO SUBTRADES

As these sections in an average technical specification will probably aggregate to approximately 75 to 80 percent of the total, the task of reading and absorbing all the information contained therein would appear ominous and almost impossible to do in the time allowed. Therefore, before starting any laborious reading one should first consider which part of the information is most pertinent (a) to the general contractor, (b) to the subcontractor (or supplier), and (c) to both the general contractor and subcontractor.

Figure 4–3 illustrates a page from a technical specification for Plastic Laminated Wood Doors. The items of most importance to the general contractor are circled, and the following is an example of how this would be transcribed in a few notes:

Notes re: Section 08200 Plastic Doors

1. Three-year guarantee, including hanging and finishing.
2. Wood solid core slab doors with plastic laminated faces.
3. Approved manufacturers: Best-Door Co., Smith Lumber Co., J. H. Jackson, Inc.
4. Excludes grilles (see Section 10), cutouts to be included.

The door manufacturer would be concerned with all the information in this technical specification, including the technical data concerning the fabrication, quality,

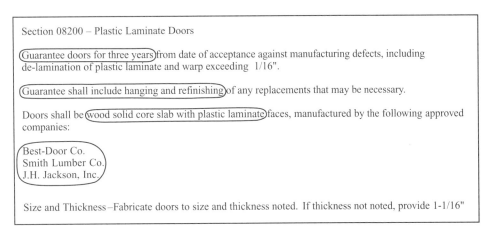

FIGURE 4–3   Page from a specification on plastic laminate doors.

door construction, materials, packaging requirements, and so on. The contractor is mainly concerned with establishing the cost of receiving, handling, and installing these doors.

The estimator will make a count of the required number of doors from the drawings and/or door schedule, grouping them according to their type and dimensions. Some suppliers also might calculate these quantities and present the contractor with a total package quotation. The majority, however, will provide a quotation that only states a unit price for each door type and will leave it to the contractor to establish the total supply cost.

The following remarks explain the significance and importance of these notes to the estimator:

1. Guarantee: It is essential to remember to check the quotations from manufacturers or suppliers to ensure that this guarantee is confirmed. Also, the estimator may consider the probability of one or more of these doors subsequently becoming defective and include a contingency amount in the tender to cover the cost of removing these doors and hanging and finishing the replacement doors. The "small print" at the back of the quotation will usually state that this work is not covered by the manufacturer's guarantee.

2. This note is merely a brief outline description of the items involved.

3. The names of the approved manufacturers remind the estimator that quotations from other manufacturers cannot be accepted for inclusion in the "base" bid amount, but could be offered separately as possible savings to the building owner if the prices are cheaper than those quoted by the approved manufacturer. (Note: This process of offering potential savings is discussed further in Chapter 14.)

4. The item regarding grilles is important. It reminds the estimator to check that the door manufacturer has allowed for making the necessary cutout in the doors to receive these grilles. Also, a check should be made that Specification Section 10A does include these items; if omitted, a query should be directed to the architect. An experienced estimator knows that the very brief words "door grilles to be included in the work of Section 10A of these technical specifications" throws onto the contractor's shoulders the responsibility for providing these items if they are not covered in any other section of the specifications.

This method of identifying and noting the items that most affect the general contractor can be applied in varying degrees to all other specialist or subtrades. The trainee or junior estimator will tend to read almost every word in a technical specification before writing down the pertinent information. He or she will probably make more notes than necessary. The ability and the confidence to recognize those items of vital importance while scanning rapidly through the technical specification can only be acquired through experience and repetition.

4.5   "WORK BY OTHERS" CLAUSES

The problem of an item (or items) of work being noted in one trade division to be provided by another trade was touched on in the example of the notes for the section Plastic Laminated Doors. These types of clauses are negative and can result in some problems if not challenged during the bid-preparation period. (It is useless to raise the issue at a later time.)

For example, a clause in the technical specification for Section 07800—Sealants might say something like this:

> Excluded from this division is the caulking and sealant work to be provided by the
> following trades:
> 03400—Precast Concrete
> 08500—Aluminum Windows

The estimator will note this statement and then check those other trade divisions. Section 03400 might clearly specify the caulking requirements for the precast concrete work, thereby confirming that the cost of this work is intended to be included in the precast concrete contractor's quotation. However, Section 08500 stays "silent" on the subject and makes no reference to this caulking whatsoever. Experience cautions the estimator into expecting that the trade contractors normally will only read those sections devoted to their own specific trades, and will usually refer to any other sections only if and when directed to do so in their own technical specification.

Prior notice of these discrepancies should warn the estimator that the following things could happen:

1. The caulking contractors will exclude the cost of this work in their quotations, in accordance with the specified instructions.
2. The aluminum window contractors will also exclude this work from their quotations, not having read any directive to do otherwise in the technical specification section applicable to their own trade.

The contractor who is negligent in pursuing this matter—assuming that all the subcontractors base their quotations in strict accordance with the requirements of their own technical specifications—is left exposed to the unhappy situation of being contractually responsible for an item of work of which the cost is excluded from the bid. Remember that the architects did not stipulate this item as being excluded from the prime contract, only from one trade division.

This kind of situation warrants the following recommended procedures:

1. Inform the aluminum window contractors that a clause relating to their trade is noted in the division for another trade. (In practice, of course, experience will prompt many of these contractors to query the omission of this work.)
2. Notify the architects regarding this omission and request the issuance of addenda to rectify this discrepancy.
3. Suggest to the caulking subcontractors that they prepare a separate quotation for this work. This is in the event that the architect does not formally clarify the matter, with the result that some window contractors will include the work and others will exclude it. This separate quotation will ensure that the general contractor will have a cost estimate for the item to include in the bid. (Alternatively, and with time permitting, this work could be "taken off" and the materials and labor priced by the contractor's estimator.)

Estimators should watch very closely for these and similar discrepancies that can occur in the various technical divisions of a specification. Most project manuals have clauses that hold the general contractor responsible for the allocation of the work to the various trades, regardless of where a specific item of work is located in the technical specification.

4.6 ITEMS RELATIVE TO NORMAL TRADE PRACTICE

The contractor's estimator should also take note of the items of work that are customarily carried out by one particular trade but are sometimes included in the specification for another trade. The specification writer may be strictly correct in the allocation of certain items according to some standard specification system (Masterformat, for example), but local or regional trade practice may decree that another trade usually performs this work.

A good example would be roof insulation. This work is generally included in the Roofing Division (Masterformat 07500) of the technical specification, but sometimes it shows up (not illogically) in the trade division for Insulation Work (Masterformat 07200). The estimator should make prebid contact with the various subcontractors for both these trade divisions to ascertain their intentions. In most cases it will be established that the roofing subcontractor's intent is to include this item because it is normal practice for them to do so, and for the same reason most of the insulation subcontractors will exclude it. However, some subcontractors in either trade may decide for one reason or another to ignore normal trade practice and quote in strict accordance with the technical specifications. The contractor's estimator should check with all the potential subcontractors in these circumstances in order to avoid the same set of circumstances that were considered in Section 4.5 concerning the problems relating to the caulking trade. These circumstances would be that (a) two contractors representing different trades will include the same item of work, or (b) neither contractor will include it.

Again the estimator is faced with the problem of either a duplication of items in the bid, which could make it less competitive, or the alternative situation of the omission of both items of cost. (It is a fair comment to say that if the bid is successful and the first condition, that is, duplication, is found to exist, it will probably be considered as a piece of shrewd strategy on the part of the estimator. Not so the opposite situation, of course.)

4.7 APPROVED TRADE CONTRACTORS OR MANUFACTURERS

Some mention was made of this in the example of note making on a technical specification for Plastic Laminated Doors. The estimator should note carefully the names of all approved subcontractors or manufacturers. He or she should also examine the other parts of the project manual (usually the General Conditions) for the exact meaning of the clause that often follows the specified names of trade contractors or products, " . . . or approved equal." The usual definition of this clause is that approval of the work or products of companies other than those named in the technical specifications must be formulated by written instructions from the architect (usually in the form of an addenda) prior to the closing of the bid. Only when this procedure is followed may the general contractor accept for inclusion in the bid any quotations from these companies; to do this without this prior written approval renders the bid liable to rejection on the grounds of informality.

3. This is similar to the first query and has been answered straightforwardly by the architect, with the promise of a confirmation by addenda. When this addendum is received, this particular item should be checked to ensure that it conforms to what was stated orally.

4. This query is of a slightly different nature. Let us assume a subcontractor brought it forth. The question relates to an item in the project manual that is ambiguously worded; its intent is not clear. It could mean one or two different things. The subcontractor has raised the question with the contractor's estimator and has requested an interpretation. In this example the estimator is following the recommended procedure by passing the query immediately to the architect. It is inadvisable for the contractor's estimator to attempt an interpretation of a hazy clause in a project manual, particularly to a third party. If the subcontractor presses for some kind of an interpretation from the contractor, then any statement made by the contractor should be qualified as being merely an opinion.

A common statement in most contract documents recognizes the status of the architect as being "in the first instance the interpreter of the contract." This applies to problems that may arise out of the documents during the actual construction phase, but it is also valid during the bidding period. Therefore, where there is doubt, query the matter.

Estimators must be aggressive in this area of communication. Every doubtful wrinkle ironed out during this phase could eliminate many future disputes and conflicts. When the bid is in the owner's hands, it is too late to ask questions about the bid documents. Keeping an organized record of queries to designers is important for checking addenda to ensure that everything queried has been answered, and that the written clarification confirms the oral statement with the same or similar wording and meaning. Also, although these query sheets do not have any contractual status, they could carry some weight in the event of an answer being given verbally but never confirmed in writing, and then later challenged by the designer.

To expostulate at a later date that "One of our people called someone at your office about four months ago . . ." is not as impressive as, "According to our records, on May 16, 1999 our Mr. Knight telephoned your Mr. Jones with this question, and he stated . . ."

Of course, if Mr. Jones no longer works at the designer's office, then the impact of this statement is somewhat deflated. He might also (in all honesty or otherwise) deny any knowledge of the incident. The record does indicate, however, that such a query was made.

4.9 ADDENDA

Addenda (or bulletins) could be considered as refinements of the original communication. They are issued by the designers to accomplish the following purposes:

Corrections of errors in the original documents.

Approval of material substitutions.

Authorization of design changes agreed to, or required by, the owner.

Response to queries from contractors and subcontractors.

Addenda often include a large amount of fussy "house-cleaning" terms to correct minor mistakes in spelling or grammar, regardless of whether such errors were glaringly obvious. Estimators gradually become conditioned to wading through a myriad of items such as " 'rump' read 'ramp,' " or "delete the sentence beginning 'Provide decorative slots to the architect's approval' and insert 'Provide decorative slats . . . etc.' "

Addenda become part of the contract documents and take precedence over the original documents. Most bid forms require that contractors acknowledge the receipt of such addenda, confirming numbers and dates of issue. The importance of ensuring that all potential subcontractors or suppliers are made aware of this additional communication is obvious. It is unwise for a general contractor to acknowledge on his bid form the receipt of Addenda Nos. 1 to 4 without ensuring that all subcontractors' quotations also confirm examination of all these addenda. The issue of addenda is another reversal of the flow of communication, which is once again coming from the designers to the contractors, for onward transmission, where applicable, to subcontractors and suppliers.

Sometimes revised drawings may supplement the addenda. The more common procedure, however, is for the written addenda to contain a number of items pertaining to drawing revisions, stating the applicable drawing and/or section numbers. The task of reading, checking, and noting all these revisions can be very demanding on an estimator's time, requiring great concentration and considerable patience. This applies particularly to a whole page or two of very minor revisions to dimensions that might have little or no influence on the actual cost (although they will become very essential during construction).

Figure 4–5 shows an example of a typical page from addenda revising the project manual. Attention is drawn to the first item in these addenda. This refers to one of the queries noted in the example of a query record sheet (see Figure 4–4). In that example a query was raised regarding the thickness and type of material to be used for underfloor fill. This answer in the addenda only refers to the material, but has not confirmed the required thickness of the bed. A further query to the architects will now be necessary.

Port Cragfield High School (Project No. PC8-81)

Addendum No. 4

Section 02220 Earthwork
    Page 6: Para. 4. Fill – Add: Provide ?/4" crushed stone fill under the concrete slabs on grade.

Section 05500 Miscellaneous Metals
    Page 6: Corner Guards – Add: Thickness of corner guards shall be 1/8".

Section 06200 Carpentry
    Page 5: Wood Railing – Delete: Wood railing at north side of Corridor No. 4.
    Page 5: Valances – Change: "solid red oak" to "oak-veneered particle board."

Section 09250 Gypsum Wallboard
    Page 1: Par. 2 – Add: Item 2.6, Install metal door frames in gypsum wallboard partitions
    (frames supplied by Section 08100 Metal Doors and Frames).

FIGURE 4–5   Addendum.

4.10 REVIEW

A great amount of communication flows back and forth during the bid-preparation period between all the concerned parties—contractors, design consultants, owners, trade contractors, and suppliers. This communication starts with the issuance of the bid documents and finishes with the final delivery of the bid into the owner's hands. One effect of this prebid communication is that it has probably improved the clarity of the bid documents, enabling contractors to prepare their bids with more confidence and probably eliminating a number of disputes during the construction period.

In summing up, it must be stressed once again that:

1. Only persistent querying and checking will dissipate haziness and discrepancies in the bid documents and make the information more definitive and decisive. In other words, when in doubt, shout.

2. Estimators should never permit sensitivity to somebody's feelings or the fear that they may be stepping on another's toes to restrict their aggressiveness in seeking necessary clarification. Certainly, it will often be obviously irritating to the designers to be subjected to a barrage of questions, but most architects would endorse the value of having things clarified in January rather than have them disputed in December. However, queries should never be made irresponsibly without a careful check to see if the matter has been clarified somewhere in the documents or in a previously issued addendum.

3. Those doubtful items that are not clarified before the bid submission will come back to haunt the contractor at a later time and could result in a reduction of anticipated profit for the project.

4. Equally, it is essential that subcontractors fully understand all information relating to their trades, so that when a contractor is expecting a quotation for "oranges" he is not presented with one for "apples." If a subcontractor has raised a query to the architect, the contractor's estimator should make sure that when an answer is received the subcontractor is satisfied with the answer. "Does that answer your question?" should be asked repeatedly.

5 | TAKEOFF: GENERAL COMMENTS

5.1 | BASIC PRINCIPLES OF QUANTITY SURVEYING

Basic rules and recommendations for taking off quantities from drawings have been affirmed and stressed in every text or reference book written on the subject; they justify some reviewing, endorsement, and repetition. The following are some of these established precepts:

1. Items should be measured as "net fixed in place" and in accordance with accepted guidelines as discussed in Section 5.2 and the examples of takeoff in the ensuing chapters.

2. Dimensions should be rounded off to:
   a. Nearest inch for measurements. Examples: 1′ 5½″ would become 1′ 6″ and 1′ 5¼″ would be written 1′ 5″. (Note: Some estimators will use a system called duodecimals. Dimensions stated in duodecimals appear in the following example: e.g., 1′ 6″ to be written 1.6, not 1.5. We prefer to use the actual decimal equivalent. These are quickly memorized when first estimating and are no slower than using duodecimals — e.g., 1′ 6″ to be written as 1.5).
   b. Two decimal places should be used for metric measurements. Examples: 456.764 would be recorded as 456.76 and 456.768 as 456.77.

3. Figured dimensions should be used in preference to scaled dimensions.

4. Dimensions relating to "deductions" or "voids" should be either written in red (pen or pencil), or enclosed in parentheses — e.g., "(4.6) × (5.0) = (23 sft)".

5. Adjustments for waste and similar factors must be added to the total net quantities of each item; they should never be considered during the actual measuring. (Refer to Section 5.3.)

6. Adherence to a systematic order of measuring and recording dimensions is essential. The dimensions should be written consistently in the sequence of length, breadth (width), and depth (height). Where there is more than a single item with the same dimensions in a specific category, a group of spread footings, for example, the dimensions should be written once and prefixed with the applicable digit. (This is commonly known as "Timesing.") For example, if a structure contained six column footings with the same dimensions, $4' 6'' \times 4' 0''$, these would be recorded as $6/4.5' \times 4.0'$.

7. Identify and record on the takeoff sheets information regarding the locations of the various items as they are identified on the drawings, such as column lines, floor elevations, room numbers, or building elevations. In fact, record and identify anything that will simplify the process of checking back on items to verify they have been taken off. The small amount of extra time necessary to do this is worthwhile and eliminates the futile and nonproductive time spent by estimators who return from lunch with complacent stomachs but their heads full of confusion as to what had been taken off before dashing off to the cafeteria.

8. Study the drawings carefully and meticulously before actually starting any takeoff, making as many notes as possible. This time will not be wasted if used constructively. Careful examination of the drawings will alert the estimator to items that are repetitious, where things start and finish, what member is supporting or is tied in with what other member, and so on. The items should be measured in a methodical order and preferably, wherever possible, the same sequence in which they will be constructed on the site. In other words, don't start at the roof and work down; or, worse, don't meander from foundation walls to suspended floor slabs, then switch to footings followed by the toppings and floor finishes, and so forth.

9. Adopt a system of marking items on the drawings as they are taken off. Use colored pencils if necessary, and do this as neatly as possible. A sinister statement in the specifications may warn estimators about possible adjustment or refund cancellation of the monetary deposit on the documents if the drawings and specifications are "unduly marked or mutilated." The meaning of "unduly marked," though, is sometimes obscure.

10. Where the company estimating system requires the transferring of the (reduced) quantities to separate summary sheets for pricing (the system recommended in this book), a distinctive check mark should be placed against the item with a colored pencil indicating that the item has been "posted." Estimators should always be on the alert against the ironic situation of having an item meticulously taken off, with all the arithmetical computations correctly made and rechecked, and then completely overlooking the item when posting to the summary. Distinctively marking each item as it is transferred will afford some protection against such omissions.

11. Formulate a takeoff method that permits a number of items to be calculated from one set of dimensions. Refer to Figure 5–1, which illustrates the recording of measurements for a group of isolated concrete footings. Figure 5–2 is a second example, this one for continuous wall footings. In the

Project	Research Center	Estimate No.	27/82
Location		By	B.E.W. Chk'd H.A.J.
Subdivision	Concrete / Formwork	Date	4/1/99

Description of Work	No. Pieces	Dimensions A	B	C	Extensions Concrete (A x B x C)	Unit	Extensions Forms (2 x (A + B) x C) (No.)	Unit	Extensions	Unit
Concrete to columns Footings (3000 lbs.)				(No.)						
Type A	7	4	4	1.17	1 4 0		1 3 1			
Type B	3	4	3.5	1	4 2		4 5			
Type C	10	4.5	4.5	1.5	3 0 3 .75		2 7 0			
					4 8 5 .75	cft	4 4 6	sft		
						/27				
					= 18.0	cyd				

FIGURE 5–1   Example of a takeoff format.

QUANTITIES

Sheet No. 1 of 1

Project	Research Center	Estimate No.	27/82
Location		By	B.E.W. Chk'd H.A.J.
Subdivision	Concrete / Formwork	Date	4/1/99

Description of Work	No. Pieces	Dimensions A	B	C	Extensions Concrete (No.)(A x B x C)	Unit	Extensions Forms (2 x(A+B)xC)(No.)	Unit	Extensions Key (2"x4") (No.)(A)	Unit
Concrete to perimeter wall footings (3000 lbs.)										
Col. Lines 1 + 4	2	150.0	2.0	1.0	6 0 0		3 0 4		1 5 0	
Col. Lines A		60.0	2.5	1.0	1 5 0		1 2 5		6 0	
Col. Lines D		60.0	2.0	.67	8 0 .4		8 3 .1		6 0	
					8 3 0 .4	cft.	8 1 6 .1	sft.	2 7 0	lft.
						/27				
					= 3 0 .75	cyd				

FIGURE 5–2   Format example with "key."

first example the single set of dimensions could be developed to provide the quantities of both concrete and formwork; in the second example the quantities for the additional item of the footing "key" were also established. This is a time saving method that avoids "double-measuring" and provides a consistent relationship between the quantities for each item. Note: the formulas involving *A, B,* and *C* are necessary if someone (calculator operator, clerk, etc.) other than the estimator is going to do the arithmetical extensions.

5.2   METHODS OF MEASUREMENT

Construction estimators are advised to formulate and agree upon a standard schedule of units and methods of measurement to be used within their own organization for taking off quantities. These schedules are to be prepared for all those trades normally taken off in the individual contractor's offices and should be adhered to as closely as possible in all estimates. Familiarity with these agreed-upon rules and methods will usually speed up the process of quantity takeoff. Less time is wasted due to an estimator agonizing about "Should this be in cubic yards, or should it be in square yards and state the thickness?" It can also simplify the task of making comparisons with similar items in previous estimates or cost reports when pricing a particular trade.

A construction company's schedule of measurements and items is also useful to site personnel; engineers, superintendents, project managers, site accountants, and others. A schedule of measurements and items ensure that "field quantities" taken off for the purpose of cost records are prepared in compliance with the methods employed by the estimators. This can guarantee a true comparison between actual and estimated quantities.

The American Society of Professional Estimators (ASPE) publishes a document called *Standard Estimating Practice.* It is self-described as being ". . . written in the language of estimators to provide not only basic and fundamental guidance for estimators, but also to define industry recognized standards . . ." This document is an excellent publication that could usefully be employed as a model for a company schedule of items and measurements, or be adopted and used without any modifications to suit company methods or procedures.

Some general contractors would prefer to identify and price separately certain items of work that in the ASPE document are suggested for inclusion in the estimated unit price, items such as scaffolding, formwork hardware and oil, and falsework. Integration of a number of activities into single items can lead to possible misinterpretations by site supervisory personnel and be a hindrance to effective cost control and accurate cost reporting. Therefore, some contractors will prepare their own schedules of measurement methods and rules, which might still follow closely the basic principles set forth in the ASPE document.

Schedules of items and measurements are included in the chapters relating to quantity takeoff for specific trade divisions. They are similar to the ASPE document and, like that document, follow as closely as possible well-established standard trade practices. Also like the ASPE document, these schedules should be considered to be flexible.

Consideration should be given to any set of estimating procedures or methods formulated in a contractor's office. Estimators must be allowed, and also allow themselves, the latitude to modify or revise any rules when good judgment indicates the justification of such revisions or modifications. The mere existence of a written rule or procedure should never become an overriding factor. Estimators should always seek to know the reason for and the logic behind each procedure rule—just knowing and being able to quote them parrot fashion is not satisfactory.

5.3 NET AND GROSS QUANTITIES

The difference between net-in-place quantities (basically what are measured on the drawings) and the gross (or "gross-on-site" might be a suitable title) quantities is something of a perennial controversy between a construction company's personnel on the site and the estimators in the office. Superintendents and foremen are conditioned by experience (not unnaturally) to consider construction materials by the method in which they are purchased, delivered, and installed. They will tend to consider these items not so much in quantity surveying terms (volumes or areas or lengths, such as board feet or linear feet), but in the more realistic context of truck or carloads, cartons, barrels, drums, rolls, sheets, and so on.

Trained and experienced estimators and quantity surveyors are equally aware of these realities, but their training and experience discipline them to be consistent in the initial establishment of the net-in-place quantities before proceeding to add adjustments as compensation for wastage and other factors. An estimator confronted with an accusation that the quantities for a specific item were "very short" will often confound a superintendent with the statement that, "There was nothing wrong with the actual quantities, it was the waste factor that was wrong." This statement is small comfort to a foreman who has been allowed only 8,000 bricks in the estimate for a structure that will require 10,000 to build. This image bears overtones of comedy, but there is some logic lurking in the wings. The estimator, by establishing the accuracy of the quantity takeoff, has also established that the waste factor was inadequate and should be adjusted for future estimates. (The alternative, of course, is for the estimator—if foolhardy enough—to accuse the foreman of undue and excessive breakage and waste.)

To attempt the establishment of an accurate and foolproof adjustment for every variable condition and material would be a time-consuming and hazardous operation. It is more sensible to determine a range of high to low percentage limitations for the different materials (based on previous experience or calculations that have proved satisfactory). These will usually satisfy most conditions.

The terms "cutting and waste" are employed in statements regarding adjustments to net quantities, but there are many other conditions that require the use of adjustment factors to develop the net quantities into the arena of actual conditions. Not all these conditions will demand consideration in the average bid, but it is important that estimators appreciate their existence and also the impact they exercise on estimates and quantities. The following are those normally encountered in building projects; they should receive consideration in the estimates:

1. Laps: The overlapping of one piece of material over another piece of the same material. One example would be welded wire mesh reinforcement. This material is usually sold in 6-foot (1830-mm) wide rolls, and most specifications require that this material be lapped a minimum of 6 inches (300 mm). This means that except for the first roll in a given area the actual surface covered will be only 5 feet 6 inches (1530 mm); therefore, the net

quantity would require an adjustment of at least 8.5 percent to provide sufficient material for the job. As this material would still be subject to further cutting and waste, it is very apparent that a minimum percentage to be added would be 10 percent.

2. Seepage: The best example for this condition would be the concrete lost due to seepage through a stone or gravel underbed. The drawings might call for a concrete slab placed on stone fill to be 6 inches (150 mm) thick net, but the actual quantity of concrete placed to achieve this thickness might be equal to 7 to 8 inches (175 to 200 mm). This condition can be compensated for in the estimate by either adjusting the net quantity with a percentage factor or by actually adding an additional 1 inch or 2 inches to the specified thickness. If this is done, it must be recorded clearly on the takeoff sheets in the "waste" columns. This will enable anyone checking the takeoff sheets to see how the adjustment was made.

3. Overbreak: When rock is excavated by either blasting or drilling, there will be spalls of breakage, and where concrete is to be placed on the rock surfaces (for footings, grade beams, slabs, etc.), additional concrete will be required to make up for the concrete filling up the broken areas. It is a similar condition to the problem of seepage, but a much greater extra thickness of concrete will be necessary to achieve the actual specified thickness.

4. Compaction: The change in a quantity of any loose material due to consolidation by compression. This usually applies to the backfilling of excavations with earth, gravel, stone, sand, or other materials; adjustment to the net quantities is necessary to compensate for shrinkage. This condition, and also the inverse condition of the swell of excavated soil, is discussed in more detail in Chapter 6.

Table 5–1 shows a schedule of suggested adjustment factors to be applied to certain materials. Excluded from this table are the factors for soil compaction and swell, which as already stated are included separately in Chapter 6. Also the adjustment for bonding in masonry work is dealt with separately in Chapter 8.

TABLE 5–1   Schedule of adjustment factors

Material	Condition	Adjustment Factor, %
Wallboards: plywood, gypsum board, fiberboard, hardboard, etc.	Cutting and waste	10–30
Wire mesh reinforcement	Laps plus cutting and waste	10–20
Lumber (this is premised on lumber being sold in lengths of 2-ft multiples)	Cutting and waste	20–30
Face brick (excludes bonding adjustment)	Cutting and waste	5–15
Concrete block	Cutting and waste	5–10
Glazed concrete block	Cutting and waste	10–20
Clay tile units	Cutting and waste	5–10
Glazed structural tile	Cutting and waste	10–20
Building paper, polyethylene, etc.	Laps and waste	5–10
Wood sheathing, T & G	Cutting and waste	10–15
Wood sheathing (diagonal)	Cutting and waste	15–25
Rigid insulation board	Cutting and waste	10–15

There are other factors to be considered for quantity adjustments not shown on the schedule in Table 5–1. For example, there is often a small wastage of ready-mix concrete materials due to spillage. Also, excess concrete in the truck has to be paid for even though it is not used. Many estimators consider these conditions are compensated for by the volume of concrete displaced by the reinforcing steel bar or other items embedded in the concrete, and that adjustments are not usually made for small openings, voids, or recesses. Other estimators lean toward the prudence of adding one to 2 percent to allow for these small discrepancies.

Although best considered at the "pricing" stage, estimators should bear in mind that many materials are sold on a "minimum purchasable quantity" basis, and when there is a considerable gap between the net requirement of a material and this minimum quantity, a compensating adjustment should be made. Sometimes the excess material could be used on another project, in which case probably no adjustment would be made. However, if it is an expensive material not often encountered in most projects, the minimum purchasable quantity should be included in the bid.

Because of all the variables applicable to the procurement and installation of materials, it should be obvious how essential is the accuracy of the net-in-place quantity takeoff. Agonizing over the most realistic adjustment factor for a given material is an exercise in futility if the net quantities are incorrect due to sloppy takeoff methods. Any investigation into the reason for a discrepancy between actual and estimated quantities should start with an examination of the original takeoff. If that stands up to inspection, the answer will either be the estimator's lack of practical knowledge about construction materials (a superintendent's opinion) or bad organization at the site resulting in excessive and unjustifiable waste (an estimator's viewpoint.)

5.4 TAKEOFF SHEETS

The examples given in the ensuing chapters for specific trade divisions will be based on the use of sheets designed for takeoff purposes only. No pricing will be done on these sheets. Each item will be taken off, the arithmetical extensions made and totaled, and then the items with the totals will be transferred to another summary sheet. An alternate method, one favored by many estimators, is to have the sheets designed for takeoff on one side, with columns for pricing at the opposite side.

There are advantages and disadvantages to both methods. When the pricing is done on the same sheet a certain amount of time is saved from not having to rewrite the quantities on the second sheet. That is certainly an advantage.

The disadvantage is that certain items applicable to a specific trade might require writing up one, two, or more sheets of dimensions. This means that an item can only be priced on the last sheet for this item (where the total quantity will be stated). An estimate for a major project will result in a huge number of sheets with the totaled and priced items occurring spasmodically throughout. With the separate summary method, all the items for a specific trade are gathered together on one or two summary sheets. This not only facilitates pricing the items; it also facilitates the checking over of the priced items by a contractor or project manager or senior supervising estimator. It could be protested, with some justification, that an item could also be omitted in the process of posting to the separate summary. That is true; but equally it is also possible to overlook an item for pricing on the "combined sheet" method.

5.5 ▌ GENERAL CONTRACTOR'S TRADES

The schedules of methods and measurements and the quantity surveying examples in this book will be limited to those trades considered as traditional for general contractors to perform with their own work forces. This no longer holds completely true, as many of these trades are now subcontracted in part or in whole. Most general contractors are prepared to do this work if subcontractors are not available or if the contractors consider they could do the work more economically than the subcontractor could and so ensure a more competitive bid. Also, the number of traditional trades that are subcontracted or worked by the general contractor varies in different regions of the country. In the western states, for example, nearly all masonry work is subcontracted, while concrete and formwork operations are still very often carried out by the general contractors' work forces.

The trades considered in this book include:

1. Sitework (e.g., excavation, grading, backfilling).
2. Concrete, formwork, and concrete floor finishing.
3. Masonry (e.g., brick, concrete block, clay tile).
4. Carpentry and millwork. (Note: It is becoming common for millwork contractors to include the installation of the millwork items in their quotations.)
5. Miscellaneous items. These would include:
   - Hollow metal doors and frames.
   - Hollow metal partitions.
   - Wood doors and frames (often included in the quotation from millwork subcontractors).
   - Miscellaneous metals (for those items to be embedded in concrete, masonry, or other work).
   - Specialties (washroom accessories, mat sinkage frames, roof hatches, toilet partitions, etc.).

5.6 ▌ DRAWINGS

The examples of quantity takeoff demonstrated in Chapters 6, 7, 8, and 10 are based on Figures 5–3 through 5–10 for a 3-story university research building.

To supplement the information shown on these drawings, brief specification notes are provided for the pertinent trade to be taken off. All takeoff examples are in accordance with the appropriate "Schedule of Items and Measurements" included in each chapter.

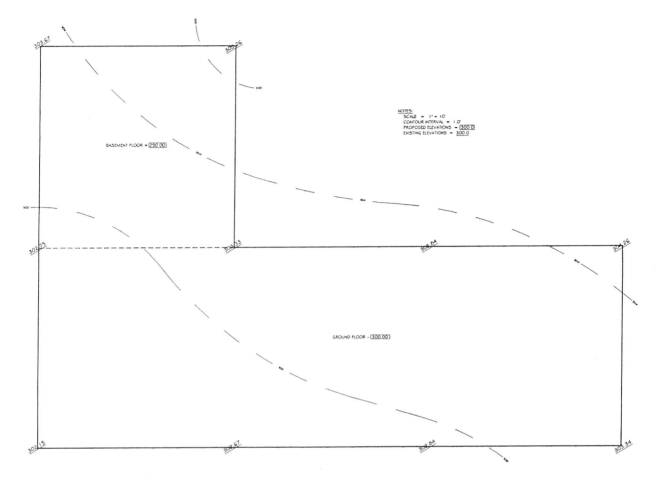

FIGURE 5–3 Plot plan.

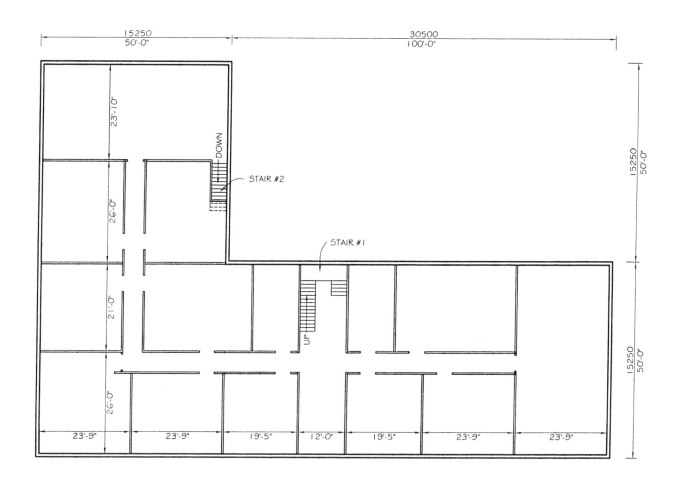

GROUND FLOOR PLAN

FIGURE 5–4   Floor plan.

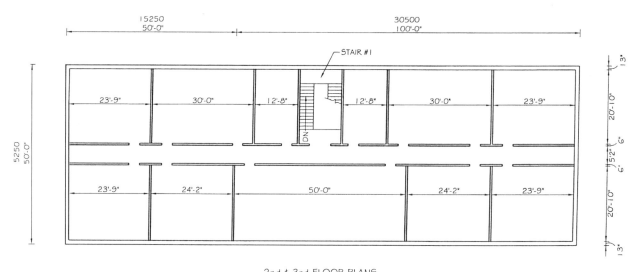

2nd & 3rd FLOOR PLANS

FIGURE 5–5   Floor plan.

54

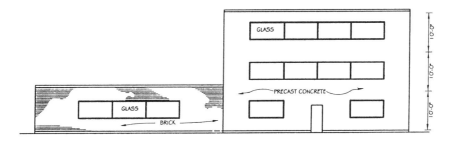

WEST ELEVATION

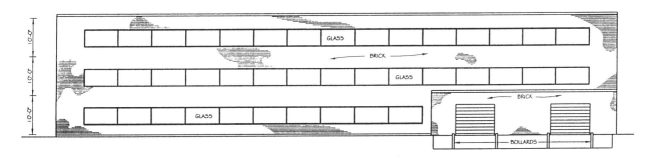

NORTH ELEVATION

FIGURE 5–6 Elevations.

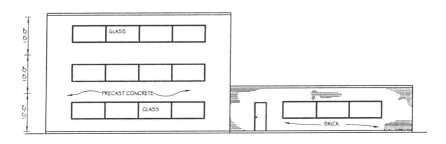

EAST ELEVATION

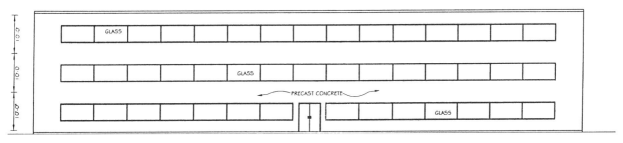

FIGURE 5–7 Elevations.

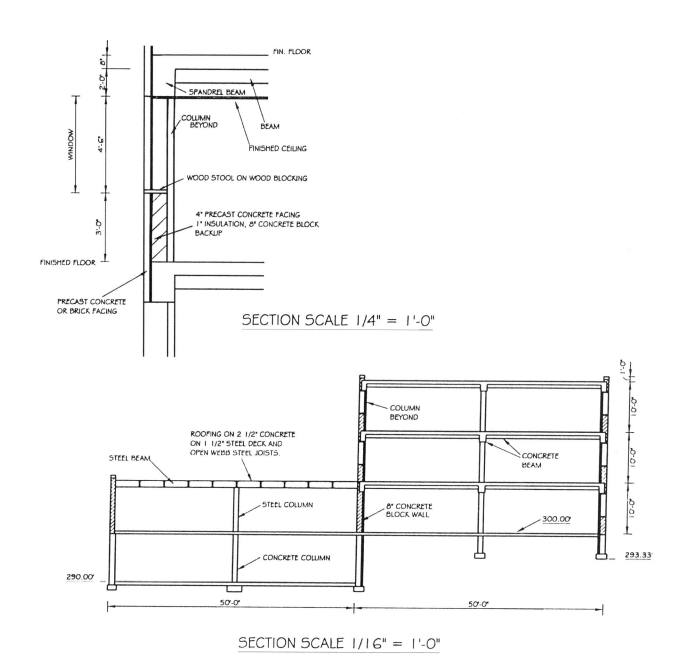

FIN. FLOOR

SPANDREL BEAM

COLUMN
BEYOND

BEAM

FINISHED CEILING

WOOD STOOL ON WOOD BLOCKING

4" PRECAST CONCRETE FACING
1" INSULATION, 8" CONCRETE BLOCK
BACKUP

WINDOW

FINISHED FLOOR

PRECAST CONCRETE
OR BRICK FACING

SECTION SCALE 1/4" = 1'-0"

ROOFING ON 2 1/2" CONCRETE
ON 1 1/2" STEEL DECK AND
OPEN WEBB STEEL JOISTS.

STEEL BEAM

COLUMN
BEYOND

CONCRETE
BEAM

STEEL COLUMN

8" CONCRETE
BLOCK WALL

300.00

CONCRETE COLUMN

290.00

293.33'

50'-0"

50'-0"

SECTION SCALE 1/16" = 1'-0"

FIGURE 5–8 Building sections.

56

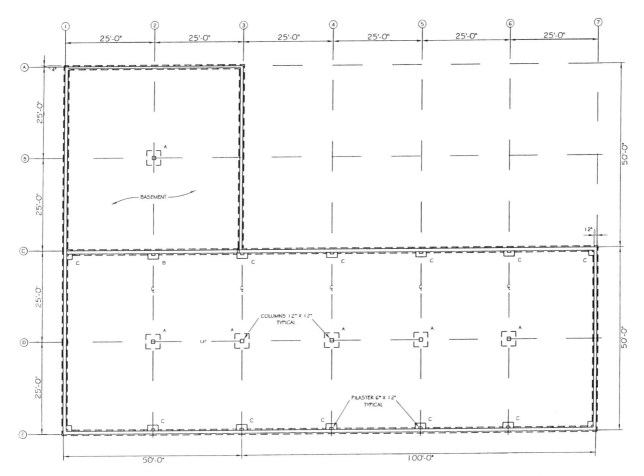

FIGURE 5–9 Foundation plan.

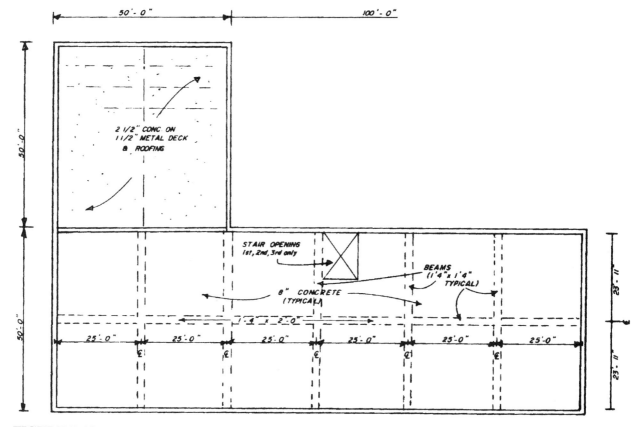

FIGURE 5–10 Structural floor plans—1st, 2nd, and 3rd floors.

6 TAKEOFF: SITEWORK

6.1 GENERAL

Sitework (site clearing and general excavation work) is one of the first operations performed on a construction project, but this does not mean that it is logically the initial trade taken off in the estimate. Experienced estimators often leave this trade until after the concrete substructure work has been taken off, and very often later than that. An early site visit is also essential before taking off sitework, and in some instances the use of a surveyor's level may be necessary for spot checks of existing grades.

Another recommendation is to have the estimator responsible for the concrete quantities also take off the excavation work. The measurement of structural work below grade will mean the recording of the locations, enumeration and size of footings, pile caps, pits, and such, all of which data will facilitate taking off the excavation and backfill for these same items.

Probably the fundamental difference between measuring the quantities of earthwork and taking off the work of other trades (concrete, masonry, carpentry, etc.) is that, with the possible exception of civil engineering projects, the actual excavation details do not appear on the drawings. What are usually shown are the details of those items for which the excavation has to be performed, be it a complete building, or foundations, pits, manholes, and other miscellaneous structures. Also, only the neat lines of the excavation are reflected in the dimensions. For excavation measurements, these basic dimensions have to be projected to provide for:

1. Additional working space.
2. Side slopes to prevent the caving in of the banks, usually legislated by jurisdictional authorities (unless a system of perimeter shoring or sheet piling is to be used to support the banks).

FIGURE 6–1 Expansion of neat-line dimensions.

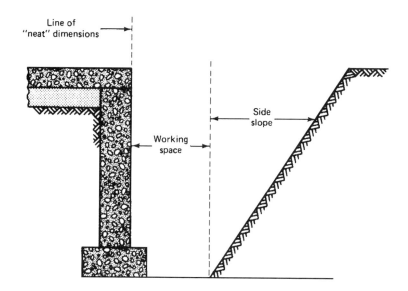

Figure 6–1 shows how these neat-line dimensions would be expanded for take-off purposes.

Another factor that affects the quantities for earthwork estimates is the swelling of the soil after it has been loosened and excavated. The factor is usually expressed as a percentage factor applied to the net-in-place (bank measure) quantities. As an example, if the appropriate adjustment factor is 15 percent, then 100 cubic yards of earth would become 115 cubic yards after excavation (loose measure volume).

Although this book primarily addresses itself to stipulated-sum bids, it is recommended that this bulking factor be dealt with by incorporating it into the estimated unit rate, rather than applying it to the net quantities. This would appear to be a reversal of all previous recommendations that adjustment factors for wastage, cutting, compaction, and so on, should be applied against the quantities. The principal reason for this inconsistency is that in building construction work (as opposed to heavy engineering works), it is usual for a general contractor to subcontract the excavation work. Excavation contractors will often only quote unit rates to the general contractors, leaving it to the contractor to compute the quantities and establish a total cost. This bulking factor will usually be included in these unit rates, and a possible duplication could occur if it was also reflected in the quantities.

Methods and equipment influence the measurement of excavation work. This applies more particularly to heavy engineering construction than to building projects. In heavy work, very often the quantity takeoff will not be started until equipment and methods have been predetermined. This book is mainly concerned with building construction, and the methods of measuring and estimating earthwork will follow the principles adopted by most general contractors. The various items will be categorized according to the type of operation (e.g., mass, trenching) or the function of the item for which excavation is required (e.g., basement, footing, pit, manhole, underfloor drainage).

These classifications naturally have some influence on the methods and equipment to be used. Certain items will preclude the use of one particular type of equipment, whereas others will lend themselves to a choice. For example, a scraper would hardly be considered practical to dig out a number of isolated column footings, whereas a major item of "cut and fill" would be suitable for that particular piece of equipment. The matter of final equipment selection is best left until the pricing stage of the estimate, rather than complicating the estimator's work at the takeoff stage. Discussions with superintendents and other supervisory personnel will yield sound advice, based on practical experience on earthwork operations. If necessary, the quantities could be regrouped into separate categories of selected equipment. For example:

Backhoe operation = 9,000 cyd

Scraper work = 14,000 cyd

And so on

6.2 SOIL REPORT

Most specifications make reference to a soil report, which has been authorized by the owner in the very early design stage. This is not always included as a bid document or considered a contract document. The usual directive in a specification states that this document is "available for inspection at the architect's office, or the office of the soil consultant."

A thorough examination of this soil report will be advantageous to the estimator before embarking on any takeoff work. It will be beneficial to make photocopies of this report (and be prepared to pay the cost if necessary). If this is not permitted, then the only option left is to make as many pertinent notes as possible during the examination of the document, time consuming as this might be. It is important to check the contractual status of information provided by this soil report. Most construction contracts allow compensation to the general contractor if actual conditions vary greatly from the information given in the soil report, particularly if the discrepancies could not be observed on a site visit. However, some specifications sound the ominous warning that "the soil report is provided for information only and the owner accepts no responsibility for the accuracy of the information contained therein."

Even if the soil borings and information are shown on the drawings or in the specifications, estimators should take note that these are often only a portion of or extracts from the official report. The complete document should be studied. One item experienced estimators look for is the groundwater table. The consultant's report will probably also make recommendations regarding methods to dispose of groundwater: drainage sumps, perimeter ditching, well-point systems, and the like.

6.3 COMPACTION

Just as an adjustment factor has to be allowed for the swell of excavated materials, another factor has to be considered for the compression or compaction of materials after being placed as fill in the structure. The recommendation for this item is that it should be measured as the compacted volume, with the neat quantities projected to include all allowances for compaction. In the unit-price type of contract, this compaction would obviously be included in the unit rate. For other contracts, where payments to the contractor are not to be based on measurements and prices, it would seem desirable to consider such material items in the context of the actual quantities to be purchased. Unless a site superintendent had been properly enlightened, there

TABLE 6–1 Backfill compaction factors	Soil Classification	Factor, %
	Soil	25–30
	Sand and gravel	20–25
	Crushed stone	15–20

could be misunderstandings about both the quantities of material required and the estimated unit cost of the material. Therefore, if 1000 cubic yards bank measure of a granular material is required, and the compaction percentage is considered to be 20 percent, the estimate should show a quantity of 1200 cubic yards priced at the unit rate quoted by the supplier. These materials are usually quoted by the ton (tonne), and need to be adjusted by an applicable conversion factor to cubic yards or meters.

Table 6–1 shows some recommended compaction factors for various material classifications. Estimators, engineers, superintendents, and soil consultants could debate interminably as to the right percentage to use for a specific condition. The only solution is to exercise the best possible judgment and to make use of whatever past experience is available.

6.4 MEASUREMENTS: GENERAL PRINCIPLES

Earthwork should be measured (with certain exceptions) in cubic yards (cubic meters) and to bank measure. Excavation should be stated separately for the following soil classifications:

1. Earth (this might be further divided into categories for hard, soft, or medium soil; clay; hardpan, etc.).
2. Rock or shale (again could be categorized as hard rock, soft shale, broken shale, etc.).

Excavation by machine should be measured to the full depth required by the drawings, and any final hand trimming or breaking should be measured separately and recorded as an "extra over."

Items that can only be excavated by hand (a different category from the trimming just described) should be measured and stated as separate items, and it is recommended that explanatory descriptions be included with the item (e.g., "hand excavation of shallow trenches"). Also included in this category are items that could not be excavated at the time of the major earthwork operations but do not carry a cubic volume sufficient to justify the float charges of bringing the equipment back to the site.

A working space allowance should be added to the basic dimensions. Recommended minimums are 12 inches (300 mm) plus the distance of the footing projection from the wall face or 2 feet 6 inches (750 mm) from the wall face, whichever is the greater. (These are only recommended minimums.)

Side slopes are expressed as a ratio based on the number of feet horizontal to the number of feet in depth.

EXAMPLE: A 1:1 slope requirement for a trench 10 ft deep means that the width of the excavation at the top will be 10 ft at each side of the trench.

TABLE 6–2 Side slope ratios

Soil Classification	Slope Ratio
Sand or gravel	1:1
Earth	1:1 to 1:2
Clay	1:3 to 1:4
Rock or shale	Nil.

These side slopes will vary according to the different OSHA soil classifications, but estimators should also check each state's jurisdictional body if it is not OSHA for any possible variation. Table 6–2 (OSHA side slope ratio) shows some recommended slopes according to soil classifications.

Excavation in confined and/or restricted areas should be stated separately. (Machine excavation might still be possible in such locations, but productivity would be greatly impeded.)

State whether excavated material is to be side-cast, stockpiled, or removed from the site. Some estimators measure everything as side-cast, and state the other two categories as extra over. The site plan should also be checked to ensure that stockpiling is practicable. There may not be sufficient space, and other vital operations might be impeded.

Small items requiring excavation of less than 10 cubic feet (300 mm³) each should be stated in cubic feet and the number of such items given. For example,

Excavate for small isolated piers (20 in number) = 55 cft

All work in rock should be measured separately and stated if to be drilled and blasted, ripped, or broken up with hand tools. The cleaning off of rock or shale surfaces must also be stated separately; this can be a very expensive item.

6.5 SCHEDULE OF ITEMS AND MEASUREMENTS: EXCAVATION

Item	Comment	Unit of Measurement
Clearing site	Includes the clearing and "grubbing" of all shrubs, small trees, brush, vegetable matter, etc.	Square yard or acre (Square meter or hectare)
Tree removal	This will include the grubbing and removal of the roots. On most projects this item will require a physical count at the site. The drawings do not usually give this information, unless there are only a few selected for removal. Keep separate as follows: ■ 12–24 inch diameter ■ 24–36 inch diameter ■ Over 36 inch diameter	Numerical
Protection of existing trees	Specifications and drawings may identify some trees that must be protected against damage during construction, and will describe the protective materials (wood boards, snow fence, etc.).	Numerical

continued

Item	Comment	Unit of Measurement
Breaking up of existing foundations	State material (concrete, masonry, stone, etc.) if known. Small items (isolated piers for example) should be enumerated. Existing foundations known to be heavily reinforced should be stated separately. If possible, state in separate categories for: ■ breaking up by tools such as a compressor ■ breaking up with hand tools ■ breaking up with excavation machinery	Cubic yard (m³)
Removal of rubble or debris	This item will include the removal from the site by trucks or garbage containers of the items previously measured for breaking up. An adjustment factor will be made to the net quantities to allow for "bulking." *Note:* Some estimators will prefer to amalgamate this item with the breaking up item rather than price it separately.	Cubic yard (m³)
Removal of miscellaneous obstructions	These would include but not be limited to: ■ fences and gates ■ manholes, catch basins, sumps ■ hydro poles, light standards and bases ■ small structures (sheds, garages, kiosks, etc.) ■ other existing obstructions	Linear foot (m) Each Each Each Each
Strip topsoil	This will be classified as either **a.** stockpiled, or **b.** removed from the site State average depth.	Cubic yard (m³)
Machine excavation	General classifications should be: ■ main building (basement) ■ excavate over site to reduced levels ■ spread footings, pile or caisson caps ■ trenches for foundations ■ trenches for mechanical and electrical trades ■ tunnels ■ manholes, catch basins, pits ■ other items *Note:* The main reason for keeping the excavation work for mechanical and electrical trades as separate items is that, although the architect's specifications may stipulate this work to be performed by these particular trades, some or all of these subcontractors may elect to exclude it in their bids, qualifying it as work to be done "by the general contractor." Estimators should always be prepared for such eventualities. They should also remember that such work usually demands pricing at a higher unit cost to allow for a slower rate of productivity due to the speed at which such services can be installed, and also for special excavation equipment if required.	Cubic yard (m³)

continued

Item	Comment	Unit of Measurement
Hand excavation	This falls into two categories:	
	a. Trimming, cleaning, and grading of surfaces after machine excavation. Trimming the sides and/or bottom surfaces of excavation for spread footings (or similar items) not exceeding 10 square feet (1 m²) could be *enumerated*.	Square foot (m²)
	b. Excavating for items that are too small, or shallow, or inaccessible for excavation by machine. These would include items such as small bases, thickening of concrete slabs under masonry walls, weeping tile, shallow trenches, curbs, etc.	Cubic foot (m³)
	Note: Handwork requiring double handling to be stated separately.	
Line drilling to rock surfaces	This is required to control the amount of work loosened or shattered by blasting. State depth and centers.	Linear foot (m)
Removal of caissons (or piling) spoil	This item is quite often identified as an "exclusion" in quotations from piling subcontractors.	Cubic yard (m³)
Stripping overburden	This is an operation within the category of machine excavation, but should be shown as a separate item. State if less than 18 inches deep (450 mm).	Cubic yard (m³)

6.6   FILL AND BACKFILL: GENERAL

As already stated, all fill and backfill operations should be measured to provide the total compacted quantities. This means that a percentage will be added to the net quantities to allow for the necessary additional volume of material.

The specifications should be checked carefully regarding the possible use of excavated materials for fill and backfill. A common phrase in a specification is that this material can be used "if approved by the architect or engineer," a statement that rarely gives any comfort or feeling of confidence to an estimator.

Where the degree of compaction is specified as a percentage (e.g., 95% Proctor) and a specific grade of material is also specified, the estimator is advised to check with the material supplier (possible gravel pits) to ascertain that the required compaction can be obtained with that material. If the suppliers express any doubts, the architect or engineer should be consulted. The contention here might be that the contractor could allow for another grade of material in the bid, which would give the specified compaction, but this material might be more costly and would affect the competitive nature of the contractor's bid.

Fills and backfill should be measured and stated separately according to the (1) material classification, and (2) compaction requirements.

Items such as small holes, pockets, bases, in fact anything with a volume of less than 3 cubic feet, should be measured separately in cubic feet and the total number stated.

Where underfloor fill or bedding is placed on rock surfaces, an additional thickness of material should be allowed for overbreak. This additional thickness could range from 3 inches (75 mm) to 6 inches (150 mm) or greater according to the estimator's judgment of site conditions.

6.7 SCHEDULE OF ITEMS AND MEASUREMENTS: FILL AND MISCELLANEOUS EARTHWORK ITEMS

Item	Comment	Unit of Measurement
Backfill	Recommended separate items for: ■ fill to grade or under slabs ■ perimeter foundations (this could be further divided into outside and inside faces if different labor and equipment methods were pertinent) ■ spread footings, pile or caisson caps ■ miscellaneous pits, manholes, catch basins ■ mechanical and electrical trenches Estimators should make some judgment (where possible) between backfill items that require placing solely "by hand," as opposed to those locations where the fill can be machine deposited into place, with handwork necessary only for trimming and compacting. All backfill at underpinning or perimeter shoring work must be stated as separate items. The placing of backfill to fill the small space left after the removal of timber lagging (mandatory in some areas) is a costly item.	Cubic yard (m³)
Underfloor fill to concrete slabs	State if stone, gravel, or sand. It may be necessary to keep separate underfloor bedding to small platforms, pits, steps, and similar. Also bedding to walkways and sidewalks should be treated as separate items.	Cubic yard (m³)
Bed and surround to drainage tile	Should be kept separate for interior and exterior locations.	Cubic yard (m³)
Spread topsoil	Stated as separate items for: ■ excavated and hauled from stockpile ■ imported topsoil It is also necessary to separate the placing of topsoil to planting beds, or plants, all of which would have to be hand placed.	Cubic yard (m³)
Sand blinding over stone or gravel	This is often required to receive a polyethylene vapor barrier. Because of the loss in stone or gravel voids, a waste percentage should be allowed, or it might be more practical to increase the specified thickness by an additional 1 inch (or more if the estimator considered it necessary.)	Cubic yard (m³)
Drainage tile	State diameter of pipe and material classification. The total length of pipe measured should include all "specials" (e.g., tapers, wye pieces, bends), but these items should be enumerated as separate items for extra over to material costs only. (This is really up to the estimator's discretion; preference might be to measure and state every item in detail.)	Linear foot (m)
Vapor barrier under floor slabs	Describe the material and allow 5 percent to 10 percent for laps.	Square foot (m²)
Timber sheeting	This would be required in locations where sloping was not practical, and would particularly apply to trench for pipes or conduits. Keep separate categories for light, medium, or heavy. Keep separate if to be machine driven.	Square foot (m²)

6.8   PERIMETER PILING AND SHORING

This is usually a mandatory requirement in large projects in the downtown areas of towns and cities where side sloping is restricted. This is an operation that is becoming increasingly common for a general contractor to subcontract to a specialist company. However, there are certain items of work that are not always included by these subcontractors, or the quotations might only reflect unit rates for the applicable items, requiring the general contractor to compute the quantities.

The following is a checklist of some items to be considered for an estimate of this work, with some recommendations regarding measurements:

1. Preboring for H-piles (state diameter and total length).
2. Driving H-piles (linear foot or meter). (Note: Items 1 and 2 would probably be quoted by a specialist contractor either on a lump sum or unit-rate basis.)
3. Lean concrete fill to piles, including subsequent removal. State in cubic yards (m^3).
4. Concrete fill to base of piles. State in cubic feet (m^3).
5. Timber lagging. State the type of wood and the thickness, and also if creosoting is required. Measure this item in square feet (m^2) and state if removal is also necessary (or state as two separate items).
6. Rakers, walers, struts, and the like. If not included by the subcontractor, these items should be measured and stated in tons (tonnes).
7. Sand fill behind lagging should be measured in cubic yards (m^3).
8. Mobile crane, welding and burning equipment, cables, slings, and the like.

Other items to be considered in their applicable trade divisions would be the excavation of the berm; concrete footings ("deadmen") for the rakers, provision of holes through the concrete wall and slabs (i.e., the formwork) for the rakers, raker and tie-back pockets (including subsequent filling in and making good); and setting and grouting of miscellaneous base plates and anchor bolts. Other items that might be excluded from a subcontractor's quotation would include:

1. Removal of lagging and upper portion of H-pile where required by a municipality.
2. Demolition and removal of sidewalks and any excavation and backfill to facilitate the removal of lagging and piles, and in some circumstances, the removal of the rakers.

In some instances the subcontractors might quote for the complete work on the basis of a unit rate per square foot, in which case only the net face area of the earth to be supported would be measured.

6.9   UNDERPINNING

Excavation work to locations where underpinning is required will be measured separately as already stated; the same will apply to applicable concrete and formwork. Other items to be taken into account with underpinning operations include:

1. Timber sheathing against the earth at each section or "pit" of underpinning. (The sequence in which these sections will be worked is usually noted on the drawings.) This sheathing can be measured in either square feet (m^2) or per board foot measure (m^3) of lumber.

2. Grouting at the point where the new wall comes into contact with the bottom of the existing wall or footing. This should be measured in cubic feet (m^3) to both the sides and the rear portion of the pit. The sheathing at the rear of the pit will need to be noted as "left in place."

6.10   DEWATERING

The rental and operation of pumping equipment for removal of water from the excavation is usually included in the estimate of site overhead or indirect job costs. For sites where the specification or soil reports indicate excessively high groundwater content, it will be necessary to consider other methods of removing the water, such as well-point installations or the provision of relief wells.

Well-point systems are provided by specialist companies, usually on a monthly rental basis. On major projects where the equipment will be required for a lengthy time period, the specialist company will often quote higher rental rates for the first, second, and third months, and a lower rate for the ensuing months. Jet-eductor equipment (if applicable) will usually be quoted separately. Other items to be considered when analyzing a proposal from a dewatering specialist would include:

1. Installation and removal of the equipment, sometimes quoted on a per diem basis.

2. Operation of the system, also on a per diem basis. If not provided by the specialist company, the estimator will have to allow for the total hours and rates of operating engineers.

3. Freight and loading charges (at the specialist company's yard).

4. Unloading and loading costs at the site. This will usually have to be done by the contractor's work force.

5. Charges for electric service.

If it is considered that the dewatering can be handled by the installation of relief or deep wells, the following items should be considered:

1. Drilling for the casings, per linear foot (m), stating the diameter.

2. Supply and placing of the casings, per linear foot (m).

3. Granular filter surround to casings, per cubic yard (m^3).

4. Pump equipment, rental or purchase.

5. Additional hose, per linear foot (m).

6. Electrical wiring, item.

7. Removal of surplus soil cuttings, cubic yard (m^3).

8. Screen sections, per linear foot (m) stating the width.

9. Attendance on pumping equipment, total man-hours.

Other dewatering systems, or variations on the systems described, are available for consideration. Soil engineering consultants and dewatering specialists should be contacted for advice and proposals.

6.11 DEMOLITION

This is also a division of sitework (Masterformat 02050), although the demolition work usually measured and priced by general contractors is for the breaking out and removal of parts of an existing structure. The complete demolition of existing buildings is usually subcontracted to demolition or wrecking contractors. Very often a new building will connect into or be adjacent to an existing building, a new hospital or university wing, for example, and the contract will require the contractor to perform renovations and alterations in that building. This work would include the breaking out and removal of partitions, ceilings, flooring, miscellaneous concrete or masonry, and similar items.

There are three separate cost factors involved in most of these items:

1. The actual breaking out, with hand tools or pneumatic or similar equipment.

2. Removing the rubble or debris to a location where it can be loaded into a truck or special garbage container. This could involve wheeling barrows along corridors, down freight or other elevators, through exits to the exterior ground level. If this was in an existing hospital, for example, where the normal activities of such an institute were to be unimpaired by construction work, the productivity factor would be exceedingly low.

3. The loading up of a truck or container, either by hand or with a front-end loader.

It is recommended that factors 1 and 2 be considered as one operation for measuring and pricing purposes. It would be difficult to allocate separate costs with any real accuracy. Factor 3, on the other hand, would often be a separate operation done periodically, and could be more easily identified for cost allocation. An exception to this ruling would occur when the debris could be wheeled to a rubbish chute for instant deposit into a truck or container.

Although a considerable amount of quantities of demolition items can be taken off from the drawings, a site visit is essential to fully appreciate all the items and work to be considered. Also, certain items may not be spelled out in the written documents but could only be inferred from the description of other work to be done. For example, the drawings and specification might contain a schedule of locations where existing ceilings were to be removed and new ceilings installed, but make no reference to other areas where the removal of ceilings would be essential for mechanical and electrical renovations.

Dustproof partitions will sometimes be shown and specified for certain locations and at defined stages of construction. More often than not, the specifications will stress the obligatory provision of these partitions, describing the construction details, but leaving the scheduling and location details to the contractor's judgment.

Items that are to be removed and later reinstalled or relocated should preferably be split into separate items, one for the removal and another for the reinstallation or relocation. Where new materials are to be installed in lieu of replacing the existing materials, they will often be specified in their appropriate trade divisions (gypsum wallboard, tile, acoustic ceilings, etc.), and the estimate should allow for this work being included in the trade contractors' quotations for those sections.

The following schedule refers to some of the items of demolition work usually performed by general contractors in projects where renovations and alterations are necessary. Large items of mechanical and electrical work or other specialized trade items (sections of aluminum curtain, for example) should be stated as lump-sum items and the appropriate trade contractors consulted if necessary.

6.12 SCHEDULE OF ITEMS AND MEASUREMENTS: DEMOLITION

Item	Comment	Unit of Measurement
Break up and remove:	*(Note: removal is to a place for loading into trucks, to a rubbish chute, or to storage)*	
Exterior masonry	State type of material (e.g., brick, block, or a combination). Keep separate walls greater than 10 feet in height.	Cubic foot (m³)
Interior masonry partition	State type of material.	Cubic foot (m³)
Existing concrete	State separately and describe according to location and function (e.g., slab, footing, wall).	Cubic foot (m³)
Strip roofing and flashings		Square foot (m²)
Ceilings	State separately for plaster, gypsum wallboard, acoustic tile, or other materials. State if suspension system included.	Square foot (m²)
Nonresilient finishes	State if tile, terrazzo, marble, quarry tile, etc.	Square foot (m²)
Glazed wood partitions		Square foot (m²)
Metal roof or floor decks		Square foot (m²)
Resilient tile and base	Allow for cleaning off of adhesive.	Square foot (m²)
Existing doors and frames	State average size and if metal or wood.	Each
Existing windows and frames	State material, also average size if enumerated.	Square foot (m²) or each
Load and remove debris	State if into trucks or containers.	Cubic foot (m³)
Dust screens	Keep separate: ■ fabrication ■ relocation ■ dismantle and removal	Square foot (m²)

6.13 TAKEOFF EXAMPLE

Figure 6–2 provides an example of quantity takeoff for earthwork. The plot plan (Figure 5–3) and foundation plan (Figure 5–9) provide most of the information applicable to this trade section. The following brief specification notes supplement the data provided on the drawings:

Strip topsoil average 6 in., stockpile on site.

Excavated material for backfill at exterior side of perimeter foundations.

Backfill at other locations: imported granular fill.

Stone underfill to concrete slabs on ground.

6-in. diameter perforated drainage pipe and fittings.

Pea gravel surround to drainage pipe.

Remove surplus excavated material from site (dump—2-mile haul).

QUANTITIES

Project	**Research Center**		Estimate No. **27/82**
Location			By **B.E.W.** Chk'd **H.A.J.**
Subdivision	**02200 - Earthwork**		Date **4/1/99**

Description of Work	No. Pieces	Dimensions			Extensions	Unit	Extensions	Unit	Extensions	Unit
					Area 1		Area 2		Area 3	
Refer to Site Plan										
					3 0 4 .2 8		3 0 3 .3 3		3 0 2 .7 5	
Gr. Flr = 300.00					3 0 3 .3 4		3 0 3 .3 4		3 0 3 .3 3	
6" slab = .50					3 0 2 .8 4		3 0 2 .8 4		3 0 2 .6 7	
299.50					3 0 3 .8 4		3 0 2 .6 7		3 0 2 .1 5	
8" stone = .67					1 2 1 4 .3 0		1 2 1 2 .6 8		1 2 1 0 .9 0	
298.83										
			Average =		3 0 3 .5 8		3 0 3 .1 7		3 0 2 .7 3	
			Less 6" topsoil		.5 0		.5 0		.5 0	
					3 0 3 .0 8		3 0 2 .6 7		3 0 2 .2 3	
			Areas 1, 2, 3		Avg. Grade					
					3 0 3 .0 8					
					3 0 2 .6 7					
					3 0 2 .2 3					
					9 0 7 .9 8 /3 =		3 0 2 .6 6			
			Less u/side of Fill				2 9 8 .8 3			
			average depth of cut (3'10") =				3 .8 3			
Basement Floor = 290.00					Area 4					
Slab + Floor = 1.17										
288.83					3 0 3 .6 7					
					3 0 5 .2 6					
					3 0 3 .3 3					
					3 0 2 .7 5					
					1 2 1 5 .6 1 /3 =		3 0 3 .7 5			
			Less 6" topsoil				.5 0			
							3 0 3 .2 5			
			Less u/side of Fill				2 9 8 .8 3			
			average depth of cut (14'5") =				1 4 .4 2			

FIGURE 6–2 Example of quantity takeoff of earthwork.

continued

Project   *Research Center*   Estimate No.   *27/82*
Location   By   *B.E.W.*   Chk'd   *H.A.J.*
Subdivision   *02200 - Earthwork*   Date   *4/1/99*

Description of Work	No. Pieces	Dimensions A	B	C	Extensions	Unit	Extensions	Unit	Extensions	Unit
					Excavation A x B x C		Hand Trim Surface A x B			
Mass Excavation to Building										
Areas 1 & 2		100' 0"								
+working space		2' 6"								
		102' 6"								
		50' 0"								
work space - 2' x 2' 6"		5' 0"								
		55' 0"								
Area 3		50' 0"								
	w/s	2' 6"								
		52' 6"								
		50' 0"								
Deduct wall		(1' 0")								
		49' 0"								
		102.42	55.0				5 6 3 8 .0	Sft.		
		52.42	49.0	3.08	3 1 4 7 2		2 5 7 3 .0	Sft.		
Area 4		50' 0"								
	wall	1' 0"								
w/s - 2' x 2' 6"		5' 0"								
		56' 0"								
slope - (14' 5" x 2) / 2 =		14' 5"								
		70' 5"								
		50' 0"								
	w/s (2)	5' 0"								
	slope	14' 5"								
		69' 5"								
		70.42	69.42	14.42	7 0 4 7 0		4 8 8 8	sft.		
adjust line "C"		(69.42)	(8.9)	(3.83)	(2 3 7 3)		(6 1 9)	sft.		
"Side Slopes for Trench Excav (Refer Sketch)										
Area 1			55.0							
	5' 6"		2/ 50.0							
4' 3"	2' 2"		2/ 7.67	7.67	4.25	5 5 5 0				
2	7 '8"		2/ 50.0	7.5	4.0	3 0 0 0				
			52.5							
Area 2			49.0							
	5 '6"		7.25	7.25	3.42	2 6 9 4				
4' 0"	2' 0"									
2	7' 6"					1 1 0 8 1 3	cft.	1 2 4 8 0	sft.		
Area 3				=	4 1 0 4	cyd.				
	5' 6"									
3' 5"	1' 9"									
2	7' 3"									

FIGURE 6–2   Example of quantity takeoff of earthwork.

continued

Project	**Research Center**						Estimate No. **27/82**					
Location							By **B.E.W.** Chk'd **H.A.J.**					
Subdivision	**02200 - Earthwork**						Date **4/1/99**					

Description of Work	No. Pieces	A	B	C	Extensions	Unit	Extensions	Unit	Extensions	Unit
Trench Excav. For Footings					**Trench Excav** **A x B x C**		**Trim Bottom** **A x 6'0"**			
Measured from elev.		298.83								
u/side foooting -		293.33								
		5.50								
Width of Wall		1' 0"								
w/s 2 x 2' 6"		5' 0"								
slope (2 x 5' 6") / 2 =		5' 6"								
		11' 6"								
		50' 0"								
2 x 5' 9"		(11' 6")		2' 6"						
		38' 6"		2' 9"						
				5' 3"						
		50' 0"								
		(6' 9")								
		43' 3"								
Line C	2/	100.0								
	2/	5.25								
		38.5								
		50.0								
		5.25								
		43.25	11.5	5.5	2 1 7 9 0		2 0 8 5			
Stepped footings	2/ 1/2	12.0	6.0	4.5	3 2 4		7 2			
1' 0"	2/2(1/2	12.0	4.5	7.83	8 3 7		1 4 4			
2 x 2' 6" = 5' 0"										
6' 0"										
293.33										
(288.83)										
4.50										
5' 6"										
1/2 x 4' 6" = 2' 3"										
7' 9"										
Adjust b/ment Excav.										
	2/	11.0	16.0	10.0	(3 5 2 0)					
1" 0"	1' 0"									
2' 6"	5' 0"									
7' 6"	6' 0"									
11'0"	10' 0"									
	16'0"									
5' 6"										
4' 6"										
10' 0"						AxB				
Perim. Col. Ftgs.	13/	5.5	2	5.5	7 8 7		1 4 3			
	2/	5.5	2	10	2 2 0		2 2			
					2 0 6 2 7	cft.	2 4 6 6	sft.		
				=	7 6 4	cyd.				

FIGURE 6–2 Example of quantity takeoff of earthwork.

continued

Project	Research Center		Estimate No. 27/82
Location			By _B.E.W._ Chk'd _H.A.J._
Subdivision	02200 - Earthwork		Date _4/1/99_

Description of Work	No. Pieces	Dimensions A	Dimensions B	Dimensions C	Extensions	Unit	Extensions	Unit	Extensions	Unit
					Excavation		Hand Trim			
					A x B x C		? X 16' 0"			
Excav Int. Col.										
Footings										
4' 0"										
2 x 1' 0" 2' 0"	5/	12.0	12.0	6.0	4 3 2 0	cf	8 0	sf		
slope										
2 x 3' 0" 6' 0"										
12' 0"										
					1 6 0	cy				
Backfill-Perimeter Foundations					Ext B/fill		Int B/fill			
					(Excav soil)		(Imported Granular)			
					A x B x C		A x B x C			
Backfill to (Assumed) New Exterior Grade										
300.00	slab									
1.50	less									
298.50										
293.33	U/side Ftg									
5.17										
1/2 x 5' 2" = 2' 7"										
w/space 2' 6" line "E"		150.0								
5' 1" line 7		50.0								
line "C"		100.0	5.08	5.17	7 8 7 9					
Deduct B/ment	2/	(10.0)	(5.08)	(5.17)	(5 2 5)					
1/2 x 14' 11" =										
7' 6" line 1		50.0	5.08	5.17	1 3 1 3					
w/s 2' 6" steps	2/ 1/2	12.0	2.5	4.5	1 3 5					
10' 0"	2/ 1/2	12.0	4.5	7.75	4 1 9					
corners	3/	5.17	5.17	5.17	4 1 4					
basement	2/	60.75								
50' 0"	50' 0"	59.8	7.25	9.67	1 2 0 7 3					
4' 9") 9' 9" 4'9")										
5' 0") 59' 9" 1'0")										
5'0") 10' 9"										
60' 9"										
4' 9" 298.50										
2' 6" 288.83	Interior	149.0								
7' 3" 9.67	2/	48.0								
		100.0	5.17	5.5			9 8 0 4			
corners	3/	(5.17)	(5.17)	(5.5)			(4 4 0)			
col line "C"		49.0	7.5	10.0			3 6 7 5			
					2 2 3 3 8		1 3 0 3 9			
298.83	Compaction = 20%				4 4 6 8		3 2 6 0	25%		
288.83					2 6 8 0 6		1 6 2 9 9			
10.0										
					9 9 3	cy	6 0 4	cy		

FIGURE 6–2 Example of quantity takeoff of earthwork.

continued

Project **Research Center**

Location _____

Subdivision **02200 - Earthwork**

Estimate No. **27/82**

By **B.E.W.** Chk'd **H.A.J.**

Date **4/1/99**

Description of Work	No. Pieces	Dimensions A	B	C	Extensions	Unit	Extensions	Unit	Extensions	Unit
					A x B x C					
B/fill to Interior Column Footings										
Total Excav Volume (sheet 4) =					4 3 2 0					
Deduct Concrete	5/	(4.0)	(4.0)	(1.17)	(9 3)					
	2/	(3.33)	(3.33)	(.67)	(1 5)					
Piers	5/	(1.0)	(1.0)	(4.83)	(2 4)					
					4 1 8 8					
compaction 20%					8 3 8					
					5 0 2 6	cf				
					1 8 6	cy				
Stone fill to U/side										
Concrete Floor Slab					*A x B x C*					
		148.0	48.0							
		48.0	49.75	.67	6 3 0 4					
Add 20% compaction					1 2 6 1					
					7 5 6 5	cf				
					2 8 0	cy				
Weeping tile at					Pipe A		Surround			
Perimeter B/ment walls							*A x B x C*			
	2/	50.0								
	2/	51.0								
	4/2/	0.08	3.5	4.75	2 0 9	lf	3 4 6 9			
						+ 20%	6 9 4			
							4 1 6 3			
						divide 27 =			1 5 4	cy
Excav Interior Trenches for					Excav		B/fill			
Mechanical Services					*A x B x C*		*A x B x C*			
		150.0								
		100.0								
	4/	50.0	7.0	4.75	1 4 9 6 3		1 4 9 6 3			
							2 9 9 3	20%		
							1 7 9 5 6			
								divide 27		
					= 5 5 4	cy		=	6 6 5	cy

FIGURE 6–2 Example of quantity takeoff of earthwork.

continued

COMMENTARY ON EARTHWORK TAKEOFF

1. Refer to Figure 6–2, Sheet 1. In this example the building area has been subdivided into four separate areas (or rectangles) as defined by the existing elevations noted on the perimeter wall lines. The average existing grade is determined for each of these areas.

   The first operation will be stripping of topsoil over the entire site (these measurements are not shown). The average depth of the topsoil is 6 inches (150 mm), and the average existing grade elevations are adjusted to allow for this preliminary operation. The thickness of the concrete floor slab and the underfloor fill are deducted from the average grade elevation (302.66) to establish the grade to which the cut will be made (298.83).

   Areas 1, 2, and 3 could have been computed as a total area, and the average grade levels and depth of cut calculated as follows (refer to Figure 6–3):

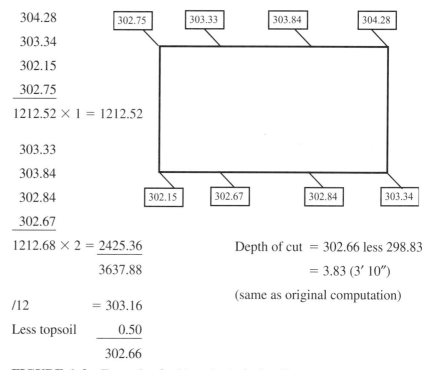

304.28

303.34

302.15

302.75
_____

1212.52 × 1 = 1212.52

303.33

303.84

302.84

302.67
_____

1212.68 × 2 = 2425.36
                 _____
                 3637.88

/12   = 303.16

Less topsoil   0.50
                 _____
                 302.66

Depth of cut = 302.66 less 298.83

= 3.83 (3′ 10″)

(same as original computation)

FIGURE 6–3   Example of grid method of takeoff.

   A more accurate computation of excavation depth would be achieved by "shooting" a series of additional levels at regular intervals at the site, and plotting the results on a grid on the drawing. Each grid would then be computed separately and the results aggregated to a total. This method is most useful for determining "cut and fill" quantities.

   In this example the excavation for the basement (Area 4) has been computed from the original ground level (average 303.75). In practice the excavator would probably excavate over all the areas to the reduced level at 298.83, and the basement would then be excavated from this level; many estimates would show the quantities computed on this basis. The "end result" in the computed quantities would be the same whichever method of measurement was followed.

2. Refer to Figure 6–2, Sheet 2. The side calculations demonstrate how the given dimensions are extended (or reduced) to provide for (a) working space, and (b) side slopes (in this instance 1:1 slopes). The calculations for line 1 at Area 3 make no mention of working space. This is because the addition of this dimension at E is offset by the required deduction at C to allow for the basement excavation in Area 4.

   The adjustment for line C is necessary to compensate for that portion of the excavation to the basement already included in the measurements for excavation to elevation 298.83 (see Figure 6–4).

   The adjustments to allow for the future side slopes to the trench excavation have been added to this mass excavation item on the assumption the excavator would be alerted to this necessity and perform the work at this time. Also, mass excavation can usually be performed at a cheaper rate than trench excavation. It has also been assumed that the exterior grading to reduce the existing levels to this new finished grade of 298.50 would be done at a later date. The sketch on the takeoff sheets (Figure 6–4) illustrates the intent of these adjustments.

3. The last item on Sheet 3 shows measurements for the additional width of the perimeter column footings. In practice an excavator would most likely dig the continuous perimeter trench to the width to accommodate these footings, and many estimators would measure the quantities on this basis. In this instance the additional volume is not very significant, but on large complex projects this could amount to a fairly substantial quantity. It must always be remembered that trenching such as this also increases the backfill quantities; this could become quite costly if a special grade of imported fill material was specified.

4. Refer to Sheets 4 and 5. The backfill measurements are from the trench bottom to elevation 298.50, which is 1 foot 6 inches below the finished ground floor level. The material to the interior side of the trenches is an imported granular fill.

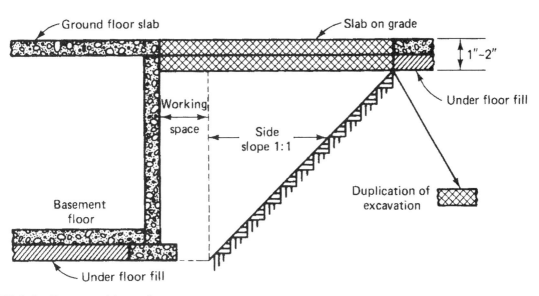

FIGURE 6–4 Basement/sitework.

5. The weeping tile and the pea gravel surrounding are not shown on the drawings. No deductions are made in the backfill and surround quantities to compensate for displacement by the piping.

6. The interior trenches for mechanical piping are not detailed on the drawings, and the examples are given for a demonstration of measuring and pricing. In practice these details would probably only appear on the Mechanical drawings, supplemented by a statement in the specifications that "excavation and backfill are the responsibility of the general contractor."

7 TAKEOFF: CONCRETE AND FORMWORK

7.1 CONCRETE: GENERAL

The various items applicable to the supply and placing of concrete should be taken off and described according to:

1. Material classification regarding strength mix, aggregate, and so on.
2. Specific function in the structure (e.g., footing, slab, beam).

A typical estimate item might be "3,000 pounds per square inch (p.s.i.) concrete in perimeter wall footings." The "3,000 p.s.i. concrete" refers to the material classification and the "perimeter wall footings" describes the structural function. If addenda to the specifications changed this item so that it now became "4,000 p.s.i. concrete in perimeter wall footings," the only difference in the estimated cost would be in the price from the ready-mix concrete supplier. The labor cost of placing the concrete would remain unchanged, as it is not affected by the change in strength mix. Equally, a second item of "3,000 p.s.i. concrete in foundation walls" would show the same price for material, but a different unit for placing the concrete than was stated for the perimeter footings.

The material cost is dependent on the specified classification for strength mix and other factors. The structural function, size, and location of the item influence the labor cost. To avoid a lot of repetitious pricing of identical material items, it is recommended that when all the items have been taken off they be regrouped into separate categories for pricing purposes as follows:

1. Concrete materials: aggregate all the items pertinent to a particular mix (say, 3,000 p.s.i. concrete) and transfer the total quantity for this material category to the estimate summary for pricing. Adoption of this method eliminates the repetition of the same material price against a large number of items and also reduces the number of arithmetical extensions to be made and checked. Also, the supplier's prices for ready-mix concrete are usually related to the quantities applicable to the particular strength mixes. This method enables estimators to quickly identify and estimate quantities of each mix when asked by the ready-mix supplier.

2. Concrete placing: collection of the items into separate categories according to their structural functions.

EXAMPLE: The quantity take-off sheets record the following items and quantities:

3000 p.s.i. concrete to perimeter footings	30 cyd
3000 p.s.i. concrete to foundation walls	70 cyd
3000 p.s.i. concrete to slab-on-grade	100 cyd
4000 p.s.i. concrete in suspended slab and beams	200 cyd
4000 p.s.i. concrete in columns	80 cyd

To facilitate pricing, these would be regrouped into the following categories:

Concrete Materials

3000 p.s.i. concrete	200 cyd
4000 p.s.i. concrete	280 cyd

Concrete Placing

Perimeter footings	30 cyd
Foundation walls	70 cyd
Slab-on-grade	100 cyd, and so on accordingly

This method of collection into categories will be further demonstrated in the examples of takeoff and pricing for concrete work.

The general unit of measurement for concrete is the cubic yard (cubic meter). Concrete should be rounded up to the nearest .5 cubic yard: e.g., 1.23 cubic yards is stated as 1.5 cubic yards. Concrete items with small quantities (less than 5 cubic yards) are also given in cubic yards, while grout in small quantities may be given in cubic feet for the cost of placing. One must be careful in pricing the placing of small quantities of concrete. In the metric system no such convenient unit as a cubic foot exists. There is, of course, nothing to prevent estimators from using the cubic foot formulas in a metric designed project if they so wish. All that is necessary is a "soft conversion" to cubic yards and then dividing by 27. Where a total quantity represents the aggregate of a number of small items spread throughout the structure (e.g., small equipment bases or pedestals) then both the concrete volume and the number of the items should be stated.

EXAMPLE: Place concrete to equipment pedestals (15 each) = 30 cft = 1.5 cyd. It will be easier to take a more realistic approach when pricing these items. The displacement of concrete by reinforcing steel or other items embedded in the concrete will not be taken into account, and no adjustment will be made to the quantities.

All work applicable to architectural concrete must be kept separate. The usual criteria for concrete work under this heading is that little or nothing will be done to the concrete after the forms have been stripped—no patching or rubbing and, sometimes, no cleaning. However, estimators should take note that, where walls in architectural concrete are of a considerable height and require to be poured in lifts, there could be a seepage of concrete at the upper lifts, which would run down to the lower part already placed and stripped. To avoid staining, this should be cleaned off immediately. Therefore, an item of cleaning should be measured in square feet (square meters); also an item for protection with polyethylene might be necessary, as additional to the cleaning.

Most ready-mix concrete suppliers quote special charges for underloads usually grouped into the categories of:

Less than 6 cubic yards

Less than 5 cubic yards

Less than 4 cubic yards

Less than 3 cubic yards

with a charge per load for each category, ranging from $10.00 to $30.00.

Also, these quotations are subject to a maximum discharge time, usually 30 minutes per load or 10 minutes per cubic meter (whichever is the greater), and a demurrage charge is made for additional time at a rate per fifteen minute interval.

Where concrete is to be placed with a concrete pump, there is an invariable additional charge per cubic yard (say $10.00) for pump mix of all mixes less than 4,000 p.s.i.

Estimators have to exercise judgment regarding the inclusion in their estimates for these special premium charges on ready-mix concrete. The decision might be made to assess them as accurately as possible and price them accordingly, or a contingency item might be included for "ready-mix premiums" providing a quantity and rate per cubic yard is established, which (hopefully) would be close to the average amount actually expended. The most important thing is to be realistic and aware that such charges exist and some money will have to be expended on them during the course of the job.

7.2 | SCHEDULE OF ITEMS AND MEASUREMENTS: CONCRETE

Item	Comment	Unit of Measurement
Concrete materials	State in separate categories of strength, mix, and aggregate. This item may require a small percentage factor to allow for waste or surplus quantity not placed.	Cubic yard (m³)
Admixtures a. admixtures integral with ready-mix concrete: air entrainment retarding admixture	State separately from the item with which it is to be integrated, and described as "Extra for . . . type of admixture."	Cubic yard (m³)

continued

Item	Comment	Unit of Measurement
b. admixtures nonintegral with ready-mix	State according to manufacturer's unit of sale (e.g., a waterproofing compound might be sold in liquid form, and would therefore be stated in gallons or quarts.) The applicable quantity would be calculated according to the manufacturer's recommendations.	Gallon, pound, etc. (liter, kilogram)
Winter delivery	This is a charge made by ready-mix companies for the heating of the concrete during certain winter months. (This varies according to the region of the country, usually within the November to May limit.) The estimator must assess all concrete quantities to be purchased and placed during this period, and state the item as being "extra over" the basic cost of the concrete.	Cubic yard (m³)
Calcium chloride	Keep separate as 1% or 2%.	Cubic yard (m³)
Placing concrete: a. wall footings b. spread footings c. pile or caisson caps d. grade beams	Where concrete is to be placed on rock or shale, an allowance should be made for additional quantity necessary to compensate for rock "overbreak." This could vary from an additional 3 to 6 inches or more, according to the estimator's judgment.	Cubic yard (m³)
Walls: a. foundation walls and pilasters b. superstructure: shear walls elevator core walls stair walls c. misc. walls to: pits loading docks ramps	The various categories are given as a recommended "checklist" and estimators may expand into additional items, or amalgamate where it is not considered the cost will differ considerably or the quantities are not significantly large. Interior foundation walls should be stated separately from perimeter walls if different placing methods are to be considered (e.g., poured with slab for example).	Cubic yard (m³)
Retaining walls		Cubic yard (m³)
Dwarf walls	Applies to walls with heights of less than 3 feet (1 m) and includes but is not limited to such items as parapets, balconies, balustrades, and similar.	Cubic yard (m³)
Columns and piers	Measured to the underside of suspended slab or soffit of beam or drop slab. Where capitals occur they should be included with this item.	Cubic yard (m³)
Skim slab on grade	This is usually not greater than 3 inches thick, and additional depth should be allowed for concrete loss (1 inch to 2 inches). Skim slabs under wall footings, small pits, etc. should be measured and stated separately.	Cubic yard (m³)
Slabs on grade or fill including but not limited to: a. floors b. ramps c. pits d. loading docks	Apply an adjustment factor to compensate for concrete loss in ground or fill, either a percentage or additional depth of 1 to 3 inches. Where placed on rock, allow additional 3 to 6 inches or more, according to the estimator's judgment of the conditions.	Cubic yard (m³)
Slab on waterproofing membrane	This slab is placed over the membrane material, which is then installed on the skim slab. There is no adjustment necessary for concrete seepage or uneven grade surfaces.	Cubic yard (m³)

continued

Item	Comment	Unit of Measurement
Suspended slabs: a. flat slabs		Cubic yard (m³)
b. beam and slab	Although the beams will be measured separately, the quantities will be added to and included with the slab quantities for pricing, as concrete for both slabs and beams is placed at the same time, and cost separation is very difficult.	
c. slabs on structural steel		
d. slabs on: metal pans, waffle pans	The normal method is to measure the slab to the gross depth and then deduct the displacement volume of the pans or waffles to arrive at the net quantity.	
e. slabs on fiber tubes	Measure as for pans.	
f. slabs with tile fillers	Measure as for pans.	
g. slabs on V-rib forms	Allowance should be made for deflection minimum 30%.	
Fireproofing structural steel a. beams		Cubic yard (m³)
b. columns	Measured to underside of slab or beam.	
Stairs	Include treads, risers, landings, soffits. Keep interior and exterior stairs separate.	Cubic yard (m³)
Exterior slabs on grade or fill	Allow for concrete loss due to seepage.	Cubic yard (m³)
Exterior steps	Allow for concrete loss due to seepage.	Cubic yard (m³)
Curbs: a. exterior		Cubic yard (m³)
b. interior	If isolated throughout building in small quantities (e.g., around showers, to lockers)	
Equipment bases a. large b. small	State number if there are many spread throughout the building. This presents a more realistic picture for purposes of pricing.	Cubic yard (m³)
Floor toppings: a. separate b. monolithic	Thickness of topping should be stated. Toppings with traprock aggregate should be kept separate.	Cubic yard (m³)
Fill to steel stair pans	State in cubic meters for metric measurements.	Cubic foot (m³)
Trenches		Cubic yard (m³)
Duct banks		Cubic yard (m³)
Manholes and catchbasins	Include walls and base.	Cubic yard (m³)
Pipe bed and surround		Cubic yard (m³)
Light standard bases	Include total number of bases.	Cubic foot (m³)
Miscellaneous Items		
Base plates, setting and grouting	State average size. Keep separate if greater than 2 ft 6 in. × 2 ft 6 in. This item will include the grout materials. Some estimators may prefer this item for grout to be measured and stated in cubic feet.	Numerical
Anchor bolt	State diameter and keep separate as follows: ■ not exceeding 3 ft in length (1 m) ■ exceeding 3 ft, not exceeding 6 ft ■ 6 ft and over	Numerical

continued

Item	Comment	Unit of Measurement
Expansion joints:		
a. less than 12 in. wide	State thickness, width, and material classification.	Linear foot (m)
b. 12 in. wide and larger	As above, but excluding the width.	Square foot (m^2)
Liquid joint filler	State width and thickness.	Linear foot (m)
Finishing formed concrete surfaces:	This item includes patching of tie holes, cleaning and rubbing of exposed concrete. Keep separate according to specification: sack rub, grinding, etc.	Square foot (m^2)
a. walls and columns		
b. soffits and beams		
c. curbs		
d. stair risers		
Steel fireproofing (mesh wrapping)	State gauge, etc. Add factor for lapping and waste.	Square foot (m^2)
Miscellaneous embedded items	This would include such items as plates, lintels, steel angles, lintel anchors, bolts, etc. Estimators should use their own judgment as to the most suitable method for takeoff and pricing. Generally a numerical count will be sufficient for plates, lintel anchors, bolts, etc. Other items may be stated in square or linear feet; and in some cases these items might be stated by weight in pounds or kilograms. It is very important to make a distinction among embedded items that must be attached to the formwork (e.g., inserts for shelf angles). These become a labor on the formwork costs.	Linear foot (m)
Floor finishing:		Square foot (m^2)
a. screed finish		
b. wood float		
c. steel trowel (hand)		
d. machine trowel		
e. hardeners	State pounds per square foot if powdered hardener. Cool hardener to be stated separately. (*Note:* State the color green as an extra over.)	
f. curing	State whether membrane curing, wet curing, polyethylene curing, etc.	Square foot (m^2)
g. stairs and landings		Square foot (m^2)
h. bases		Linear foot (m)
i. saw cuts	State separately if filled.	Linear foot (m)
j. stair nosings		Linear foot (m)

7.3   FORMWORK: GENERAL REMARKS

One of the basic principles that estimators learn regarding the measurement of formwork to concrete structures is that it is not (with some few exceptions) the formwork that is measured, but the concrete. To be precise, it is the surface of the concrete that will be in contact with the forms, known as the contact area. This is another of those items that often confuse the practically minded site personnel, who if requested to take field measurements will often measure the actual area of the forms. In many cases this will project above or beyond the concrete structure that they envelope, resulting in a difference in quantity from that stated in the estimate.

As the drawings only show the "finished product" of a formed concrete structure, the contact area is all that can be accurately measured. Contrary to what was recommended for other materials, the adjustment factors for cutting and waste will be included in the unit prices and not in the quantities. The conversion of the contact area to the actual lumber and plywood requirements is usually achieved in the pricing of formwork, as will be demonstrated in Chapter 12.

Experienced estimators appreciate that certain factors that might influence the cost of formwork do not necessarily affect the cost of placing the concrete, and the opposite is also true. For example, it is universally accepted that formwork to a curved or circular surface is more expensive than to a straight surface; but the cost of placing the concrete to a curved wall (as an example) will be the same as for a straight wall. The configuration of this particular item has no significant influence on its labor cost.

However, the placing of concrete in a wall less than 6 inches (150 mm) in width might be costlier than in a wider wall, but the formwork cost would be the same in each case. Also, a slab with a sloping surface (especially if the angle was fairly acute) would provide some premium costs to both the formwork and the concrete placing, and also may require forming on the upper face.

Estimators must also be correct in the pricing of embedded items, distinguishing those that are fastened to the formwork separately from other items (i.e., inserts attached or items requiring support within the forms, such as pipes and flanges).

The general unit of measurement for formwork is the square foot of contact area, sfca (square meter of contact area), but there will be many items that can be more realistically measured and priced on a linear foot basis, and some that should just be enumerated. As in concrete, where total quantity in square feet represents a considerable number of small items in a particular category, this numerical quantity should be stated with the item.

Formwork to exposed architectural concrete work is very expensive and should be kept separate according to the specification classifications. Structural items requiring formwork to "one side only" should be kept separate in the different classifications according to the nature of the unformed surface (e.g., rock, existing structure, timber lagging, or existing walls).

Formwork in locations where stripping is difficult should be identified and so noted. Items where the formwork is to be "left in place" will also be kept separate.

Formwork to underpinning should be measured and stated separately.

Keep separate formwork to items "curved on plan," sloping surfaces, and other irregular shapes. Certain shapes may require a different approach when measuring, often requiring a base item for an imaginary straight and regular profile, and an item is taken off separately for the achievement of the "shape" by a system of boxing out. There are different options open to estimators for measuring these specialty formwork items. Estimators will adopt the method that provides the simplest and fastest method for takeoff and can be priced realistically. There are also different methods of actually constructing such items. Estimators should discuss these items with carpenter foremen, and then measure them in accordance with the proposed method of construction.

It will be noted that the items just discussed could be those "exceptions to the rule" of strict contact area.

The CIQS Method of Measurement for Concrete (which includes formwork) states:

a) Formwork shall be measured in square feet of "contact area" (meters) . . . and shall include erection, oiling, transporting, falsework, stripping, cleaning and all necessary form hardware.

Contractors' estimators might prefer to treat some of those items separately. This would apply most particularly to:

1. **Oil:** As this could not be considered as a "reuse" item, there might be some confusion when embodying it in the unit price (which usually reflects the reuse factor). Preferably, it should be stated in gallons (calculated on the manufacturer's recommendations regarding area coverage per gallon), or it can be given in square feet of covered area (which would be identical to the contact area). However, the cost of applying the oil will be included in the unit cost for labor.

2. **Form hardware:** This is sometimes referred to as "formwork accessories" and often means different things to different estimators. It generally represents such items as rough hardware (e.g., nails, screws), tie wire, and form ties. Many estimators are satisfied to use some tested and tried formula based on the total cubic volume of formed concrete or the net area of the formwork. Others may consider this satisfactory for the nails and wire, but not a realistic approach to assessing the cost of the ties. Form ties can be calculated very accurately, but it becomes a time-consuming task when faced with innumerable items of different heights and widths, and it is a rare estimator that is not short of time. However, as these materials are not subject to reuse (except possibly some portions of interior disconnecting ties), they should be considered separately and excluded from the unit price for formwork materials.

3. **Falsework:** This can be included with the item and in the price, but once again the reuse consideration might persuade an estimator to keep this separate.

7.4   SCHEDULE OF ITEMS AND MEASUREMENTS: FORMWORK

Item	Comment	Unit of Measurement
Wall footings Spread footings Pile, caisson, or caps Grade beams	State separately where concrete is placed on rock or shale where cutting will be required, unless a leveling bed has been applied.	Square foot (m²)
Walls: a. foundation walls	Generally all walls should be summarized in the following categories:	Square foot (m²)
Superstructure b. shear walls c. elevator core walls d. stair walls	■ not exceeding 12 feet high ■ 12 feet to 18 feet high ■ exceeding 18 feet high	
Miscellaneous walls to: a. pits b. loading docks c. ramps		Square foot (m²)
Retaining walls	Battered walls to be stated separately.	Square foot (m²)
Dwarf walls	Applies to any walls less than 3 feet high.	Square foot (m²)

continued

Item	Comment	Unit of Measurement
Pilasters	Item to include side and face (Adjustments will be required to the wall form area for the area equivalent to the pilaster face.)	Square foot (m²)

FIGURE 7–1 Form-work takeoff—pilaster.

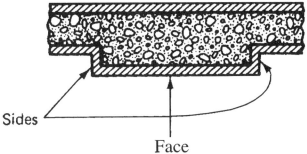

Item	Comment	Unit of Measurement
Noncircular columns	Measured to the underside of slabs, beams, drops, and capitals. Keep separate where of unusual shape (elongated, triangular, etc.)	Square foot (m²)
Circular columns	State diameter and material (metal or fiber material.)	Linear foot (m)
Suspended beams	To include sides and soffits (adjust slab soffit area.) State separately for: ■ spandrel beams (include slab edge) ■ isolated beams ■ beams greater than 3-foot depth	Square foot (m²)

FIGURE 7–2 Form-work takeoff—suspended beam.

Item	Comment	Unit of Measurement
Up-turned (kick) beams	Sides only.	Square foot (m²)
Suspended slabs: a. flat slab b. beam and slab c. slab on structural steel d. slab on metal pan joists e. slab on plastic dome forms f. others g. canopies h. balconies	No deductions to be taken for openings less than 20 square feet. Slabs located at a height greater than 12 feet to be kept separate and the average height stated; also keep separate slabs located at a height of 30 feet or more above the floor below. Slabs less than 3 feet high will be kept separate. Miscellaneous small and isolated suspended slabs to be so noted.	Square foot (m²)
Fireproofing structural steel: a. beams b. columns	Refer to comments regarding concrete beams and columns	Square foot (m²)

continued

Item	Comment	Unit of Measurement
Drop slabs	To include soffit and edge (adjust slab area)	Square foot (m²)

FIGURE 7–3 Form-work takeoff—drop slab.

Item	Comment	Unit of Measurement
Column capitals	State average dimensions. Keep separate if in metal or part of assembly with metal column forms (circular).	Square foot (m²) or numerical
Suspended stairs and landings	Item to include landing soffits and edges, risers, stringers, sloping soffits, etc.	Square foot (m²)
Steps and stairs on grade	Item to include risers, stringers, edges.	Square foot (m²)
Curbs a. interior b. exterior		Square foot (m²)
	Combined "curb and gutter" to roadwork to be kept separate.	
Equipment bases a. lamp standard bases b. pedestals	State the number where total quantity represents numerous small items.	Square foot (m²) Square foot (m²)
Parapet walls		Square foot (m²)
Balustrades		Square foot (m²)
Edges to slabs: a. not exceeding 12 inches high	"Suspended" edges to be given separately.	Square foot (m²) Linear foot (m)

FIGURE 7–4 Form-work takeoff—smaller edge to slab.

b. 12 inches high or more

Square foot (m²)

FIGURE 7–5 Form-work takeoff—"outside" form to a wall.

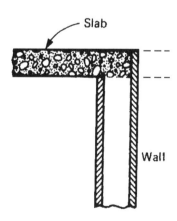

continued

Item	Comment	Unit of Measurement
Construction joints: a. bulkheads to slabs b. bulkheads to walls		Square foot (m²)
c. key	State if to be "split" for waterstop.	Linear foot (m)
Boxings	Measured to contact area, keep separate to special shapes. Provide sketch if necessary.	Square foot (m²)
Chases	State average dimensions.	Linear foot (m)
Chamfers, drips, etc.	State average dimensions.	Linear foot (m)
Double forms (masonry shelves, etc.)	Measured to contact area.	Square foot (m²)
Hanches, nibs, small projections, etc.	State as "extra over" if already included in the contact area measurements for a specific item, e.g., a wall.	Square foot (m²) or linear foot (m)
Metal pan joist forms: straight tapered closed end	State width and depth (deduct the cubic "void" volume from the concrete.)	Linear foot (m)
Waffle (dome) pans	State dimensions (the cubic volume of these units can be deducted from the total gross volume of the concrete.)	Numerical
Filler tile Soffit tile End piece	Keep separate and state different tile sizes. (*Note:* this tile joist construction is not as common as it was several years ago.) The net cubic volume of the tile may be computed as a concrete displacement factor.	Numerical Numerical Numerical
Anchor slots	State if filled.	Linear foot (m)
Miscellaneous items to be fastened to formwork	Refer to comments regarding "embedded items" in concrete. A numerical count will apply to most of these items, but the estimators must include in this division only those parts of a component *actually attached to the formwork*. Example: With a shelf or spandrel angle bolted into special inserts, only the *inserts* for these items should be taken as an attachment to formwork. The angle itself would be taken with another trade (e.g., Miscellaneous Metals or Structural Steel). Some estimators prefer to "weight" each item and then aggregate all the weights into one single item for pricing, stated in pounds or kilograms.	

7.5 | TAKEOFF EXAMPLE

Figure 7–6 provides an example of quantity takeoff for concrete and formwork. The building section (Figure 5–8), foundation plan (Figure 5–9), and structural plans for the first, second, and third floors (Figure 5–10) provide most of the information

Project **Research Center**
Location _____
Subdivision **03300 Concrete**

Estimate No. **27/82**
By **B.E.W.** Chk'd **H.A.J.**
Date **4/1/99**

Description of Work	No. Pieces	A	B	C	Extensions	Unit	Extensions	Unit	Extensions	Unit
					Concrete		*Forms*		Area 3	
Isolated Col Ftgs					*A x B x C*		*2 x (A+B) x C*			
3000 LBs (25 Mpa)										
Type A	5/	4.0	4.0	1.17	9 4		9 4			
B	2/	3.33	3.33	.67	1 5		1 5			
					1 0 9		1 1 2	sft		
					= 4	cyd				
Continouous Wall Ftgs										
3000 Lbs (25 Mpa)					*Concrete*		*Forms*		*Key*	
<u>*Perimeter*</u>					*A x B x C*		*2 x A x C*		A	
100.0										
50.0										
150.0 x 2 = 300.0										
2x2x50.0 = <u>200.0</u>										
500.00										
Ftg protection										
2x4x .33 = <u>2.67</u>										
502.67										
D D T Corners										
4x 1.67 = <u>(6.67)</u>										
		496	108	0.67	5 5 5		6 6 5		4 9 6	
<u>*Add*</u> Type C ftgs	11/	33.0	1.33	.067	2 9		4 4		3 3	
3.0 .83	4/	1.33	1.33	.067	5		7		5	
<u>1.67</u> <u>.67</u>	15/	3.0	3.0	.17	2 3		1 5			
1.33 .17										
<u>Int. Wall Ftgs</u>										
2 x 25.0 = 50.0										
2x .33 = <u>.67</u>										
50.67										
DDT2x <u>(3.33)</u>										
1x .67) 47.33		47.33	1.67	.67	5 3		6 3		4 7	
Stepped ftgs	2/	4.5	1.67	1.33	2 0		2 4			
					6 8 5		8 1 8	sft	5 8 1	lft
					= 2 5	cyd				
Riser Forms (stepped ftgs)					*A x B*					
	2/	4.5	1.67		1 5	sft				

FIGURE 7–6 Example of quantity takeoff for concrete and formwork.

continued

				Project	**Research Center**				Estimate No. __27/82__
Location					By __B.E.W.__ Chk'd __H.A.J.__
Subdivision __03300 - Concrete__					Date __4/1/99__

Description of Work	No. Pieces	A	B	C	Extensions	Unit	Extensions	Unit	Extensions		Unit
		Dimensions							**Pilaster Forms**		
					Concrete		Forms		sides	face	
					A x B x C		2 x A x C		2xAxC	BxC	
Foundation Walls					Concrete		Forms		Pilaster Forms		
4000 lbs (30 Mpa)											
Wall Heights:											
Top of wall 300.00											
Top of ftg 294.00											
6.0											
B/ment Wall	300.00										
less slab	.67										
	299.33										
top of ftg	289.50										
	9.83										
Line "C"	4/	25.0									
Line "E"		150.0									
Line 1 & 7	2/	50.0	1.0	6.0	2 1 0 0		4 2 0 0				
DDT Corners	2/	(1.0)	(1.0)	(6.0)	(1 2)		(2 4)				
Basement	3/	50.0	1.0	9.83	1 4 7 6		2 9 5 2				
corners	2/	(1.0)	(1.0)	(9.83)	(2 0)		(3 9)				
Stepped Ftgs	2/	4.0	1.0	1.5	1 2		2 4				
	2/	4.0	1.0	3.0	2 4		4 8				
	2/	4.0	1.0	4.5	3 6		7 2				
Int B/ment Wall	2/	25.0	1.0	9.83	4 9 2		9 8 4				
	2/	(1.0)	(1.0)	(9.83)	(2 0)		(3 9)				
Pilasters	10/	.6	1.0	6.0	3 0				6 0	6 0	
	2/	.6	1.0	9.83	1 0				2 0	2 0	
	3/	.5	.5	6.0	5				1 8	9	
		.5	.5	9.83	3				1 0	5	
					4 1 3 6	cft	8 1 7 8		1 0 8	9 4	
							(9 4)			1 0 8	
							8 0 8 4	sft		2 0 2	sft
					= 1 5 3	cyd					
Piers below grade					Concrete		Forms				
4000lbs (30MPa)					A x B x C		2x(A+B)xC				
	5/	1.0	1.0	5.5	2 7		1 1 0	sft			
					= 1	cyd					

FIGURE 7–6 Example of quantity takeoff for concrete and formwork.

continued

91

Project	**Research Center**		Estimate No.	**27/82**
Location			By **B.E.W.** Chk'd **H.A.J.**
Subdivision	**03300 - Concrete**		Date **4/1/99**

Description of Work	No. Pieces	Dimensions A	B	C	Extensions	Unit	Extensions	Unit	Extensions		Unit
					Concrete A x B x C		**Forms** 2x(A+B)xC				
Columns - 4000 lbs (30 Mpa)											
10.0											
slab (.67) ext.	3/16/	1.0	1.0	7.33	3 5 2		1 4 0 7				
9.33 int	3/5/	1.0	1.0	8.0	1 2 0		4 8 0				
BM 2.0 adj s.o.g.	5/	1.0	1.0	.5	3		1 0				
7.33 B/ment		1.0	1.0	9.83	1 0		3 9				
					4 8 5	cft	1 9 3 6	sft			
					= 1 8	cyd					
Spandrel Beams - 4000lbs (30 Mpa)					concrete A x B x C		**Forms** soffits A x B		sides 2xAxC	slab edges Ax8"	
4' facing	3/2/	150.0									
6" facing	3/2/	50.0	1.0	2.0	2 4 0 0		1 2 0 0		4800	804	
10" x 2 = 1.67	3/4/	(1.67)	(1.0)	(2.0)	(4 0)		(2 0)		(80)	(13)	
					2 3 6 0	cft	1 1 8 0		4720	791	
										4720	
										1180	
					= 8 7	cyd				6691	sft
Interior beams - 4000lbs (30MPa)					concrete		**Forms** soffits A x B		sides 2 x A x C		
150.0											
Sp.BM & facing											
2x 1.33 (2.67)											
147.33	3/	147	1.33	1.33	7 8 6		5 8 8		1	1 7 9	
	3/5/	46.0	1.33	.67	6 1 5		9 2 0			9 2 0	
					1 4 0 1		1 5 0 8		2	0 9 9	
BM = 2.0 50.0									1	5 0 8	
less slab (.67) (1.33)					= 5 2	cyd			3	6 0 7	sft
1.33 48.67											
2 x 1.33 (2.67)											
46.0											

FIGURE 7–6 Example of quantity takeoff for concrete and formwork.

continued

92

Project	Research Center		Estimate No.	27/82
Location			By B.E.W.	Chk'd H.A.J.
Subdivision	03300 - Concrete		Date	4/1/99

Description of Work	No. Pieces	A	B	C	Extensions	Unit	Extensions	Unit	Extensions		Unit
Susp. Slab (flat plate)					Concrete		Forms		Set		
- 4000 p.s.I. (30MPa)					A x B x C		A x B		Screeds		
									A x B		
50.0 50.0											
1.0 (.67)											
51.0 49.33		50.67	49.33	.67	1 6 7 5		2 5 0 0	sft	2500	sft	"A"
facing (.33)											
50.67					= 6 2	cyd					
Susp Slab (BM & slab)					Concrete		Set Screeds		Soffit Forms		
-4000 p.s.I. (30 Mpa)					A x B x C		A x B		A x B		
100.0											
50.0											
150.0											
2 x .33 (.67)											
149.33	3/	149.3	49.33	.67	1 4 8 0 7		2 2 0 9 9		"B"	22099	
									DDT Spam	(1180)	
					= 5 4 8				"int"	(1508)	
Add: Sp Beam (P.3)					8 7					19411	sft
Int Beam					5 2						
					6 8 7	cyd					
L/Wt Conc fill to Metal Deck					Concrete		Set Screeds				
					A x B x C		A x B				
Concrete 2"		49.33	50.0	.33	8 2 2		2 4 6 7	sft	"C"		
Rib 1 1/2"											
3 1/2" - 4"					= 3 0	cyd					

FIGURE 7–6   Example of quantity takeoff for concrete and formwork.

continued

Project	**Research Center**	Estimate No. __27/82__
Location		By __B.E.W.__ Chk'd __H.A.J.__
Subdivision	__03300 - Concrete__	Date __4/1/99__

Description of Work	No. Pieces	Dimensions A	B	C	Extensions Concrete A x B x C	Unit	Extensions Set Screeds A x B	Unit	Extensions	Unit
Slab on Grade (30 Mpa)										
150.0										
-2 x 1.0 2.0										
148.0		148.0	48.0				7 1 0 4			
		48.0	49.0	.5	4 7 2 8		2 3 5 2			
Add for seepage - 1"		148.0	48.0							
		48.0	49.0	.08	7 8 8					
					5 5 1 6		9 4 5 6	sft	"D"	
					= 2 0 4	cyd				
Exp joints to slab or grade					A					
(1/2" x 6" A.I.F.B.)										
	2/	148.0			2 9 6					
	2/2/	48.0			1 9 2					
	2/	49.0			9 8					
Around columns	6/	4.0			2 4					
					6 1 0					
Slab edges forms (NE 12")					A					
B/ment	2/	48.0			9 6					
	2/	49.0			9 8					
stair openings	2/2/	17.0			6 8					
	2/	11.83			2 4					
B/ment stair	2/	4.0			8					
	2/	9.0			1 8					
					3 1 2	Lft				

FIGURE 7–6 Example of quantity takeoff for concrete and formwork.

continued

Project __Research Center__

Location _____

Subdivision __03300 - Concrete__

Estimate No. __27/82__

By __B.E.W.__   Chk'd __H.A.J.__

Date __4/1/99__

Description of Work	No. Pieces	Dimensions			Extensions	Unit	Extensions	Unit	Extensions	Unit
		A	B	C						
					Concrete A x B x C		Forms A x B		Finish A x 1'.5"	
Concrete stairs (30 Mpa)										
Soffitt		21.25	4.0	.33	2 8		8 5		3 0	
Steps	16/1.5 /	4.0	.83	.58	1 6					
Forms risers	16/	4.0	.58				3 7		9 1	
stringer		21.25	.92				2 0		1 2 2	sft
boxing		21.25	.92				2 0			
bearing		4.0	.67				3			
					4 4		1 6 5	sft		
					= 2	cyd				
					Bulkhead form A		Key A		Waterstop A	
Construction Joints (vertical)										
Assume 40'.0 pours										
Total wall length - 298.0										
divide 40										
=7.5	8/	6.0			4 8		DO		DO	
	4/	9.58			3 8		DO		DO	
					8 6	lft	8 6	lft	8 6	lft
					Bulkhead A		Key A			
Ditto (horizontal)										
s.o.g.	5/	47.5			2 3 8		2 3 8			
		150.0			1 5 0		1 5 0			
					3 8 8	lft	3 8 8	lft		

FIGURE 7–6   Example of quantity takeoff for concrete and formwork.

continued

Project | *Research Center* | Estimate No. *27/82* | By *B.E.W.* Chk'd *H.A.J.* | Date *4/1/99* |

Location
Subdivision *03300 - Concrete*

Description of Work	No. Pieces	Dimensions A	B	C	Extensions Walls/cols A x B	Unit	Extensions Soffits A x B	Unit	Extensions	Unit
Clean Patch & Rub										
<u>*Exposed concrete surfaces*</u>										
Int. walls - B/ment	2/	48.0	9.33		8 9 6					
	2/	49.0	9.33		9 1 4					
col		4.0	9.33		3 7					
soffitt		48.0	49.0				2 3 5 2			
Ext. - above grade		150.0								
	2/2/	50.0								
		150.0	2.0		1 0 0 0					
					2 8 4 7	sft	2 3 5 2	sft		
Concrete floor finishes							*Summary of Screed areas*			
				Area	"A" P4		2 5 0 0			
				Area	"B"		2 2 0 9 9			
				Area	"C"		2 4 6 7			
				Area	"D" P5		9 4 5 6			
							3 6 5 2 2	sft		

Description of Work	Dimensions A	B	Extensions Finishes Machine Trowel (plain)	Extensions Ditto (hardener)	Unit	Roof finish	Curing	Unit
Total Area Screeds (above)			3 6 5 2 2				36522	sft
roof areas	150.0	50.0				7500		
	50.0	50.0				2500		
						10000		sft
hardener floors	48.0	49.0		2 3 5 2	sft			
			3 6 5 2 2					
Deduct *roof finish*			(1 0 0 0 0)					
hardened areas			(2 3 5 2)					
			2 4 1 7 0	sft				

FIGURE 7–6 Example of quantity takeoff for concrete and formwork.

continued

Project	**Research Center**						Estimate No.	**27/82**			
Location							By **B.E.W.**	Chk'd **H.A.J.**			
Subdivision	**03300 - Concrete**						Date **4/1/99**				

Description of Work	No. Pieces	A	B	C	Extensions	Unit	Extensions	Unit	Extensions	Unit
					Concrete A x B x C		Forms 2 x (A+B) x C		Finish A x B	
Equipment Pads (25 Mpa)										
	3/6/	2.5	1.75	.67	5 2		1 0 3	sft	7 9	sft
					= 2	cyd				
Masonry Shelf - 4" x 6"					A					
	3/	50.0			1 5 0	lft				
Inserts for Shelf Angles at Spandrell Beams (2'.0" c/c)										
100/2 =	50	+2			5 2					
2 x 150/2 =	152	+2			1 5 4					
					2 0 6	ea				
Anchors for precast concrete Facing Panels (4'.0" c/c)										
North elevation	3	x 150 / 4	=	113 + 3	1 1 6					
East and West Elevation	2 x	3x50 / 4	=	75 + 6	8 1					
					1 9 7	ea				
							say 2 0 0	ea		

FIGURE 7–6 Example of quantity takeoff for concrete and formwork.

continued

Project _Research Center_

Location _____

Subdivision _03300 - Concrete_

Estimate No. _27/82_

By _B.E.W._   Chk'd _H.A.J._

Date _4/1/99_

Description of Work	No. Pieces	Dimensions A	Dimensions B	Dimensions C	Extensions	Unit	Extensions	Unit	Extensions			Unit
					Concrete A x B x C		Finish A x B					
Concrete fill to Metal Stair Pans												
(25 Mpa)	2/16/	4.5	.83	.17	2 1		1 2 1					
Landings	2/	12.0	4.5	.17	1 8		1 0 8					
					3 9	cft	2 2 9	sft				
							Wall Forms	Slab Edge	Key		Hand ?	
					Concrete A x B x C		2 x A x C	(A+B) x2	A		A x B	
Sump Pits (25 (Mpa)												
Base		9.83	8.25	.5	.4 1			3 6	lft		8 1	sft
Walls	2/	9.83										
	2/	6.92	.67	4.5	1 0 1		3 0 6	sft	3 4	lft		
					1 4 2							
					= 5	cyd						

FIGURE 7–6 Example of quantity takeoff for concrete and formwork.

continued

applicable to this trade section. The following brief specification notes supplement the data shown on the drawings:

3000 p.s.i. concrete to footings, pits, and bases.

Lightweight concrete fill to metal roof deck.

4000 p.s.i. concrete to all other items.

Air entrainment to all concrete mixes excluding lightweight concrete.

Rub exposed concrete surfaces.

½-in. asphalt impregnated expansion joint junction of slabs and walls.

Concrete slab finishes:

    plain trowel to floor slabs

    60-lb nonmetallic hardener to basement floor

    wood float roof surfaces

    membrane curing

Waterstops at construction joints below grade.

Shelf angle inserts at spandrels.

Anchor slots (provided by Section 04200 Masonry).

Formwork to comply with Publication ACI 347-78.

COMMENTARY ON CONCRETE TAKEOFF

1. The side notes (under "description of work") show the buildup of the figures recorded in the dimension columns. The wall lengths noted on the drawings are extended for the footing projections; where duplication has occurred, deductions are made for doubling up at the corners (see Figure 7–7).

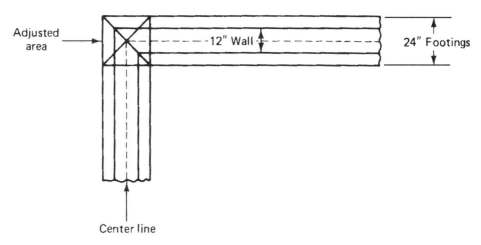

FIGURE 7–7 Commentary—concrete takeoff (footings).

Another method used by many estimators is the center line method for measuring walls and footings which, once the center line is calculated, eliminates the need for further adjustments to the dimensions (as noted on sketch).

2. The column footings, type C, have been included on Sheet 1 with the perimeter wall footings. These could have been included with the takeoff item for column footings with formwork measured to the four sides, particularly if there was a significant difference between the depth of these footings in comparison with the wall footings. In this instance the difference is small.

3. The dimensions for the stepped footings are a deviation from the normal sequence of length, breadth and height. For simplification reasons the height (4 feet 6 inches) is taken first, multiplied by the footing width (1 foot 8 inches), the third dimension being an assumed thickness equal to two times the normal footing thickness (8 inches $\times$ 2 = 1 foot 4 inches). The riser forms are measured separately.

4. The side notes on Sheet 2 (Foundation Walls), show the computations to establish the wall heights.

5. In accordance with the method prescribed in the Schedule of Items and Measurements, the pilaster forms are measured for sides and face, with the face area deducted from the wall face area.

6. The columns (Sheet 3) are measured from top of slab to the underside of beams.

7. The spandrel beams are measured using the full dimensions for the concrete walls as shown on the drawing, with adjustments made for the thickness of the face brick.

8. Also, no adjustments are made for doubling-up at the corners or for the intersection of interior beams.

9. The suspended slab soffit areas (Sheet 4) are adjusted for the beam soffits where applicable.

10. The slab on grade (Sheet 5) has been measured to the net slab thickness of 6 inches, and an additional measurement for an assumed 1 inch of loss through seepage. This adjustment could also have been achieved with a percentage factor based on experience and judgment.

11. The construction joints for the foundation walls (Sheet 6) allow for concrete pours to 40 feet of wall length. The measurement of this item would usually result from discussion with field superintendents or construction managers, or from the estimator's own judgment of what was reasonable. Also the specifications would probably state some restrictions on length of pours.

12. The item for rub exposed concrete (Sheet 7) is measured to the interior walls, columns, and slab soffits in the basement. The exterior rubbing is measured for that portion which extends from the finished grade (assumed at 300.00) to the top of the wall.

13. The concrete floor finishes are developed from taking the total "screed" area for the predominant finish (i.e., machine trowel) and deducting from this area the separately measured areas for the other types of concrete floor finishes.

14. The equipment pads (Sheet 8) are not shown on the drawings; the number and dimensions are assumed to provide an example of measuring these items.

15. The inserts set into the concrete (into the formwork to be strictly correct) at the spandrel beams to receive the shelf angles are usually supplied and installed by the general contractor. The shelf angle will be supplied by either the structural steel or miscellaneous metals subcontractor (with the contractor's installation measured with the miscellaneous work for those trade divisions).

16. The anchors for the precast concrete wall panels will be supplied by the precast concrete subcontractor to the general contractor for installation in the formwork.

17. The steel stairs (Sheet 9) extend from the ground floor to the second and third floors. They would be supplied and installed under Section 05500 Metal Fabrications, but the concrete fill to the treads (pans) will be the responsibility of the general contractor. This is one item where the unit of a cubic foot is preferable. A large number of treads are included in one cubic yard (or cubic meter) and the cost of placing the concrete is often as much per cubic foot as per cubic yard. (They could, of course, be measured and priced as a cost per tread.)

18. The sump pits (like the equipment pads) are not indicated on the drawings and are included as an example of measurement and costing.

8 TAKEOFF: MASONRY

8.1 GENERAL

The general trade practice in the United States is to express the quantities of the major masonry materials (i.e., brick, block, tile, etc.) in terms of pieces (or thousand piece units). A two-stage procedure is therefore necessary to establish these quantities:

1. Normal measuring to establish wall areas (square feet or m^2).
2. The computation of the masonry units by multiplying the wall areas by a factor applicable to the size of the unit plus thickness of the mortar joint.

This means that the accuracy of the quantities depends not only on the measurements taken off the drawings but also the computation of the factor. An accurate quantity survey of a major masonry project can be spoiled by the careless application of an inaccurate factor.

To take off and price estimates for masonry work on the measured net wall areas for each specific material would appear at first to be the simplest method, but the problems just stated (factors, bonding, waste, etc.) do not disappear if ignored. They must be reflected in the unit rates, and the possibility of errors is not lessened; in fact, they might be harder to detect. Also, as previously stated, for purposes of purchasing and cost control the estimate should reflect as closely as possible the actual methods by which these materials are sold and installed.

Superintendents do not normally issue purchase orders or requisitions for so many square feet (square meters) of bricks or blocks; these materials are purchased on the basis of the number of units required. It is advisable, therefore, to prepare and price the estimate accordingly. To provide merely the wall or partition areas of the different materials merely transfers the operation of calculating the required number of units, plus the wastage and bonding factors, to superintendents, purchasing agents, or some other people. In reality, it is the estimator who is considered to have the best training and expertise to do this work effectively.

Before considering the problems in detail relating to bonding and wastage factors, it is necessary first to review some of the following basic principles to be observed when taking off quantities for masonry work:

1. The quantities will be taken off net in place.
2. Circular work should be stated separately.
3. No deductions should be made for openings less than 10 square feet (1 m^2) in area.
4. State the nominal dimensions of the materials, and keep separate according to specified classification and type.
5. Keep separate the work in the following categories:
   - Exterior cladding ("skin") to the building
   - Interior partitions and furring
   - Exterior masonry work (retaining wall, landscaping, etc.)
   - Fireproofing to structural steelwork
   - Load-bearing walls
   - Foundation walls below grade
   - Renovation work to existing masonry (including filling in of openings in areas where doors or windows have been removed)
   - Miscellaneous categories

8.2   SCHEDULE OF ITEMS AND MEASUREMENTS: MASONRY

Item	Comment	Unit of Measurement
Face brick	Describe material and classification, type of bond, and pointing requirements. State as extra over the numerical quantities of brick units pertaining to: ■ "snapped headers" ■ brickwork in decorative patterns ■ brick on edge ■ arches ■ special shape units (bullnose, splayed, etc.) ■ stack bond ■ other special requirements Glazed brick to be stated as separate category.	Thousand pieces
Common brick	Describe material classification, function ("backup," beam filling, etc.)	Thousand pieces
Firebrick	Describe according to manufacturer's literature.	Thousand pieces

continued

Item	Comment	Unit of Measurement
Concrete block masonry	Separate categories for: ■ low pressure units ■ autoclaved units ■ lightweight units State as extra over for: ■ solid and/or semisolid block ■ headers ■ specials: bullnose, sash units, piers, bond beams, etc. ■ exposed faces (i.e., not covered by plaster, drywall, or other materials.) There is an additional labor cost where block is to remain exposed. *Note:* It is the exposed faces that have to be measured (enumerated). A block unit in a wall that is exposed on both sides will have two exposed faces. The alternative method is to measure and record the units in categories for: ■ block unexposed ■ block exposed one side ■ block exposed two sides This can slow down the takeoff process. In the following takeoff examples, the method prescribed is faster and just as effective for establishing a reasonably accurate cost factor. Cutting blocks to fit around structural steel columns shall be enumerated and described as an extra over.	Piece
Structural clay tile	State separately for: ■ smooth surfaces ■ scored surfaces ■ rugged surfaces ■ other surfaces ■ furring tile ■ partition	Piece
Structured glazed tile	Keep separate for: ■ header units ■ stretcher units ■ universal units *Note:* Special fittings may be measured according to group numbers and described as extra over.	Piece
Glazed concrete block	Refer to the comments regarding concrete block and glazed structural tile.	Piece
Gypsum masonry	State thickness	Piece
Mortar	To be stated separately according to specified mix proportions. Additives to be stated as extra over. Colored mortar to be described as extra over. Fire temperature and fireclay bonding mortar to be kept separate.	Cubic yard (m^3)
Dampcourses, flashings	Describe specified material classification and (where applicable) weight per square foot (m^2)	Square foot (m^2) or linear foot (m)
Cleaning down masonry	Keep separate according to the materials to be cleaned (brick, block, tile, etc.). Describe cleansing solution specified. These same measurements can be used for enumerating the "exposed faces" of block or tile, by applying a block or tile factor to the measured area.	Square foot (m^2)

continued

Item	Comment	Unit of Measurement
Miscellaneous embedded items	Keep separate according to function and/or size. Include (but not limited to): ■ anchor bolts ■ bearing plates ■ sleeves ■ brackets ■ other similar items	Piece
Rake out and point mortar joints	This item will be measured when and where the specifications require joints to be raked out and pointed with mortar materials. Mortar specifications to be stated, and the area measured will be the net area of exposed masonry work requiring the raking and pointing.	Square foot (m²)
Anchor slots	This item may appear in two parts of the estimate: masonry and formwork. It applies to masonry work in direct contact with cast-in-place concrete. It is generally simpler to measure this item with the masonry (the structural drawings rarely show masonry or other materials applied against the concrete) and then transfer the item to the formwork summary. It can appear in both divisions: the material supply in the masonry section, and the installation with the formwork section.	Linear foot (m)
Anchorage material	Classify and describe as per the specification. Various categories will include (but not be limited to): ■ dovetail anchors (stated if dowelled) ■ ties (stated if corrugated) ■ cavity wall ties ■ others *Note:* Bronze, brass, or stainless steel anchorage materials to be stated separately.	Piece (or 1000 pieces)
Lintels: Steel	State if built up in multiple sections	Linear foot (m)
Precast concrete	Give width and depth	Linear foot (m)
Reinforced masonry	This applies particularly to concrete block or structural clay tile masonry. The item should be measured as an extra over, which will provide the additional cost of a bond or lintel beam, reinforcing rods, and concrete fill. Keep separate for different thicknesses.	Linear foot (m)
Control joints	This item usually applies to a rubber control joint, and should be separated into flange widths.	Linear foot (m)
Masonry reinforcement: Reinforcing steel bars	This item should exclude reinforcing to masonry lintels, which is included with the item.	Pound (kilogram)
Prefabricated rods or mesh	State overall wall thickness. Give all classification details, whether standard, heavy duty, extra heavy duty, etc., and other information pertinent to identification in manufacturer's literature and price list.	Linear foot (m)
Prefabricated corners and tees	Give pertinent information as required for rods or mesh.	Piece
Expansion joints	State thickness and material classification.	Square foot (m²)
Weep hole plugs		Per hundred pieces
Cavity wall insulation	State thickness and type of material	Square foot (m²)

106

8.3 ▐ MASONRY EQUIPMENT

Apart from the items already covered in the schedule of measurements, there are also items of equipment to be considered. These would include the following:

Mortar mixers: rental cost per month

Scaffold frames: rental per month, plus the cost of erection and dismantling

Masonry saws and blades: rental per month

Forklift: rental per month

Hanging scaffolds: this should be divided into:

- rental per month of machine
- erection and dismantling of outriggers and scaffolds
- overhead and winter protection

Winter heat and protection: this would probably be measured and priced in the estimate for site overheads, and would include for:

- space heaters, including fuel and handling
- tarpaulins (including any necessary framework or supports)

Note: The item for erection and dismantling of scaffold frame units may be expressed as square feet (square meters) of wall area, and an appropriate unit rate applied. Some estimators measure the total length of each "lift" of scaffolding; that is, a partition 65 ft long requiring 2 lifts of 5 ft scaffolding would be expressed as "130 ft of scaffold in lifts of (approximately) 5 ft."

8.4 ▐ CONVERSION FACTORS: GENERAL

The factor by which the square foot (m^2) area of a wall constructed of a particular masonry material is multiplied to arrive at the required number of masonry units is not difficult to calculate. To establish a factor, certain basic information about the material must be known.

This basic information includes the obvious ones of length, width, and height; but because the masonry units in a structure are separated by another material, mortar, the thickness of the mortar joint has also to be taken into account. As the general trade practice is to base the calculations on the number of units per square foot area of wall or partition, only the face dimensions of length and height are necessary. The thickness of the unit is not necessary for this calculation, unless (as will be explained later) the unit is placed in such a manner that the thickness now replaces the length for the face area (e.g., headers).

The thickness of a unit would, of course, be essential if the factor was to be based on the cubic volume of the masonry work, a practice followed in certain regions or by some estimators. However, this book will be restricted to the factors per wall area, rather than volume.

For example, for brick in a wall 4 in. (one brick) thick, with mortar joints specified as ½ in., the factor is derived by dividing 1 sft by the length of the brick, plus ½ in., multiplied by the height of the unit, again plus ½ in.

EXAMPLE: Face brick, size 8⅝ in. × 2⅝ in. high in a wall, laid in stretcher (running) bond, with ½-in. mortar joints.

$$\frac{1 \text{ sft}}{(8\frac{5}{8} + \frac{1}{2}) \times (2\frac{5}{8} + \frac{1}{2})} = 5.63 \text{ bricks/sft}$$

To express a similar example in metric dimensions: face brick size 190 mm × 57 mm high, stretcher bond, with 10-mm mortar joints:

$$\frac{1 \text{ m}^2}{(0.190 + 0.10) \times (0.57 + 0.10)} = 74.6 \text{ bricks/m}^2$$

A basic factor can be calculated for each kind of masonry material, utilizing only the dimensions for length, height, and mortar joint thickness. Given an accurate measurement of the wall or partition area (within the parameters outlined in the schedule of measurements) the resultant quantities derived from the multiplication of this area by the appropriate factor will be an equally accurate enumeration of the masonry units actually laid in a specific location. However, once the condition of a single wythe of brick transforms into a condition where greater wall thickness and full headers for bonding are necessary, the calculations become a little more complex. The bonding of solid brick walls affects both the face brick factors and the backup (common) brick factors. The bonds most commonly used are:

Flemish bond: alternate headers and stretchers in each course.

English bond: alternate courses of headers and stretchers.

Headers every fifth course: (self-explanatory): five courses of stretchers to one course of full headers.

Headers every sixth course: same principle as for fifth-course headers.

Full English bond every sixth course: alternate courses of stretchers and "snapped" headers, except for each sixth course, where full headers will be used.

Full Flemish bond every sixth course: similar to the variations on English bond for sixth-course headers.

The calculation of quantities of brick per square foot (m²) is made by applying a correction factor to the basic factor for a brick laid in stretcher bond.

The following are the correction factors to be applied for the types of bond already mentioned:

Flemish bond: 33⅓ percent

English bond: 50 percent

Full headers, fifth course: 20 percent

Full headers, sixth course: 16.7 percent

Full English bond every sixth course: 16.7 percent (Note: The main consideration here is for wastage factors because of "snapped" headers, and corresponding increased labor costs.)

Full Flemish bond every sixth course: 5.5 percent

It is important to remember that the correction factors applicable to the specified bonds must be utilized as additions to the basic factors for face brick, and as deductions from the factors for backup brick, if another (i.e., common) brick is to be used. Table 8–1 provides a table of factors for a limited selection of bonds, brick sizes, wall thickness, and mortar joints dimensions, and Table 8–2 offers a corresponding table for metric dimensions. It should be noted that the dimensions shown

TABLE 8–1 Brick quantities: American.

		Quantities per Square Foot			
Brick Type and Size	Type of Bond	Mortar Joint (in.)	Facing 4 in.	Backup 4 in.	Backup 8 in.
(a) Modular:					
3⅝ × 2¼ × 7⅝ in.	Stretcher	⅜	8.00	–	–
		½	6.44	–	–
	Flemish (full headers)	⅜	10.66	5.34	13.34
		½	8.60	4.31	10.76
	English (full headers)	⅜	12.00	4.00	12.00
		½	9.68	3.23	9.68
	Full headers, fifth course	⅜	9.60	6.40	14.40
		½	7.74	5.16	11.61
	Full headers, sixth course	⅜	9.34	6.67	14.67
		½	7.33	5.38	11.83
(b) Ontario:					
4 × 2⅝ × 8⅜ in.	Stretcher	⅜	6.00	–	–
		½	5.63	–	–
	Flemish (full headers)	⅜	8.00	4.00	10.00
		½	7.51	3.76	9.39
	English (full headers)	⅜	9.00	3.00	9.00
		½	8.45	2.82	8.45
	Full headers, fifth course	⅜	7.20	4.80	12.80
		½	6.75	4.51	10.14
	Full headers, sixth course	⅜	7.00	5.00	11.00
		½	6.57	4.69	10.32
(c) Quebec:					
3¾ × 2¼ × 8 in.	Stretcher	⅜	6.87	–	–
		½	6.16	–	–
	Flemish (full headers)	⅜	9.16	4.60	11.47
		½	8.21	4.11	10.27
	English (full headers)	⅜	10.31	3.44	10.31
		½	9.24	3.08	9.24
	Full headers, fifth course	⅜	8.25	5.50	12.37
		½	7.39	4.93	11.09
	Full headers, sixth course	⅜	8.02	5.72	12.59
		½	7.19	5.85	12.00

TABLE 8–2   Brick quantities: metric

Brick Type and Size	Type of Bond	Quantities per Square Meter			
		Mortar Joint	Facing 90 mm	Backup 90 mm	Backup 190 mm
(a) Modular:					
90 × 57 × 190 mm	Stretcher (running)	10 mm	74.6		
	Flemish (full headers)	10 mm	99.6	49.8	124.4
	English (full headers)	10 mm	111.9	37.4	111.9
	Full headers, fifth course	10 mm	89.5	59.7	134.3
	Full headers, sixth course	10 mm	87.1	62.1	136.7
(b) Ontario:					
101.6 × 60.33 × 212.73 mm	Stretcher (running)	10 mm	63.8		
	Flemish (full headers)	10 mm	85.0	42.6	106.4
	English (full headers)	10 mm	95.7	31.9	95.7
	Full headers, fifth course	10 mm	76.6	51.0	114.8
	Full headers, sixth course	10 mm	74.5	53.2	117.0
(c) Quebec:					
95.25 × 57.15 × 203.20 mm	Stretcher (running)	10 mm	69.9		
	Flemish (full headers)	10 mm	93.2	46.7	116.7
	English (full headers)	10 mm	105.2	35.0	105.0
	Full headers, fifth course	10 mm	83.9	56.0	126.0
	Full headers, sixth course	10 mm	81.6	58.3	128.3

in Table 8–2 for Ontario size and Quebec size are "soft conversions" to metric, and item (a), Table 8–1, gives soft conversions from metric to American. It must also be emphasized that the factors shown in these tables exclude any allowances for waste or breakage. Mathematical purists might contest some of the factors regarding absolute arithmetical accuracy, and, admittedly, in many instances they have been "rounded off" to the nearest decimal; they remain, however, reasonably accurate for estimating purposes.

8.5 ▊ CONCRETE BLOCK MASONRY

The factors for establishing the required number of concrete block units per square foot are calculated in the same way as for brick materials. The length and height dimensions for a standard imperial-sized concrete block are 15⅝ inches × 7⅝ inches.

The factor per square foot for block laid with ⅜-inch mortar joints will be

$$\frac{1 \text{ sft}}{(15\frac{5}{8} + \frac{3}{8}) \times (7\frac{5}{8} + \frac{3}{8})} = 1.13 \text{ units/sft}$$

Using ⅝ inch joints,

$$\frac{1 \text{ sft}}{(15\frac{5}{8} + \frac{5}{8}) \times (7\frac{5}{8} + \frac{5}{8})} = 1.08 \text{ units/sft}$$

Expressed in metric dimensions, the imperial-sized block is 390 mm × 190 mm. The factor per square meter using 10-mm joints will be

$$\frac{1 \text{ m}^2}{(0.390 + 0.10) \times (0.190 + 0.10)} = 12.5 \text{ units/m}^2$$

8.6 STRUCTURAL CLAY TILE MASONRY

The factors needed to establish quantities of structural clay tile masonry units are calculated as demonstrated for concrete block masonry. There are a greater variety of sizes available in this type of masonry material than for concrete block. The following are some of the normal length and height dimensions:

Smooth face tile: 5 inches × 11⅝ inches
Partition tile: 11⅝ inches × 11⅝ inches

The factor per square foot for the above units, using ⅜-inch joints, will be:

$$\text{Smooth face tile} = \frac{1 \text{ sft}}{(5 + ⅜) \times (11⅝ + ⅜)} = 2.23 \text{ units/sft}$$

$$\text{Partition tile} = \frac{1 \text{ sft}}{(11⅝ + ⅜) \times (11⅝ + ⅜)} = 1 \text{ unit/sft}$$

8.7 STRUCTURAL GLAZED TILE

The basic dimensions of length and height for a stretcher unit are 11¾ inches long × 5¼ inches high, and the factor per 1 square foot (¼-inch joints) would be 2.2.

8.8 FIREPROOFING TILE FOR STRUCTURAL STEEL BEAMS

This type of steel fireproofing (tile) is most uncommon these days. The modern system of spray fireproofing is more common. The tile is confined to the sides and flanges of structural steel beams and girders; the conversion factor should be calculated on the basis of the number of pieces per linear foot of beam (or flange).

EXAMPLE: A steel beam side is fireproofed as follows:

Sides, 1 piece per lft of beam side
Flange (shoe tile), 2 pieces per lft of flange
Soffit, 1 piece per lft of beam soffit

The sides would be calculated using the factor per one side, multiplied by 2. The same would apply to the flanges.

8.9 MORTAR

There are two types of factors most commonly used for calculating mortar quantity requirements. One factor gives the quantity of cubic yards of mortar per square foot of wall area, stating the mortar joint thickness and the brick dimensions. The other is a factor based on the cubic yards of mortar per so many units of masonry (e.g., 1000 bricks), again taking brick and mortar joint dimensions into consideration.

Basically, all factors are obtained by calculating the total cubic volume of the wall and then deducting from this figure the total net volume of the masonry units; the amount remaining will be the net volume of mortar required. Note the two words "net volume."

It is not the calculation of this net volume that is difficult. The real challenge is deciding upon the most realistic waste factor. Bricklayers are only happy when the estimate provides sufficient quantity of mortar to lay all the bricks plus a little bit left over to splatter at the estimators' feet when they visit the site. However, it is a difficult material to work with, and the estimated quantities should reflect the realities of actual job conditions. A percentage factor of 25 percent to 40 percent is not unreasonable.

Table 8–3 provides factors for the calculation of mortar needed. These factors are net and do not include any percentage for waste.

8.10 MASONRY TIES AND ANCHORS

These items, like mortar, cannot be measured or calculated directly from the drawings; in most cases they do not even appear on the drawings. They are best calculated on the basis of so many pieces per square foot of wall. Specifications usually give enough information regarding the spacing of these ties to make such calculations.

TABLE 8–3 Mortar quantity factors

Brick	Cubic Feet of Mortar per 1000 Brick	
	⅜″ Joint	½″ Joint
4″ Standard Modular (3⅝″ × 2¼″ × 7⅝″)	8.06	10.89
Ontario (4″ × 2⅜″ × 8⅜″)	9.67	13.03
Quebec (3¾″ × 2¼″ × 8″)	8.65	11.66

	Cubic Yards of Mortar per 1000 Block
Concrete Block (15⅝″ × 7⅝″)	
	⅜″ Joint
4″ block	1.1
6″ block	1.6
8″ block	2.2
10″ block	2.6
12″ block	3.3

*These factors based on estimating data prepared by the Clay Brick Association of Canada.

Dovetail anchors, which are attached to anchor slots, can easily be calculated when the total linear length of slot is measured.

8.11 REVIEW

At the beginning of this chapter, it was stressed that preparation of masonry quantities underwent two stages to arrive at the enumeration of the units, followed by adjustments for waste and bonding. It is worth repeating that, if proper care is not used in all these operations, significant errors can result. A normal masonry takeoff is not complicated; measurements of wall areas can be made quite accurately. A good takeoff can be useless if the correct factors are not considered and applied; things go quickly from bad to worse if bonding corrections are inaccurate (or forgotten); then, finally, lack of judgment may result in an unrealistic factor for waste.

There is nothing wrong with using set printed tables, but estimators must develop their expertise in checking such tables and understanding how they were prepared. They should also prepare their own tables for materials or sizes not included in the printed ones. Research into actual projects should highlight some practical information regarding material waste, based on data regarding the quantities actually purchased and the quantities installed in the structure.

8.12 TAKEOFF EXAMPLE

Figure 8–1 provides an example of quantity takeoff for masonry. Floor plans (Figures 5–4 and 5–5), elevations (Figures 5–6 and 5–7), and the building section (Figure 5–8) show most of the information applicable to this trade section. The following brief specification notes supplement the data shown on the drawings:

Face brick, modular size, red rug, laid in 6th course headers.

⅜-in. joints, Type "N" mortar.

Lightweight concrete block—for backup and interior partitions.

Dampcourses and flashings: 2-oz laminated copper paper.

Cavity wall ties—Z-bars ³⁄₁₆-inch wire.

Dovetail anchors, hot-dipped galvanized, 16 gauge—$1'' \times 3\frac{1}{2}'' \times \frac{3}{8}''$

Anchor slot (supply to formwork trade for installation).

Cavity wall insulation—1-in. polystyrene type 4.

Stone coping at parapet, fixed with $\frac{1}{2}''$ diameter $\times 1'$-$6''$ anchors.

Concrete fill to block lintels, two No. 4 reinforcing bars.

Clean down exposed masonry (muriatic acid).

COMMENTARY ON MASONRY TAKEOFF

1. The side notes show the computations of the drawing dimensions and levels to arrive at the wall heights. The face brick at the low-rear portion of the building extends below the floor slab and sits on a shelf formed in the concrete wall.

Project   *Research Center*   Estimate No. 27/82
Location   _____   By *B.E.W.*   Chk'd *H.A.J.*
Subdivision *04200 Masonry*   Date *4/1/99*

Description of Work	No. Pieces	Dimensions A	Dimensions B	Dimensions C	Extensions	Unit	Extensions	Unit	Extensions	Unit
							Clean Down			
					Face Brick		*Face Brick*			
					A x B		*A x B*			
Face brick - exterior walls (6" course headers)										
modular	3/8"	*Joint*								
1 - storey area										
roof 310.0										
gr.fl. (300.0)										
10.0										
parapet 1.0										
slab & shelf 1.0										
12.0	3/	50.0	12.0		1 8 0 0		*DO.*			
North Elevation										
3 x 10.0 = 30.0										
parapet 1.5										
31.5		100.0	31.5		3 1 5 0		*DO.*			
2 x 10.0 = 20.0										
parapet 1.5										
21.5		50.0	21.5		1 0 7 5		*DO.*			
DDT. Windows	2/	(137.75)								
		(89.58)								
	2/	(29.5)	(4.5)		(1 9 0 8)		*DO.*			
Overhead Door	2/	(10.0)	(8.0)		(1 6 0)		*DO.*			
Ext Door		(3.0)	(7.0)		(2 1)		*DO.*			
					3 9 3 6	*sft*	3 9 3 6	*sft*		
Factor = 6 course hdrs = x9.34 =					3 6 7 6 2					
				Add 5% waste	1 8 3 8					
					3 8 6 0 0					
					= 3 8. 6	*M pcs*				
					Coping		*Anchors (2'.0" c/c)*			
					A					
Stone coping at parapet										
	2/	150.0			3 0 0		300 - 0			
	5/	50.0			2 5 0		2	= 150 + 2	1 5 2	
					5 5 0	*lft*	2 5 0			
							2	= 125 + 5	1 3 0	
									2 8 2	*pcs*

FIGURE 8–1   Example of quantity takeoff of masonry.

continued

Project *Research Center*   Estimate No. *27/82*
Location _____   By *B.E.W.*   Chk'd *H.A.J.*
Subdivision *04200 Masonry*   Date *4/1/99*

Description of Work	No. Pieces	Dimensions A	B	C	Extensions	Unit	Extensions	Unit	Extensions	Unit
							Cavity Insulation A x B			
					Block 8" A x B					
Concrete Block Backing to										
Face Brick & P.C. Concrete										
50.0										
2 x 1.0 (2.0)		2/150.0								
48.0		2/ 50.0	31.5		1 2 6 0 0		DO.			
		(48.0)	10.0)		(4 8 0)		DO.			
Deduct										
Spandrel beam	3/2/	(150.0)								
& slab edge	3/2/	(50.0)			(3 4 6 7)		DO.			
		(100.0)	(2.67)							
Drs. & W/Ws	2/2/	(137.75)								
		(89.58)								
	2/	(59.33)								
31.5	5/	(39.42)								
(7.0) *4" brick*	2/	(10.0)	(4.5)		(4 3 9 3)		DO.			
24.5 *8" block*		(10.0)	(8.0)		(8 0)		DO.			
12"	2/	(3.0)	(7.0)		(4 2)		DO.			
corners	4/	(1.0)	(24.5)		(9 8)		DO.			
1 storey bldg	3/	50.0	9.33		1 4 0 0		DO.			
Deduct										
doors/windows	2/	(29.5)	(4.65)		(2 6 6)		DO.			
	2/	(10.0)	(8.0)		(1 6 0)		DO.			
		(3.0)	(7.0)		(2 1)		DO.			
					4 9 9 3	sft	4 9 9 3	sft		
		x 1.13 = 5642					4 9 9	10% waste		
		+ 5% waste	282				5 4 9 2	pcs		
				5924	pcs					
Dampcourse (16 oz.)					A					
	2/	150.0			3 0 0					
	5/	50.0			2 5 0					
					5 5 0					
					+10% 5 5					
					6 0 5	lft				

FIGURE 8–1 Example of quantity takeoff of masonry.

continued

Project	Research Center	Estimate No.	27/82
Location		By	B.E.W.	Chk'd	H.A.J.
Subdivision	04200 Masonry	Date	4/1/99

Description of Work	No. Pieces	Dimensions A	B	C	Extensions	Unit	Extensions	Unit	Extensions	Unit
					A					
Flashing over windows & doors										
windows	2/2/	137.75			5 5 1					
		89.58			9 0					
	2/	59.33			1 1 9					
	5/	39.42			1 9 7					
	2/	10.0			2 0					
	2/	29.5			5 9					
o/head doors	2/	9.83			2 0					
single door	2/	4.25			9					
main entrance		9.83			1 0					
					1 0 7 5	lft				
					A					
Anchor slots (supplied to formwork trade)										
748.0										
297.0										
100.0										
1145.0										
÷ 2 = 573										
+ 5										
+ 6										
+ 1										
585	585/	2.67			1 5 6 2					
ext. columns	12/	7.25			8 7					
	2/3/	7.25			4 4					
	2/12/	7.25			1 7 4					
	2/2/4/	7.25			1 1 6					
					1 9 8 3	lft				
Dovetail anchors										
		585 x 2			1 1 7 0					
		58 x 7.25								
	2				2 1 0					
					1 3 8 0					
						say 1400 pcs				

FIGURE 8–1   Example of quantity takeoff of masonry.

continued

Project _Research Center_

Location _____

Subdivision _04200 Masonry_

Estimate No. _27/82_

By _B.E.W._   Chk'd _H.A.J._

Date _4/1/99_

Description of Work	No. Pieces	Dimensions A	B	C	Extensions 6" Block A x B	Unit	Extensions 4" Block A x B	Unit	Extensions	Unit
Interior Concrete Block Partitions										
150.0 23.0										
(2.0) 19.0										
148.0 12.0										
(54.0) 54.0										
94.0										
(5.0)										
89.0										
gr. fl. corridor		94.0								
10.0 21.0		89.0								
(.67) 26.0	2/2/	20.83								
9.33 3x6" 1.5	3/	5.0								
48.5	2/	48.5	9.33		3 5 3 0					
doors	15/	(3.5)	(7.0)		(3 6 8)					
partitions	10/	20.83								
stair		14.83	9.33				2 0 8 3			
2nd & 3rd floors	2/2/	148.0								
	2/2/	20.83	9.33		6 3 0 1					
doors	2/15/	(3.5)	(7.0)		(7 3 6)					
partitions	2/8/	20.83	9.33				3 1 1 1			
					8 7 2 7	sft	5 1 9 4	sft		
			x 1.13 =		9 8 6 2		5 8 6 9			
			+ 5% waste		4 9 3		2 9 3			
					1 0 3 5 5	pcs	6 1 6 2	pcs		
					A					
Extra-over Concrete & R4esteel to Lintels										
	46/	5.6			2 5 3	lft				

FIGURE 8–1   Example of quantity takeoff of masonry.

continued

Project	Research Center
Location	
Subdivision	04200 Masonry

Estimate No. 27/82

By __B.E.W.__ Chk'd __H.A.J.__

Date __4/1/99__

Description of Work	No. Pieces	Dimensions A	Dimensions B	Dimensions C	Extensions	Unit	Extensions	Unit	Extensions	Unit
					Lintel Block A		Bullnose Unit A			
Special Concrete Block Units										
	46/	5.5			2 5 3					
	5/	9.33					4 7			
					2 5 3		4 7			
							x 1.5		= 7 0 pcs	
				x .75 =	1 9 0	pcs				
Exposed Block Surfaces					Clean Block A x B				Extra for Exposed faces	
		19.0	9.33		1 7 7					
		(3.0)	(7.0)		(2 1)					
		9.83	9.33		9 2				248 x 1.13 = 280 pcs	
					2 4 8	sft				
Scaffold Frames										
in 5'.0" Lifts										
I storey high										
2 lifts	3/2/	50.0			3 0 0					
7 lifts	7/	100.0			7 0 0					
5 lifts	5/	50.0			2 5 0					
interior (1 lift)		1030.0			1 0 3 0					
					2 2 8 0	÷ 7 =	3 2 6 frames			
Cavity Wall Ties										
10.0	3/	50.0	10.17		1 5 2 5					
(1.33) solid		100.0	22.0		2 2 0 0					
8.67		50.0	15.67		7 8 4					
1.5					4 5 0 9	sft				
10.17										
					1 per 2 sft = 4509 = 2255			say	2300	pcs
					2					

FIGURE 8–1 Example of quantity takeoff of masonry.

continued

Project   *Research Center*

Location

Subdivision *04200 Masonry*

Estimate No.   *27/82*

By   *B.E.W.*   Chk'd   *H.A.J.*

Date   *4/1/99*

Description of Work	No. Pieces	Dimensions A	B	C	Extensions	Unit	Extensions	Unit	Extensions	Unit
					A					
Extra-over - labor										
to brick sills										
	2/	137.75			2 7 6					
		89.58			9 0					
	2/	29.5			5 9					
					4 2 5	lft				
Mortar (Type "N")										
Brick factor	8.06 c ft/1000		=	39 x 8.06	=		11.6			
				27						
Conc block 4"	(1 cyd/1000)		=	6.1 x 1			6.1			
6"	(1 1/2 cyd/1000)		=	10.4 x 1.5			15.6			
8"	(2 cyd/1000)		=	5.9 x 2			11.8			
							45.1			
					Add 25% waste		11.2			
							56.3 cyd			

FIGURE 8–1   Example of quantity takeoff of masonry.

continued

119

2. Openings in the wall are deducted from the gross area using the net door dimensions (i.e., the extra width for frames is not included).

3. The factor to determine the number of bricks is obtained from Table 8–1.

4. The dimensions on the drawings are from corner to corner and are correct for the face brick measurements, but it should be noted that the block backup (sheet 2) extends from the inside face to inside face. This would be 150 feet (100 feet + 50 feet) less 2 × 4 inches = 8 inches.

5. The anchor slots (sheet 3) are measured the full depth of the spandrel beam at 24 inches on center, with extra slots allowed at the ends. The slots to the columns are measured for three sides.

6. The dovetail anchors are measured on the basis of two per anchor slot in the spandrel beams, and at 24 inches centers at the columns.

7. In this example the measurements for the interior concrete block partitions (sheet 4) are developed from the dimensions noted on the drawings (with some overlapping at intersections, etc.). In practice, however, and particularly for a very large project with many floors and rooms divided by partitions, this is one item where time limitations would advocate the use of a scale or a "measuring wheel."

8. The length of the block lintels (sheet 5) are developed as follows:

Width of opening	3 feet 6 inches
Plus 2 × 1 foot	2 feet 0 inch
	5 feet 6 inches

For the purpose of the estimate this is accurate enough, but it should be pointed out again that the dimension of 5 feet 6 inches does not allow for the width of the doorframe.

9. Only special jamb and bullnose units have been measured, although many other special shapes and sizes would be required. For bidding purposes it is sufficient to establish (by some method or other) an approximation of the premium cost of these items. On this example a linear measurement has been taken for the height of the jambs, and the lintel, and the number of units per foot established. A more detailed estimate of quantities of each type of unit would have to be made for actual purchasing purposes.

10. The extra cost of laying block which will remain exposed is measured as recommended in the schedule of items and measurements, that is, taking the "cleaning" area multiplied by the factor to establish the number of pieces, to which the estimated premium labor cost would be applied.

11. The scaffold frames are measured on the basis of linear feet per each 5 feet lift of scaffold. The total length is then divided by 7 feet to establish the number of scaffold frames to be erected and dismantled. This is based on using 7-foot braces. The actual number of frames to be purchased or rented would be the minimum number required for the project according to the estimator's judgment.

12. The extra over for the brick sills (sheet 6) is measured in linear feet and the cost will be based on 3 bricks per foot.

13. The mortar quantities are based on the factors shown in Table 8–3. Note that 25 percent waste is added to the net quantity.

9

TAKEOFF: MISCELLANEOUS METALS AND STRUCTURAL STEEL

9.1 GENERAL

The term "miscellaneous metals" is a time-honored expression for work that is now encompassed within the Masterformat sections of 05500 Metal Fabrications. Miscellaneous metals are smaller fabricated pieces (generally rolled shapes) used to attach material together, provide protection (as do bollards), and serve the other hundred smaller steel uses. Structural steel pieces, on the other hand, are the steel components used to form the major structural systems or parts of the structural systems in buildings in combination with other materials. Structural steel can further be defined as larger rolled shapes that make up the beams, columns, and other structural members of a steel frame building system. These structural shapes are generally all rolled pieces (I-beams, wide flanges, tubes, channels, plates, angles, etc.) produced at large steel manufacturing plants and shipped to fabricators for fabrication into beams, columns, and other structural components. Miscellaneous Metals and Structural Steel form the largest amount of work within the section, but other areas are also included. They are ornamental work, handrails, aluminum products, decking and sheet siding, and bar joists to name a few.

Ornamental work has become a specialized area within this division, but the generalized market for this type of work was lost in the 1950s. The market consisted of handrails, guard rails, gates, and the like. Ornamental work uses small bar stock as its basic component (although today small steel tube material is also used).

Often miscellaneous metals are used in support of other structural components. Metal fabricated hangers, connectors, clips, and gussets are all used to connect concrete to wood or steel, wood to steel, masonry to wood or steel, and even steel to steel. Not all miscellaneous metal items are a part of the building structure. They can be used to guard other items (i.e., corner guards, handrails, and bollards), or just to satisfy aesthetic purposes.

Sheet metal decking and bar joists are additional items in Division 5. Often decking is installed by ironworkers, but in some instances it is installed by the sheet metal trades. Decking can be supplied by the same fabricators supplying the structural and miscellaneous metal portion of a work but is not required to be. Decking is not an item that is fabricated, but is purchased from a decking manufacturer. Bar joists also are not fabricated from the traditional steel fabricator, but manufactured by a supplier specializing in the manufacture and design of bar joists.

9.2   FABRICATORS

Not all fabricators have the ability to produce all sections within Division 5. Individual pieces may be unprofitable to build in some shops. These fabricators just exclude those items during the bidding, leaving it to the general contractor to include the left-out items or add them into the estimate. Other things that also will further restrict a fabricator's ability to produce the items within this section are overall size of a piece, length and weight of a piece, and the metal of choice. (Aluminum is difficult to weld and needs a craftsperson trained and certified.) It should be mentioned early in this chapter that preengineered metal buildings are not included in this CSI Division 5, but are in a later division under the CSI Masterformat. Preengineered structures are not built by the same type of fabricators that are quoting on miscellaneous metals and structural steel specified in Division 5.

9.3   SPECIFICATIONS

Most specifications will require shops to maintain certifications on welders in certain circumstances and often will request shop drawings on the items to be made or welded. Installation drawings are also a requirement for the installation process. Additionally, these specifications will cover other critical information needed by the estimator to be able to understand and determine the cost of this work, to align the different fabricator quotes, and finally, to price the work.

Some of this other specified information may describe coatings to be applied to the steel items. These coatings take the form of galvanizing or paint (most often just priming). These two coatings are substantially different in costs, and if not quoted properly could negatively affect the estimate. The workmanship of the welding and grinding will also be described in the specification and can impact the costs.

This division among the trades requires a great amount of investigation and analysis by the estimator. Many items often appear on the drawings that are not clearly defined in the specifications as to which trade is responsible for their supply and/or installation. All the estimator knows with any certainty is that it is the general contractor who must bear the responsibility of ensuring that the costs of these items are included in the bid total. The quotes for metal trades often differ from those of other vendors/subcontractors in that they are specific to items that will be provided by the fabricator. Many other trades will quote a full division and will use the terms "per plans and specifications" to denote compliance to the section or subsection. The miscellaneous metals and structural steel fabricators create lists of items to be delivered and indicate whether they are to be furnished only, furnished and installed, or installed only. It is common practice for the subcontractor specializing in metal work to provide the general contractors with a pre–bid proposal clearly listing all the items that will be included in subsequent quotes, and noting those items that will be "supplied only." This practice is of great assistance to the contractor's estimator, who can prepare sheets for analyzing the different quotes and proceed to take off and price those items to be installed by the contractor. Even without these pre–bid proposal lists, an experienced estimator can identify most of the latter items. They usually apply to all items embedded in concrete or built in to masonry or wood work.

9.4   SCOPE ALIGNMENT

The need for scope alignment is quickly noted as one lists the many different items that fall within Division 5. To do this task, the estimator must also have a complete list of all the miscellaneous metals, structural steel, ornamental metals, handrails, and so forth required for the project. It should also be noted that, when reviewing the miscellaneous metals and structural fabricator quotes, items not to be furnished as well as items outside the scope of Division 5 and listed in other specification sections are quite often listed specifically. This trend of specifically listing all items probably came about from misunderstandings of what was considered miscellaneous metal and what was fabricated from steel, for example, re-bar or light gage framing. These items were never meant to be included in the scope of work for these fabricators, but because of their material makeup were misinterpreted to be part of their work. Figure 9–1 shows an example of a miscellaneous metal quote that illustrates these points concerning which items will be supplied only and which will be both supplied and installed. Generally, most items of work that can be identified as "embedded" fall under the category of "supply only."

Some items may only be identified in the specification by an all-embracing label like "Miscellaneous Steel Angles, Channels, etc." or similar terms, and there will be a brief description of the items followed by the statement "as shown and detailed on the drawings." This will entail an unavoidable meticulous examination of all the drawings (architectural, structural, mechanical, and electrical) to establish the location and quantities of such items. Estimators should examine details of metal window assemblies and work around elevators where it is quite common to find miscellaneous angles and the like, which may not be defined as being part of those particular trade divisions.

It is recommended that estimators first list all the items noted in the specification for this trade; next, measure and record the quantities of the "supplied" items; and then add to the list all those items that are detailed on the drawings but not identified in the specifications. These should also be drawn to the attention of the trade contractors, although sometimes this process is reversed by the trade contractors alerting the general contractors.

Markworks Steel Fabricators, Inc.
P.O. Box 148
162 South Ross Street
Auburn, Alabama   36849
(334) 844-9200

Proposal No.   98-203   Date   June 16, 1998

THIS PROPOSAL SUBJECT TO TERMS AND CONDITIONS ON THE BACK HEREOF WHICH TERMS AND
CONDITIONS ARE REFERRED TO AND MADE A PART HEREOF.

Project Name:
Location:
Bid Date:
Bid Time:

We propose to provide a complete Miscellaneous Metals and Structural Steel package in accordance with the following terms and conditions:

1. Documents used to prepare bid:
    Drawing Numbers:
    A 101 through A 135, S 101 through S 25 . . .

Specification Sections:
    05000
    05120
    05500

2. Addenda and Dates:
    Number 1, Dated May 20, 1999
    Number 2, Dated May 25, 1999

3. Furnish, Fabricate, and Deliver only
    a. Embedded angle at dock leveler—detail E on sheet S 15
    b. Angle brace—detail P on sheet S 12
    c. Lintels
    d. . . .

4. Furnish, Fabricate, Deliver, and Erect (Structural Steel)
    a. Columns
    b. Tapered girders
    c. Beams
    d. . . .

5. Furnish, Fabricate, Deliver, and Erect (Miscellaneous Metals)
    a. Tube frame at rollup door—detail R on sheet A 45
    b. Elevator ladder—detail C on sheet A 56
    c. . . .

6. List of Conditions
    a. This quotation is firm for acceptance within 60 days.
    b. Prices are firm for delivery before August 30, 1999.
    c. Prices are based on truckload shipments (LTD's will require special arrangements and additional
       compensation).
    d. All truckloads are to be standard size shipments (8′ × 40′). No over width and no over length.

FIGURE 9–1   Pre-bid proposal.

    e. Unless specifically noted otherwise, all structural and miscellaneous steel is to cleaned per SSPC-SP2 and to receive one coat of our standard shop primer (red oxide).

    f. Detailed shop drawings and erection drawings are included in the bid price. However, unless specifically noted otherwise, review of shop drawings by a registered professional engineer is to be considered as an extra cost to this proposal.

    g. We do not include intermediate or finish coats of paint. No special protection, packaging, or crating included.

    h. Liquidated damages will not be accepted.

    i. Fabrication of like items (total quantities) will occur at the same time regardless of delivery requirements. Deviation will be cause for additional costs.

    j. Our bid includes all domestic pricing on required bolts, nuts, washers, and other fasteners. Please make note of the uncertain and sometimes untimely availability of certain domestic bolts, nuts, washers, and other fasteners. If this occurs to any such items required on this project, we will be turning to you for direction as to how to proceed.

    k. Contract structure: the customer will issue 1) a purchase order to Markworks Steel Fabricators, Inc. for the materials; 2) a subcontract to the steel erection company for the installation of the material as outlined above. The sum of the purchase order and the subcontract will be equal to the amount shown below as "Base Bid." The steel erection company (to be chosen by Markworks Steel Fabricators, Inc.) will erect per the scope shown above and is bondable (at a rate of 1.5%).

    l. Terms: Net 30 days, no retainage allowed.

    m. This proposal shall become a part of any purchase orders and subcontracts resulting from this quote or any related quotations.

7. Exclusions (unless specifically noted otherwise)

    a. Grout and Grouting

    b. Touch-Up Paint, Touch-Up Painting, or Touch-Up Galvanizing

    c. Lightgage Metal Framing, Stainless Steel, Re-bar, and Non-Ferrous Items

    d. Field Measurements

    e. Carpenter's Hardware

    f. Material Embedded in Precast Concrete and/or Connection Material for Precast Concrete (precast to precast, precast to masonry, precast to cast in place concrete, precast to steel, precast to wood, etc.)

    g. Detention Hardware, Equipment, Connections, or Accessories

    h. Material or work found on bidding documents other than those documents specifically listed in section "1" of this proposal

    i. Cost of bond or bond premium

    j. Testing, Survey, or Inspection

    k. Demolition

    l. Expansion Joint Covers

    m. Glued Laminated Timber Connection Material and Bolts

    n. Metal Deck and Weld Studs (Section 5300)

    o. Post for Signs (C-202, C203, C204)

    p. Ornamental Fencing (Detail 3 on C-502)

    q. Card Reader Post (C-503)

    r. Wire Partitions

    s. Anchor Bolts for Mechanical Equipment

    t. Hilti Anchor @ dowels (Detail 4, on S-405)

    u. Concrete for Bollards or Pan Stairs

    v. Backcharges—If any changes or alterations are required to our work which will result in backcharges, we must be notified in writing of the nature and approximate cost involved and be given the opportunity to review the changes before they are made or we will not accept the backcharges.

    w. Federal, state or local excise, sales, usage or similar taxes now in force or which may be levied. If Seller is required to pay any of such taxes directly, the amount shall be added to the contract price.

FIGURE 9–1 Pre-bid proposal.

continued

8. Price

Base Bid _____

Alternate No. 1 _____

Alternate No. 2 _____

Bid price for "Furnish, Fabricate, and Deliver Only" items are material FOB trucks jobsite.

If you have any questions please call.

By: Jim Borland

Vice President, Sales

FIGURE 9–1   Pre-bid proposal.

9.5   SCHEDULE OF ITEMS AND MEASUREMENTS: MISCELLANEOUS METALS AND STRUCTURAL STEEL

Item	Comment	Unit of Measurement
Miscellaneous metals	The following list represents those items most commonly considered as embedded items, or items usually quoted on a "supplied only" basis by the trade contractor. The method of fixing should be stated with each item. If sleeving is required, the sleeves should be enumerated and the material into which they are to be set described. (Strictly speaking, the setting of sleeves into various materials should be transferred to and included with the applicable trade divisions.) *Note:* Check for sleeves embedded in concrete that might require fastening to, and holes cut in, the formwork.	
Miscellaneous steel: angles, shelf angles, channels, plates, etc.	State function and /or location ("lintels to masonry," "loading dock nosing").	Linear foot (m) or pound (kilogram)
Covers and frames to:		Numerical
a. manholes and catch basins	State size, material.	
b. trenches	State size, material.	
c. sumps and other pits	State size, material.	

continued

Item	Comment	Unit of Measurement
Sills, stools, thresholds	State all dimensions.	Linear foot (m)
Miscellaneous brackets for the fixing of other items of work (wood railings, vanity units, etc.)		Numerical
Expansion joint covers and assemblies		Linear foot (m)
Corner guards		Numerical
Gratings and frames	Note if to be filled with concrete.	Square foot (m²)
Supports for ceiling-hung toilet partitions		Pound (kilogram)
Lateral supports for masonry partitions		Pound (kilogram)
Bollards		Numerical
Channel door frames	Not hollow metal frames.	Pound (kilogram)
Metal fabricated pit ladders		Numerical
Ornamental work	Handrails, gates, security doors	Numerical
Handrails	Both aluminum and steel tube handrails	Linear foot (m)
Metal stairs	Fabricated: stringers, risers, and landing	Numerical
Structural steel work	Rolled, buildup, and tube shapes used as structural pieces: ■ Beams ■ Purlins ■ Trusses ■ Columns (both solid and tube shapes) Including base plates, gussets, etc.	Pound (kilogram) and numerical
Aluminum products	Expansion joint covers, trench covers, opening frames	Numerical
Structural decking and sheet siding	Rolled in specialty manufacturing plants (a purchase-and-install item for this subcontractor or may be subcontracted to a specialist that does only this work)	Square foot (m²)
Bar joists	Generally fabricated in specialty manufacturing plants (a purchase-and-install item for this subcontractor)	Linear foot (m) and numerical

9.6 | SCOPE ALIGNMENT PROCESS

One of the largest and most important parts of an estimate consists of the many items that will be subcontracted. In some instances, the general contractor may even opt to subcontract all of the project work to specialty contractors and not do any fabricating or installing with its own forces. On bid day a contractor will receive many different quotes for virtually the same work. The first step in aligning the quote so that the quotes can be compared is called scope alignment. The authors have decided to describe the process of scope alignment in this chapter on miscellaneous metals and structural steel because of its complexity and also because scope alignment is needed on virtually every project involving the metal trades. As mentioned previously, fabricators and installers of miscellaneous metals and structural steel do not bid complete

---

SECTION 05500

METAL FABRICATIONS

PART 1 - GENERAL

1.01   SUMMARY

    A.   Section Includes: Metal fabrications for standard and custom-fabricated items, as indicated on the Drawings.

    B.   Related Sections:
        1.   Section 05120 - Structural Steel.
        2.   Review Division 1 - General Requirements, which contain information and requirements that apply to this Section.

1.02   ENGINEERING REQUIREMENTS

    A.   Design Concept: Metal Fabrication requirements shown by the drawings are intended to establish basic dimensions, alignment of members, profiles of members and relationship of items to other building components.
        1.   Engineering Requirements: Engineer the designated items, including supporting members, connections and anchorage to building structure, making necessary additions and modifications to any specified proprietary system manufacturer's standard details as may be required to comply with specified performance requirements, while maintaining the basic design concept.
            a.   Structural Design: Prepared by a structural or civil engineer licensed in the jurisdiction of Governing Authorities, including calculations and drawings as necessary for review and approval by Governing Authorities.

    B.   Performance Requirements: Comply with Reference Standards, requirements of Governing Authorities and requirements specified herein.
        1.   Structural:
            a.   Wind Load: As required by Governing Authorities for applicable heights.
            b.   Horizontal Force: 20 psf minimum, but not less than requirements of Governing Authorities.
                1)   Screens and Similar Open Assemblies: Assume 20 psf over full height and width of screen (no open area).
            c.   Maximum Deflection of Members: 1/360 of span when tested in accordance with ASTM E330.

FIGURE 9–2   Section 5500 Metal Fabrication (partial specification).

sections, as do many of their counterparts in other sections. Fabricators come in many sizes and have different capacities to build items needed, and some do not have the necessary skills to fabricate all the items within this section. The numerous items of metal described in this chapter vary in size from small items of steel to very large and heavy steel items along with items of other metals (e.g., aluminum handrails).

    A starting point is a listing of work to be performed under or covered by the specification sections, in this case Division 5 (Masterformat). Figure 9–2 is a copy of early parts of the section on miscellaneous metals.

Fire Arms Control Building
Project No. 99-134

Scope Alignment – Miscellaneous Metals

Spec. Section Number	Description	Our Plug Number	Sub. Name & Phone No.	Sub. Name & Phone No.
05500 Iron	Metal Fabrication	$ 250,000	Stockton Steel	Kraftwerk
			(209) 978-7801	(503) 394-5948
	Pipe railings		√	√
	Pit ladder		√	√
	Edging angles		√	
	Bollards		√	√
	Corner angles		√	√
	Ceiling supports		√	√
	Tube frame for roll-up door			√
	Floor angles		√	√
	Original quote		$ 245,000	$ 263,000
	Total cost with plug numbers			

FIGURE 9–3   Scope alignment—initial plug sheet.

A specification section review and listing of work is the starting point for this examination. It is also the beginning of the list of work that is generated by an upcoming bid because as subcontracts are developed by the general contractor they will specifically link the specification and the subcontract together. A plug sheet (Figure 9–3) should be started that lists all work to be done under the sections. Additionally this sheet should contain rows that allow the noting of any addenda that are included, whether sales tax will be included or excluded, whether materials are furnished only or furnished and installed, and lastly a column for freight costs (FOB, etc.). These columns are crucial in the comparison and analysis the estimator will be doing on the different quotes, as to what they are providing. All of the column information will directly impact the discussion on whom the estimator will use. The object of the plug sheets is to make sure that the estimate is complete and that one is comparing apples to apples in deciding which bidder to use. Scope alignment can be defined as comparing the scope of each subcontractor doing like work, in order to recognize whether each will include a scope similar to all others bidding the same specification section.

The second step in the process of scope alignment is the entering of the items that each subcontractor has quoted on. In most cases one will find that 80 or 90 percent of the work will be the same.

The final step in scope alignment is to contact each subcontractor and clarify their individual quotes. Some estimators will use the convention that if an item of work is obvious and not needing confirmation or clarification, a check (✓) mark is

Spec. Section Number	Description	Our Plug Number	Sub. Name & Phone No.	Sub. Name & Phone No.
	Fire Arms Control Building Project No. 99-134 Scope Alignment – Miscellaneous Metals			
05500 Iron	Metal Fabrication	$ 250,000	Stockton Steel (209) 978-7801	Kraftwerk (503) 394-5948
	Pipe railings		√	√
	Pit ladder		√	√
	Edging angles		√	*add $ 1,000*
	Bollards		√	√
	Corner angles		√	√
	Ceiling supports		√	√
	Tube frame for roll-up door		*add $ 23,000*	√
	Floor angles		√	√
	Original quote		$ 245,000	$ 263,000
	Total cost with plug numbers		$ 268,000	$ 264,000

FIGURE 9–4   Scope alignment—filled-out plug sheet.

placed next to the item. At this time, each fabricator/subcontractor would be called and the unchecked items either confirmed to be in the quote or outside the scope of that fabricator's quote. Any questions by the estimator on the additional exclusion or contract clarifications made by the subcontractor in his quote should also be addressed. All subcontractors must be aligned with the same addenda at a minimum. When using the term "align," the authors intend the process of adding estimated amounts to each subcontractor in any area in which the subcontractor may be deficient. The issue of sales tax also should be aligned at this time. If a fabricator is not quoting a specific piece, details, or work, it is left blank and later a plug number (an estimated amount representing the estimator's best calculation of the cost of the work) is inserted to allow an apple to apple cost comparison (Figure 9–4). These plug numbers can come from the estimators themselves or better, from another subcontractor that is willing to price the item separately for the estimator. In most cases, this breakout of a single item is not a quote to fabricate and/or install that piece of work. Most subcontractors are more than willing to help in scope alignment in this fashion, but generally not to provide a single item later during the progress of the project. An example is illustrated in Figure 9–4 under the item of "Tube frame for roll-up door." The plug number of $23,000.00 was obtained from the general contractor's estimator and placed in the quote of Stockton Steel. Note that this estimator used italicized number/underlined, to represent an exclusion and the plug number from another subcontractor. Use of clouds is another way to represent or to highlight these numbers.

9.6 REVIEW

Division 5 work is one of the most complicated groups of work to incorporate into an estimate. Division 5 covers many different items within the section, but what complicates the process is that each individual fabricator/supplier/subcontractor will only provide a part of the work specified for this section. This means that the estimator must know the complete scope of the work within this section and then must make a detailed comparison between all the companies quoting the work. In some instances the general contractor will not receive any coverage on an item or a group of items. The estimators must then fill in the missing parts with their own pricing. The other part of the quoting process that makes the estimator's job more complicated is the lack of conformity between furnish and install, furnish only, install only, and not furnishing or installing of items within the Division 5 work. It is one thing for estimators to price materials they may not be familiar with, but then having to price the labor that has been excluded is truly challenging.

It is also recommended that estimators note the applicable drawing and detail numbers on both the takeoff sheets and the summary sheets for pricing. This facilitates any rechecking required, and also simplifies the problem of adequately describing an item: "2 × 4 in. (50 mm × 100 mm) blocking as per detail A.6/21" is much simpler to locate and understand than, say, "2 × 4 blocking at perimeter ceiling recess for valance in gymnasium."

The quantities for the rough carpentry items that are applicable to or required for finished carpentry or millwork should be measured with those items. This will avoid the irritating chore of working twice through the same drawings and details.

10.2 MEASURING ROUGH CARPENTRY WORK

Lumber is sold on the foot board measure (bft) basis, with the existing American dimensions expressed in "soft conversion" metric terms. The metric substitution for the board foot (bft) is the cubic meter (m^3). It is recommended that most items be measured and priced in linear or running feet and then converted to board feet; this applies particularly to the cost of installation, as will be demonstrated in Chapter 12. Exceptions will be found to this rule where smaller quantities are used, but generally this rule is always used for large quantities of structural framing (roofs, floors, walls, etc.) where it could be more realistic to establish unit costs per board feet for both material and labor.

All items should be measured net in place, but consideration must be given to basic construction requirements that are rarely shown or indicated on the drawings. These would include:

1. Allowances for bearing on walls, columns, beams, and the like.
2. Additional studs at corners, openings, and so on.
3. Diagonal bridging.
4. Studs and plates at partitions.
5. Overlapping of the various members.

All items should be kept separate according to lumber dimensions, classification, and grade, for example, "No. 2 Spruce, Construction Grade." The number of dressed sides should also be stated.

Items that require drilling for bolts or any system of fixing other than nailing, screwing, or gluing should be stated separately.

Adjustment factors should be applied to the net lumber quantities as allowances for cutting and waste. It was stated in Chapter 5 that most estimators do not have the time to accurately plan and categorize all the miscellaneous items of lumber into a practicable list of purchasable lengths. As long as good judgment is exercised in the assessment of each individual condition, these percentage factors can provide reasonably adequate gross and purchasable quantities.

Plywood and other wallboards should be measured in square feet, and here again factors must be applied to allow for cutting and waste. (Items with very small quantities could be expressed in terms of the minimum number of sheets required.)

Lumber requiring pressure treatment should be kept separate, or, alternatively, the various items can be priced as "untreated" and then added and expressed in one single total as "extra over" in board feet ("extra over for pressure treatment—500 bft").

All blocking and the like, which are in short pieces, should either be enumerated or the number stated in the description; for example, "2 × 4 in. blocking at metal windows (in 20 pieces) + 82 lft." This enables the estimator to realistically price the cutting and fitting in place.

10.3 SCHEDULE OF ITEMS AND MEASUREMENTS: ROUGH CARPENTRY

Item	Comment	Unit of Measurement
Miscellaneous roof carpentry	Keep separate for: ■ cants ■ blockings ■ curbs ■ copings and parapets ■ others (Built up or laminated in place work to be identified separately.)	Linear foot (m)
Strapping and furring	Keep separate for: ■ exterior walls ■ interior partitions ■ bulkheads ■ soffits ■ other surfaces	Linear foot (m)
Window blockings	If in short pieces less than 5 feet (1.5 meters) long, state the number in the description. Include detail or section number with item.	Linear foot (m)
Blocking and furring to finished carpentry work	Separate into categories such as: ■ paneling ■ counters and cupboards ■ shelving ■ railings ■ doorframes ■ others	Linear foot (m)
Structural framing	Main categories: ■ roofs: rafters, ridges, eaves, ties ■ floors and ceilings: joists, bridging, plates, trimmers, girders, etc. ■ walls and partitions: studs, plates, lintels, etc. Allow for bearing into walls, beams. Extra members at the end of each span, "doubling" at corners, intersections, openings or under partitions, etc.	Linear foot (m) or board foot

continued

Item	Comment	Unit of Measurement
Wallboards	State: ■ thickness ■ material classification ■ number of finished (sanded) surfaces Keep separate categories for: ■ subfloors ■ wall sheathing ■ soffits ■ fascias ■ parapets ■ circular or sloping surfaces Wallboards in strips less than 12 inches wide should be stated in linear feet.	Square foot (m²)
Plywood sheathing	Main categories: ■ floors ■ walls and partitions ■ roofs Keep diagonal works separate; add applicable waste factor to net quantities. State if tongued and grooved, rabbet edged.	Square foot (m²)
Building paper	Describe material.	Square foot (m²)
Roofing felt	Describe material.	Square foot (m²)
Vapor barriers	Describe materials.	Square foot (m²)
Miscellaneous blockings	State location, function, and drawing detail numbers. Small quantities: state number of pieces.	Linear foot (m)
Rough hardware: ■ anchor bolts, ■ joist hangers, metal angles, brackets, etc.	State diameter and length. State material, gauge, size, etc.	Numerical Numerical
Miscellaneous rough hardware	This includes nails, screws, spikes, etc. Usually the total weight is established by applying a factor based on the number of pounds per thousand board feet. This "rule of thumb" formula will usually provide an adequate sum of money to include in the estimate.	Pound (kilogram)

10.4 FINISH CARPENTRY

The finish carpentry work reviewed here refers to the items in a modern building that are usually supplied by a millwork subcontractor; therefore, the estimating methods and procedures to be discussed will in most cases be restricted to the receiving, handling, and installation only of this work. It is not unusual for some subcontractors to quote this trade on the basis of both supply and on-site erection; but most contractors still take off and price finished carpentry work for the following reasons:

1. The estimated cost of installation can be added to a supply only quotation to make a proper comparison with the complete package quotations.

2. There may be certain items excluded from the quotations; by having a complete takeoff and all work priced, the contractor can estimate the value of these omissions. (The rough carpentry work to which this work is attached will also usually be excluded from these quotations.)

The Masterformat includes two divisions: 06200 Finish Carpentry and 06400 Architectural Woodwork. The distinction between these two divisions is best interpreted as one of quality. Cabinet work, for example, might be specified in both sections, but the specification in 06400 (Architectural Woodwork) would generally require the work to be custom-made and of a very high quality. This section is usually quoted by special subcontractors, nearly always on the basis of complete supply and on-site erection in accordance with the specification.

There are no reliable shortcuts to estimating the cost of millwork or finish carpentry installation. Rule of thumb formulas such as allowing a percentage of the material cost to cover the cost of installation usually produce hit and miss results. All items should be measured and listed for pricing. However, it is possible to group items into categories that provide common cost factors.

A good example is fitments (counters, cupboards, storage units, etc.). One factor influencing the installation costs of these items is the amount of cabinet hardware required.

EXAMPLE: Assume two counter units, each with similar dimensions and each with plastic laminate tops. Counter 1 has two cupboard doors, three shelves, and three drawers at one end. Counter 2 has two drawers and two shelves open to view (no doors). The cost of installing this counter will be less than installing counter 1, because there is less hardware, such as hinges, knobs, shelf brackets, and drawer guides.

If categories are established such as these, the total length of all counter units pertaining to a selected category can be measured and summarized accordingly; this method should accelerate the takeoff process considerably. The alternative is to take each counter or cupboard as a separate item, stating the dimensions. Whichever method is followed, the drawing or detail numbers should be shown on the summary sheets.

All other items (trim, stair rails, paneling, fascias, sills, etc.) should be taken off in detail. Specifications often contain items that some (or all) millwork suppliers will exclude from their quotations, and without a complete estimate it will be sheer guessing to evaluate the cost of the excluded items.

Estimators should also be alerted to the interface items that:

1. Form integral parts of specific finish carpentry or millwork units but are specified under other divisions, such as brackets, metal legs, glass shelves, angle supports, and stainless steel trim; or

2. Are the same type items as in item 1, but are included in the finish carpentry specifications, although local or regional trade practices might influence the exclusion of these items from subcontractors' quotations.

In both cases these items should be taken off, but consideration must be given as to the division in which they should be summarized and priced. If metal brackets for wood stair rails are included in the division for Miscellaneous Metals, for example, then the quantities of these brackets should be included in the list of items for that division (i.e., Miscellaneous Metals). Most subcontractors or suppliers bidding that trade will include these items in their quotations. If, however, contrary to normal trade practice, they have been included in the finish carpentry section of the specifications, then estimators can either list them under that division or under whatever division they consider as being the most likely to quote prices on these items.

All finish carpentry items located more than 10 feet above floor level should be measured and stated separately, and the average height stated. This would particularly apply to wood ceilings or valances.

The number of items included under the division of Finish Carpentry and Millwork is almost limitless, and the following Schedule of Items and Measurements covers only those items common to most buildings. The rules of measurement laid down can be followed for all other items not specifically listed. The function of the building (school, hospital, residential, etc.) dictates the items and quality of finish carpentry to be included.

10.5 SCHEDULE OF ITEMS AND MEASUREMENTS: FINISH CARPENTRY

Item	Comment	Unit of Measurement
Counters and cupboards	If by the linear foot (meter) then state width and height. If numerical then state all dimensions. State material for tops (plastic laminate, wood, linoleum, etc.) State whether floor or wall mounted, or ceiling hung. Open shelf units, or similar units requiring a minimum of hardware should be stated separately. Give drawing or detail numbers. State if "cut-out" for sinks required.	Linear foot (m) Numerical
Trim	State material, dimensions, location, and/or functions (to doors, windows, paneling, etc.)	Linear foot (m)
Paneling	Keep separate according to classification, soffits and sloping surfaces to be stated separately. State any requirements for grain or book matching.	Square foot (m²)
Ceiling strips	State type and dimensions of the material, also the spacing centers and methods of fixing. Keep separate to sloping soffits.	Linear foot (m)
Stairs	Items to include treads, risers, nosings, wall strings, etc. State number of treads and risers, width, etc.	Numerical
Benches:		
■ Less than 6 feet long	State width, height, and location	Numerical
■ Longer than 6 feet	State width, height, and location	Linear foot (m)
Mop rails		Linear foot (m)
Base and nosing		Linear foot (m)
Sills, valances, wall	State material and dimensions of partition caps, copings, window stools, etc.	Linear foot (m)
Shelving:		
■ Widths up to and including 12 inches		Linear foot (m)
■ Greater than 12 inches wide		Square foot (m²)

continued

Item	Comment	Unit of Measurement
Handrail	State separately for stairs. State all pertinent information: ■ material ■ dimensions ■ fixing Keep laminated work separate.	Linear foot (m)
Glazed partitions	Item will include framing and trim. Partitioning greater than 10 feet high to be stated separately.	Square foot (m²)
Miscellaneous rough hardware	Includes for nails, screw, small bolts, brackets, etc. Keep separate any special requirements for stainless steel, brass, etc.	Pound (kilogram)

10.6 DOORS AND FRAMES

These can be taken off (counted) from the drawings or, preferably, from a "door schedule" where one is provided. These schedules will either be shown on the drawings or included in the specifications, or may even (particularly on a large project) be issued in a separate book.

General contractors usually take off quantities for the doors and frames in order to establish the handling and installation costs of these items. Masterformat sections 08100 Metal Doors and Frames and 08200 Wood and Plastic Doors cover the items most applicable to this work. For many years it was customary for the millwork contractors to include the supply of wood and plastic doors in their quotations. Many still maintain this custom, according to local or regional practice, or possibly because of a millwork supplier's belief that this could provide a marketing advantage. It is, however, becoming more common for the door manufacturers to quote directly to the general contractor. However, regardless of who actually supplies the doors, the contractor still has to estimate the costs involved in receiving, unloading, storing, handling, and hanging them, including the preparation for and installation of the finish hardware.

The main concern to an estimator between these two sources of supply is that if the millwork supplier includes for the doors it will be on a lump-sum basis. The door manufacturer, though, will usually state a unit price for each type and size of door, to be multiplied by the estimated quantities to establish the total amount to be included in the bid.

The Masterformat sections 08250 Door Assemblies and 08300 Special Doors apply to specialty items where almost without exception the specialist companies undertake the responsibilities of fabrication, supply, and on-site installation. However, to be familiar with the requirements when checking the quotations, the total number and sizes of these door assemblies should be established. The doorframes should be noted as separate items because the door manufacturers usually do not supply them.

11 PRICING THE ESTIMATE: BASIC PRINCIPLES

11.1 GENERAL

The pricing of an estimate falls into the following categories:

> Material costs
> Labor costs
> Equipment costs and rentals
> Unit rates (from subcontractors)
> Firm price quotations from subcontractors

Each category demands special consideration to be given by the estimator in regard to procedure and methodology. The element of risk to the contractor also varies with each category. In the categories of material costs and unit rates, for example, the main risk is in the accuracy of the contractor's quantities to which the unit prices will be applied. The category of labor costs is vulnerable to an error in the quantities plus the additional risk of an underestimated ("low") unit rate for the work. For example, the estimate includes an item of 3,000 cubic yards of concrete with a strength mix of 3,000 pounds per square inch (p.s.i.). The most competitive price received from a ready-mix concrete supplier is $70 per cubic yard, this price being guaranteed "firm" for 30 days. The estimated rate for placing this concrete is $10 per cubic yard. The material unit price, $70, is guaranteed providing a purchase order is issued within the stated time limitation. The unit rate for labor, $10, is an estimate of cost and not guaranteed. If the actual quantity of concrete proves greater than its estimated quantity, then both the material and labor costs will increase because of this error. However, the labor cost would be increased even further if the actual unit cost for placing the concrete was greater than the estimated cost. Assuming the actual quantity of concrete to be 3,150 cubic yards and the reported placing rate to be $12, the following comparison between estimated and actual costs illustrates the differential in risk percentage between material and labor costs:

Estimate	Actual	Increase
Material:		
3,000 cyd at $70 = $210,000	3,150 cyd at $70 = $220,500	5%
Labor:		
3,000 cyd at $10 = $30,000	3,150 cyd at $12 = $37,800	26%

The risk in the category of equipment costs and rentals is one of judgment applicable to the selection of the type of equipment for a particular operation, and an over-optimistic assessment of the production output per hour or day to be anticipated from that piece of equipment. Also, a badly organized project often has items of equipment lying idle for long periods but still subject to rental costs.

11.2 MATERIAL PRICES

Material prices are obtained from the following sources:

1. Quotations from material manufacturers and/or building supply companies. These quotations may be in the form of signed letters, or are telephoned into the contractor's office and (usually) confirmed in writing.
2. Catalog or price lists distributed to general contractors and updated periodically.

Whenever possible, and particularly for those materials where large quantities are applicable, competitive quotations should be solicited from a number of suppliers. Standard price lists are quite satisfactory for the less contentious items, but are usually higher than quotations prepared for a specific project.

The contractor's principal risk in the material prices of a bid has already been identified as relating to the estimated quantities. Other risks could evolve from lack of proper understanding or interpretation of the quotations (however bona fide) from reliable supply or manufacturing companies. The following are some points to be considered when checking quotations:

1. Ensure that the material quoted is in accordance with the specification requirements. If the specification for a particular material contains an amount of technical data relative to weights, gauges, dimensions, and similar matters, and the quotation also contains such information, a careful check is essential to ensure that the data are the same in both instances. It is important to know that the apple as quoted is the apple as specified. Very often a specification will supplement the data with a manufacturer's catalog or model number, and even if this number is identified and repeated in a quotation, there could still be a problem if there are variations in the supporting technical data. The best thing to do here is to query both the architect and the supplier to clear up the discrepancy.

2. Check that the material will be delivered to the project site. Any wording other than "FOB Job Site" suggests that additional amounts for freight should be considered.

3. Check the supplier's time limitations on the placing of the order. The knowledge that a quotation is "good for 30 days" provides small comfort to an estimator if the bid itself has to remain open for the owner's acceptance for 60 days or longer. A query should be made immediately to the supplier. Most firms are prepared to be reasonable about this matter when the problem is explained.

4. Check the quotation regarding sales or other taxes. Certain types of projects (hospitals, schools, and other public buildings) are often exempt from certain taxes, and the supplier should be queried if the status of the taxes in the price has not been clarified in the quotation.

5. Check all the small print at the bottom or reverse side of a quotation for any other pertinent qualifications. These are often the "ghosts" that will haunt the contractor later if not challenged and dispelled at the time of the bid.

Figure 11–1 shows a typical quotation from a building supply company covering a miscellany of items. Figure 11–2 is an example of a quotation from a ready-mix supplier.

J. A. J. BUILDING SUPPLIES CO., LTD

SAN ANTONIO, TEXAS

MATERIAL PRICES

Masonry Materials

Concrete block:

	Price per Piece	
	Standard	Lightweight
4 in. (10 cm)	.44	.48
6 in. (15 cm)	.50	.54
8 in. (20 cm)	.56	.60
10 in. (25 cm)	.70	.74
12 in. (30 cm)	.76	.80

Masonry cement	$2.66 per 66 2/3 lb bag
Dovetail brick anchors	$120.00 per 1,000 pieces
Flashing (copper coated paper 2 oz)	$28.00 per 100 sft
Premixed grout	$25.00 per 55 lb bag
Rigid polystyrene insulation:	
1.5 × 16 × 96 in.	$5.75 per sheet
2 × 16 × 96 in.	$6.90 per sheet
Brick sand	$1.00 per 100 lb bag

All prices include federal and state sales tax.

FIGURE 11–1 Typical quotation from a building supply company.

<table>
<tbody>
<tr><td colspan="2"><u>J. H. J. CONCRETE SUPPLY COMPANY</u></td></tr>
<tr><td colspan="2">Ready-mix concrete delivered to the site.</td></tr>
</tbody>
</table>

Strength	Price
3000 p.s.i. (20 Mpa)	$48.00 per cyd
4000 p.s.i. (25 Mpa)	$51.50 per cyd
5000 p.s.i. (35 Mpa)	$57.00 per cyd
Extra for winter heating (November 1 to April 15)	$3.00 per cyd
Extra for air entrainment	$1.50 per cyd
Calcium chloride (2%)	$1.00 per cyd
Underload charges:	
5 cyd and less than 7 cyd	$10.00 per load
4 cyd and less than 5 cyd	$15.00 per load
3 cyd and less than 4 cyd	$20.00 per load
Less than 3 cyd	$25.00 per load

Above prices are inclusive of federal and state taxes.

FIGURE 11–2   Quotation from a ready-mix supplier.

11.3 | LABOR UNITS

Few general contractors would disagree with the statement that the estimated cost of labor in a bid is the biggest exposure to risk. The only item that the contractor can predict with certainty is the prevailing hourly rate that has to be paid to the company's on-site labor force. Large projects of long duration will also require speculation regarding labor rate escalations that may occur during that period.

As already stressed in Section 11.1, the contractor is not only vulnerable to the risk of an error in the quantities (although proper adherence to good quantity surveying practices will temper this risk), but also to "tight" unit rates that reflect an output that may not (or cannot) be achieved. Cost reporting systems can provide useful information regarding the actual unit rates established on the site, but these unit prices are only historical data. They are not in the same category as material prices in a signed quotation from a supplier or a subcontractor. Cost reporting systems are beneficial guides for subsequent estimating, but they carry no guarantee and they also need to be properly understood and interpreted. Also, where actual costs appear excessively high or low, the perennial problem of misallocation of costs has to be considered a possibility.

An experienced estimator's leading question regarding a reported unit price for labor is always, "What was the current labor rate at the time?" Two similar projects might report a unit cost of $12.32 per cubic yard for placing concrete to foundation walls, but if these projects were built in different regions, or at different times, then the hourly labor rates would probably also be different. Assuming the current labor rate in Project A is $22 per hour, and on Project B it is $24 per hour, the output per labor-hour at each project would be:

Project A = $12.32 per cubic yard ÷ $22 per hour = 0.56 labor-hour per cubic yard

Project B = $12.32 per cubic yard ÷ $24 per hour = 0.51 labor-hour per cubic yard

Project B achieved a better output per labor-hour for this labor item than did Project A. If Project A had attained the same output as the other project, the unit price reported would have been $11.22 ($22 × 0.51) and not $12.32.

Estimating the cost of labor is basically the assessment of the quantity of work that can be achieved by a worker or a crew of workers within a specific time span. The factors to be considered in making this assessment include:

1. The size and mix (e.g., carpenter and two helpers) of the work crew.
2. The time duration to be considered (e.g., hour, day, week).
3. The total hourly (or daily) cost of the crew.
4. The anticipated output of work in that time duration.

EXAMPLE:
   Crew composition: 6 laborers
   Hourly rate per laborer: $19.00
   Time duration: 8 hours (48 labor-hours)
   Productivity for 8 hours: 160 units

   Unit rate (48 labor-hours × $19.00 per hour) ÷ 160 = $5.70 per unit

This could also be expressed as a labor-hour factor:

   48 labor-hours ÷ 160 units = 0.3 labor-hour per unit

With this information, an estimator can establish a unit price by multiplying the hourly labor rate by the labor-hour factor.

EXAMPLE:
   Labor rate = $19.75
   Unit rate   = $19.75 × 0.3 = $5.93 per unit

Competency (and also confidence) in computing the estimated labor costs is attained by the development of the following knowledge and skills:

1. Familiarity with the methods and systems used for the various construction operations, and most important, an appreciation of how such methods and systems relate to and influence costs.
2. Analytical on-the-spot observation of construction operations, checking crew sizes, equipment, and approximate assessment of output.
3. Understanding the factors that limit productivity in some items of work while promoting it in other items. For example, placing concrete to large

repetitive floor slabs in a multistoried structure can be organized to provide a high output per labor-hour, while the footings in the substructure will be limited to a much lower output however economically the work is planned and carried out.

A label with the one word "experience" can be affixed to all those three prerequisites, but how to channel that experience effectively is equally, if not more, important when estimating the cost of labor. This applies also to how such methods relate to and influence costs. Possessing know-how about the methods of specific construction operations is one thing, but this know-how is useless to estimators if they cannot translate it into the language of costs.

Some other factors that influence productivity are:

1. Climatic conditions: Inclement weather can seriously impair productivity, and the time of the year in which certain work will be carried out must be taken into consideration, as well as the geographical location of the project. Northern Montana in January provides a different open-air work environment from California during the same month, yet the working conditions in July for both regions might not be dissimilar. Extremes in heat or cold, rain, snow, and gusting winds all have an effect on workers' output and proficiency.

2. Labor conditions: In certain regions there may exist a shortage of skilled or semiskilled construction trades people. Also, the experience of those workers who are available may be limited to small projects with fewer scheduling pressures and requirements than the larger jobs. Both factors can retard productivity, and estimators should investigate the local labor situation when bidding on projects in new and unfamiliar locations.

3. Supervision: Intelligent planning and good organization of a project always open the way to optimum output from the labor force, and these elements are provided by the superintendents, project managers, foremen, and other supervisory personnel. Inefficient supervision will usually result in bad planning accompanied by a drop in productivity, but construction companies do not usually retain inefficient supervisors on their payrolls for a very long period. Many successful contracting companies adhere to the philosophy that it is foolhardy to bid on a project if there is no experienced superintendent available for the job. The situation could exist, however, of the availability of a seasoned superintendent with an excellent company record of profitable projects, but without experience on the kind of building for which the bid is being prepared. ("Jake's topnotch at schools or hospitals; no one to touch him. But he's never done a large industrial plant like this.") In this case a factor for supervision might be advisable, but this is a decision that should be made after discussion with company management. Generally, estimators should think positively and base their estimates on the ready availability of first-class supervision.

One essential truth to be hammered into young estimators when they first start pricing estimates is that they are not expected to accurately predict the actual field unit cost down to the last cent for each item in the bid. If and when there is an exact match between estimated and actual unit rates, it is often due to either coincidence (luck) or some fancy "juggling" with figures.

There will usually be a fluctuation of rises and falls in all the unit rates, but everyone—field personnel, management, and estimators—always look hopefully toward the final cost as representative of a victory of the falls (cost underruns) over the rises (cost overruns).

Another harsh truth for neophyte estimators is that, in the opinion of the field personnel who have to build the structure, all estimates (and estimators) fall into two categories: bad and very bad. The distinction between these two categories is that, in the first case, the estimated cost was met or improved upon only by the good organization and hard work of the site personnel. In the second case the estimated cost was so ridiculous and impossible to achieve that it was not the fault of the field staff that money was lost.

These statements may seem facetious, but one point should be emphasized seriously: the category designated in the field as "bad" pinpoints the target at which estimators should be aiming when computing prices. This target is the maximum output that is possible, feasible, and reasonable for any given operation, dependent on the necessary ingenuity and effort of the work crew. An experienced estimator attempting to assess the quantity of units (for whatever) that could be installed by a worker in an 8-hour day would consider the options this way:

- 160 units: reasonable, quite possible
- 200 units: optimum, not impossible
- more than 200 units: unreasonable, unrealistic

With the exception of uncontentious items of small quantities, estimators would usually opt for the second option as the target to be considered. The name of the game is always to be competitive, but at the same time also to be practical and constructive. After analyzing previous costs, preparing some price buildups, and testing the results by discussion with other people (estimators, managers, superintendents, etc.), the estimator may decide that 190 units per 8-hour day is the best that could be achieved, and the unit price would be based on that output factor.

Estimators should always attempt to strip unit costs back to this essential factor of output. To retain a catalog memory of hundreds of unit prices for various items can be very impressive (and also useful if suddenly requested to provide some quick "ball-park" guesstimates in a short amount of time), but it is more important to know what these units actually mean and what items of work they actually include. Two estimators from different companies talking "shop" might remark that $10 a cubic yard is a good average unit price for placing concrete to a floor slab on earth. The system in the one company might be to include the screeding and troweling of the slab in that unit, and the second company's system might treat these operations as separate cost items; in other words, apples are not being compared with apples. One company's units might include equipment costs, whereas the second company might consider these under separate headings.

Where labor unit prices are concerned, estimators must seek out the labor-hour productivity that lies behind them. Mention was made of the usefulness of on-the-spot analytical time and method studies. These studies can pinpoint the methods used, the crew composition, and the output accomplished within a certain time. Experienced estimators form the habit of doing cost checks like this anytime they see a particular operation in progress. Any number of "sidewalk superintendents" can gawk incomprehensibly through an opening in a hoarding at what appears to be a chaotic muddle of workers, dirt, and equipment. Experienced, responsible estimators discipline themselves to quickly identify the various activities, to note the number of workers involved and the equipment used, and to assess the quantity of work performed in the time duration of the observation.

A more constructive on-the-spot observation method and system, covering a time duration of 4 hours, would be reported as follows:

Operation: Place concrete to suspended slab and beams

Method: Mobile crane and buggies

Crew: 8 laborers, 1 foreman

Equipment: Mobile crane

Buggies: 4 hand-powered type

Average time cycle for buggying (loading, wheeling, depositing, reloading): 3 min

Concrete delivered by ready-mix truck: 8 cyd capacity

Number of trucks observed in 4-hr period: 10 = 80 cyd

This type of record is useful for future estimating purposes, but it must be remembered that this particular observation study covered only 4 hours of the whole operation and did not reflect any initial setting up time, cleanup at completion, or any lost-time factors. It may also have been taken at the peak period and did not reflect a possible lower average output. The productivity reported for that specific time cycle was 80 cubic yards averaging 20 cubic yards per hour. An adjustment factor would be necessary to reduce the optimum output down to the average output for the entire operation. Assume this factor to be 10 percent; the observed output would be modified to

$$
\begin{array}{ll}
 & 80 \text{ cyd} \\
\text{Less } 10\% & \underline{8 \text{ cyd}} \\
\text{Average} & 72 \text{ cyd} \div 4 \text{ hr} = 18 \text{ cyd/hr}
\end{array}
$$

This information can be reduced to a single labor-hour per unit factor:

9 labor-hours ÷ 18 cyd = 0.5 labor-hour per cyd

With a current laborer's rate of $19.00 per hour, the estimated unit price per cubic yard would be $19 × 0.5 = $9.50. Considerable time can be saved if these labor-hour factors are used for pricing rather than building up a detailed analysis in the same manner as the observation report, particularly if only a single category of workers is being considered (e.g., laborers).

What about a mixed crew, such as so many bricklayers with so many helpers? Consider a crew of six carpenters and two laborers—the carpenter's rates are higher than the laborer's rates of pay. Except for large, highly contentious items in an estimate, when the prices should be tested by using two or three different approaches or methods to compute the costs, it will generally be sufficiently realistic and accurate to consider the carpenter-to-laborers mix in a crew as coming under these categories:

1. Ratio of 1:1: one carpenter, one helper
2. Ratio of 2:1: Two carpenters, one helper (or four carpenters, two helpers, and so on). This could also be expressed as two-thirds skilled labor, one-third semiskilled.

3. Ratio of 3:1: Three carpenters, one helper (or six carpenters, two helpers, etc.) This could be expressed as three-quarters skilled labor, one-quarter semiskilled.

There are obviously more possible mixes than the three stated, but for estimating purposes these will be sufficient. A more in-depth price buildup would be recommended for a large item of work with excessive quantities where every cent in a unit rate could make a significant change in the total cost. To use single labor-hour production factors for mixed crews requires the establishment of composite rates.

EXAMPLE:

Carpenter's rate $=$ $25 per hr

Laborer's rate $=$ $19 per hr

The composite hourly rate for the ratios stated would be:

1:1 $=$ ($25 per hr + $19 per hr) $\div$ 2 = $22.00 per hr

2:1 $=$ [(2 $\times$ $25 per hr) + $19 per hr] $\div$ 3 = $23 per hr

3:1 $=$ [(3 $\times$ $25 per hr) + $19 per hr] $\div$ 4 = $23.50 per hr

To compute the unit rate cost of an operation where a crew of, say, four carpenters and two helpers would be reasonable, the estimator would identify an appropriate labor-hour/output factor and multiply the factor by a composite rate for a 2:1 ratio.

Estimators should build up their own tables of labor factors for the various construction operations. The source of information to prepare these tables would be observation studies, cost reports, or discussions with field supervisors, foremen, carpenters, and the like. Many excellent books on the market also provide much useful data.

The following examples illustrate different formats for these tables, all based on formwork to foundation walls, and all assuming the same output and crew composition.

Method 1: Output per Specific Time Cycle

Specific time: 8 hr

Crew: 2 carpenters at $25 per hr $=$ $50 per hr

                1 helper at $19 per hr $=$ $\underline{\$19 \text{ per hr}}$

                                      $69 per hr

Average output: 175 sft

Computation: ($69 per hr $\times$ 8 hr) $\div$ 175 sft = $3.15 per sft

Method 2: Time Cycle per Specific Quantity

Specific quantity: 100 sft

Average time: 9.2 hr for carpenter

                    4.6 hr for helper

Computation: (9.2 hr $\times$ $25 per hr) + (4.6 hr $\times$ $19 per hr) $\div$ 100 sft

                 = $3.17 per sft

Method 3: Labor-hour Factor/Composite Rate

Using data from Method 2:

Crew ratio: 2:1 (two carpenters, one helper)

Composite rate: ⅔ × $25 per hr   = $16.67 per hr

⅓ × $19 per hr   = $ 6.33 per hr

$23.00 per hr

Labor-hour factor: 13.8 (total labor-hours) ÷ 100 sft = .138 labor-hour per sft
(using composite rate for 2:1 ratio)

Computation: .138 labor-hour per sft × $23.00 per hr = $3.17 per sft

It will be noted that there is a difference of about one cent between the unit price in method 1 and methods 2 and 3, which is not significant unless it was to be applied to an exceedingly large quantity.

Estimators can prepare tables or price analyses in any format they prefer. The advantage of method 3 is that a lot of data can be included in a small space, and these reference tables, once compiled, enable estimators to make quick computations. If these labor-hour factors are further divided and grouped into categories according to low, average, or optimum productivity, the estimator can exercise judgment on each item according to its merits. Using the same example of formwork to a foundation wall, the table would show the item in this fashion:

| | | | Productivity | |
| | | | High | Low |
Item	Crew Ratio	Per Average	Decrease by:	Increase by:
Formwork to foundation walls	2:1	.138	10–20%	10–15%

Note: The labor-hour factors, whether designated average, high, or low, are all-inclusive of setup time, peak output, and down time. The categories low, average, and high refer to the conditions imposed by the influences of repetitive work, climate, supervision, and so on. The estimator will take these factors into consideration and use judgment in regards to the adjustments. In the example shown, the judgment might be to consider a factor between average and high, and the mean of these two factors would be used.

Unit rates given in project cost reports can be used to calculate these labor-hour factors, but it must be stressed that these unit rates do not provide the information regarding a mixed trade crew; this can only be obtained by actual observation or after discussion with the site personnel. Labor-hour factors derived from these costs can be achieved by dividing the hourly rate of the principal trade into the unit price:

EXAMPLE:

Unit price in cost report = $2.25 per sft

Carpenter's rate   = $25 per hr

Computation: $2.25 per sft ÷ $25 per hr = .09 carpenter hr per sft

If this factor is to be used in future estimating, it must only be applied to the current hourly rate for a carpenter. If the applicable rate for a carpenter is $24.75, then the revised unit rate will be $24.75 × .09 = $2.23. If a crew ratio was assumed as 2:1 and an existing composite rate established as $23.50, then the factor would be $2.25 per square foot ÷ $23.50 = .10 labor-hour per square foot, and this would be applied against the revised composite rate.

A contentious item with a large quantity, say several hundred thousand square feet of formwork or more than 5,000 cubic yards of concrete, should be first computed with the labor-hour factor per square foot or cubic yard, and then tested with other methods such as:

1. Preparing a detailed price buildup for a typical day, assessing crew requirements, output, and other factors.

2. Calculating the cost of the completion operation, say for a typical "pour," from start to finish, including setting up, cleanup, and so on.

These check methods will probably produce different unit prices; the estimator is then confronted with a decision-making process as to which to select for use in the bid. Discussion with other people (estimators, managers, and superintendents) will be required.

The hourly rates used for pricing labor items in a bid should be the basic rate (i.e., exclusive of labor premiums such as unemployment insurance, vacation pay, and other benefits). These vary from trade to trade and region to region. They are best calculated as a percentage to be added to either:

1. Total labor cost of each trade summary (e.g., excavation, concrete), or

2. Total labor cost for complete project as shown in the main bid summary

The advantage of method 2 is that the estimator has only to make this adjustment once rather than five or six times on the individual trade summaries, with the chance of forgetting to do it on one of them. Also method 2 permits the use of a specific item on a standard printed general estimate summary, which would eliminate the possibility of the item being overlooked.

11.4 EQUIPMENT

Certain items of construction equipment may be contractor-owned, and other equipment rented as and when required. The examples given in this book will be based on the assumption that rental rates will apply to both categories (i.e., rented or owned).

Most construction equipment companies distribute lists or books outlining the equipment available, accompanied by a schedule of rental rates on an hourly, daily, weekly, or monthly basis. (Note: Many companies list a 4-week rental in lieu of monthly rate, and estimators should not confuse the two as being the same thing.)

The following are some points that should be checked when assessing an equipment company's schedule of rental rates:

1. Do the rates include operators where applicable (e.g., excavation equipment, cranes)?

2. Do the rates include repairs or fuel?

3. What is the minimum rental period? (This is usually a minimum of 4 hours.)

4. Are there any additional pickup and/or delivery charges?

5. What accessories are included or will be an additional charge (hoses, conduits, etc.)?

6. What taxes are included or must be added?

Making the best possible decision regarding the choice of equipment for specific uses on the project is something estimators should not hesitate to discuss with job superintendents and other field personnel. Practical experience can foster good advice, and second or third (or fourth) opinions are invaluable, especially from people who are continually exposed to these matters. Sometimes, and particularly if opinions differ greatly about the pros and cons of certain equipment, the estimators may have to make the final decision themselves. Also, the equipment companies can provide a lot of data regarding the suitability of certain equipment for the various operations, output, fuel requirements, and so on. Most important, never base any decisions regarding equipment solely on the optimistic "rose-colored" statements in promotional literature. Production factors in such literature are often applicable only to peak periods of highly repetitive work under ideal conditions.

Sometimes before a decision is made regarding the choice of equipment, an analysis will be necessary showing comparative evaluation of costs. This particularly applies to items where the use of equipment could reduce the crew size and, at the same time, increase output, but estimators must convince themselves that the comparative cost will be economical.

EXAMPLE: Placing concrete to concrete walls where it is not possible to chute directly from the ready-mix truck.

Method 1: Buggy the concrete into place.

Size of crew: 1 at truck

3 wheeling

1 vibrating

1 screening

Total: 6 crew people

Average output: 10 cyd per hr

Cost: 6 laborers at $19 per hr = $114 per hr

3 buggies at $0.67 per hr = $2 per hr

Total: $116 per hr

$116 per hr ÷ 10 cyd per hr = $11.60 per cyd

Method 2: Place concrete with mobile crane and bucket directly into walls.

Size of crew: 1 at truck

1 vibrating

1 screening

Total: 3 crew people

Mobile crane (incl. operator, fuel, etc.) = $50.00

Average output = 16 cyd per hr (peak period might be 20 to 25 cyd)

Costs: 3 laborers at $19 per hr = $57 per hr

Mobile crane = $50 per hr

Total: $107 per hr

$107 per hr ÷ 16 cubic yards per hr = $6.69 per cyd

Obviously, method 2 provides the most economical solution. Apart from cheaper unit cost for placing the concrete, the crane could also be used for hoisting reinforcing steel, formwork, and other items. When it is decided to perform all the main concrete placing items in the structure (excluding floor toppings, equipment bases, curbs, etc.) with the use of a mobile crane, the crane cost should be computed on a monthly rental basis for the scheduled duration of the structural operations. This will be more accurate than assessing the rental period on the basis of hours per cubic yards of concrete.

11.5   SUBCONTRACTORS' UNIT PRICES

Most subcontractors prepare lump-sum quotations for the work of their specific trades, but there are certain trades where some quotations should be anticipated as being submitted on a unit-price basis. These trades would include (but not necessarily be limited to):

Excavation and grading (including backfilling operations)

Asphalt paving and concrete curbs

Sodding and seeding

Concrete floor finishing

In some cases the subcontractors bid on this basis as a declared and fixed trade practice. Sometimes, though, due to lack of sufficient time to prepare a lump-sum quotation, or difficulties in procuring the drawings for takeoff purposes, trade contractors provide only unit rates for the work of their trades.

As has already been stated, the principal risk to general contractors with this type of quotation is the same as with material prices, that is, the possibility of a serious error in the quantities. However, with these unit prices some other hazards also need to be considered. Quotations for construction materials can be checked against the specification, and the prices confirmed as representing the specified requirements. Unit prices for subtrade work usually include the cost of materials, equipment, and labor, and cannot always be so readily identified with the specifications.

Estimators should check closely with subcontractors as to what is and what is not included in their unit prices if they choose this method of submitting a quotation. For example, an excavation subcontractor who quotes a rate for bulk excavation may have to be queried regarding the disposal of the excavated material; does the rate include for trucking away, or for spreading on the site, or just "sidecasting"? Equally, unit rates for backfill operations should be explicit regarding compaction and that the fill material corresponds to what is demanded in the specification. Also, even if subcontractors have been pressed for time to prepare a proper takeoff and estimate, their unit prices should be received with caution if they cannot demonstrate that they have seen the drawings and properly read and understood the specifications.

The subcontractor may query the general contractor regarding the quantities applicable to the items of work on which he or she intends to quote. This information should be given when requested, and if it is not requested it is a good idea to check that the subcontractor is aware of the magnitude of the quantities involved. Quantities do have an impact on the estimated rate. A postbid written confirmation from a subcontractor stating that a unit rate for "bulk excavation by machine" was applicable only to a minimum quantity of 100,000 cubic yards is unlikely to soothe the feelings of an estimator who has estimated the maximum quantity to be 70,000 cubic yards.

11.6 | EXAMPLES OF PRICING

The following chapter will provide examples of pricing the estimates for the various trade divisions already considered in the quantity takeoff examples. A schedule of labor-hour/output factors is provided for each trade as background to the pricing demonstrated. In addition, basic labor rates are provided for the applicable trades, which will remain consistent throughout the various examples; also, the additional payroll charges, fringe benefits, and the like are shown.

12 PRICING THE ESTIMATE: EXAMPLES

12.1 GENERAL

The examples of pricing estimates of selected trades as demonstrated in the following pages are in accordance with the principles and methods discussed in the last chapter. The purpose is to display some of the options and methods an estimator would consider when determining unit rates that are competitive but also realistic.

The prices shown are applied to American units, and appropriate factors are presented for conversion to metric units. Each specific trade specimen is supplemented by explanatory comments where some additional clarification appears necessary.

The quotations from the various material suppliers are not illustrated. It is assumed that the material rates noted on the estimate sheets are the most competitive rates received from a number of suppliers. For the most part, the unit prices for labor are based on average productivity per labor-hour as shown on supplied schedules. Comment is made on operations where output might be above or below the average. For certain major items where large quantities and repetition of work prevail, a more in-depth analysis of the crew makeup and production is discussed in the supplementary comments for each trade section.

12.2 LABOR RATES

The following are the hourly labor rates used to establish the unit prices for carpenters and laborers, from which the composite rates are developed. Also shown are various labor charges applicable to each trade. These include statutory labor charges (unemployment insurance, worker's compensation, and so on) and some typical benefits as defined in union agreements according to trade and locality. The estimated unit costs reflect only the basic hourly rate for each trade. The labor burdens will be expressed as a premium percentage on the total estimated cost of labor. It should be noted that rates will vary greatly depending on union vs. nonunion rates, commercial rates vs. residential rates, and prevailing wage rates vs. nonprevailing wage rates. This text uses the following only as examples, and the problems use rounded rates so that the reader can better follow the calculations. When using labor unit rates, the estimator must be consistent not to include labor burden if it is later added to the total labor amount. Always check unit rates for this factor so that this potential doubling is eliminated from the estimate.

Carpenter:

	Basic rate	$24.30 per hr	
	Vacation pay	.51 per hr	
	Taxable Wage		$24.81
Benefits	Heath & Welfare	$2.70 per hr	
	Pension	$1.01 per hr	
	Apprenticeship, Misc.	.43 per hr	
			$4.14
Insurance	W.C.I.	$5.99 per C	
	PL, BI, & PD	$2.74 per C	
		$8.73 per C	$2.17
Payroll Tax	F.U.T.A. (F.U.I.)	.80%	
	S.U.T.A. (S.U.I.)	2.30%	
	F.I.C.A.	7.65%	
		10.75%	$2.67
	Total Burden		$8.98
	BURDEN PERCENTAGE	36.2%	
	COST OF LABOR-HOUR		$33.79

Laborer:

	Basic rate	$16.61 per hr	
	Vacation pay	2.20 per hr	
	Taxable Wage		$18.81
Benefits	Heath & Welfare	$3.00 per hr	
	Pension	$1.51 per hr	
	Apprenticeship, Misc.	.28 per hr	
			$4.79

Insurance	W.C.I.	$5.99 per C	
	PL, BI, & PD	$2.74 per C	
		$8.73 per C	$1.64

Payroll Tax	F.U.T.A. (F.U.I.)	.80%	
	S.U.T.A. (S.U.I.)	2.30%	
	F.I.C.A.	7.65%	
		10.75%	$2.02
	Total Burden		$8.45

BURDEN PERCENTAGE   44.92%

COST OF LABOR-HOUR $27.26

Labor rates for other trades are noted on the estimate sheets where applicable.

12.3 COMPOSITE LABOR RATES

The pricing examples include many items where mixed crews of craftpersons and helpers would be required. In these instances "composite rates" have been established and used. The schedules of labor-hour factors (Section 12.4) show some suggested crew ratios on which the following composite rates are based. It should be noted that these rates are used as examples and do not match the previous examples of wage rate calculations.

1. Crew ratio 1:1. The composite rate will be the average of the aggregated rates of the craftperson and helper:

Carpenter	$25
Laborer	19
Total	$44

   Composite rate = $22.00

2. Crew ratio 2:1. The composite rate represents two-thirds of the craftperson's rate plus one-third of the helper's rate:

Carpenter $\frac{2}{3} \times$ $25	$16.67
Laborer $\frac{1}{3} \times$ 19	6.33
Composite rate =	$23.00

3. Crew ratio 3:1

Carpenter $\frac{3}{4} \times$ $25	$18.75
Laborer $\frac{1}{4} \times$ 19	4.75
Composite rate =	$23.50

A word of caution: the anticipated productivity for each operation as expressed in terms of labor-hours per unit of measurement is always related to the output by the principal craftperson in the crew (e.g., carpenter, electrician). The helper's role is supportive to the work of the craftperson. Some operations require more support than others do, which is indicated by the crew ratios. However, in some regions, union agreements demand certain operations of work to be performed by craftsmen, whereas in other areas they would be performed by helpers; stripping of formwork would be a good example. Normally, the greater proportion of carpenters in a crew signifies a higher output of production; but where additional carpenters are only replacing helpers or laborers, there will be no improvement in production. The additional cost of using carpenters in lieu of laborers increases the amount of the composite labor rate, but usually not more than about 2 percent on a union job. On a job where rates are substantially different between these two occupations, this percentage goes up. It should also be noted that often apprentices are substituted for laborers at a potentially lower rate than laborers.

Another significant factor to be considered is the hourly cost of a foreman, where one is required. Most construction companies include the foreman's time as a direct labor cost, and the composite rates would require adjustment to reflect the foreman's hourly rate. The suggested adjustment factors to be applied to the composite rates are

1. Working foreman (i.e., one who will also be using the tools of the trade): add 1 to 2 percent to the composite rate, or divide the extra hourly cost of the foreman by the number of workers in the crew, including the foreman.

    Example: Foreman's premium rate $1.50 per hr

                     Total crew: 8 people

                     Premium on composite rate $1.50 ÷ 8 = $0.19

2. Nonworking (general) foreman: increase the composite rate by 12 to 15 percent, or divide the full hourly rate paid to the foreman by the number of workers in a crew excluding the foreman.

    Example: Foreman's rate $26.50 per hr

                     Total crew: 7 people

                     Premium on composite rate $26.50 ÷ 7 = $3.79

Note: More than likely the foreman would be responsible for the supervision of more than one crew, in which case his or her time could be spread over a greater number of workers, reducing the premium on the composite rate.

12.4   SCHEDULES OF LABOR-HOUR FACTORS

The following schedules (Tables 12–1 through 12–12) show the labor-hour factors applicable to a series of construction operations for selected trades. These are provided to illustrate the data on which the estimated labor units in the pricing examples are founded, and also as a suggested format for estimators to produce their own labor units based on cost records and analytical on-site observations from within their individual company organizations.

The factors shown against each operation are based on average output per labor-hour. Where production output could be anticipated to be greater or less than the average applicable percentages, adjustment factors are shown. The supplementary

TABLE 12–1   Schedule of labor-hour factors: excavation and fill

				Adjust for Higher or Lower Productivity	
			Metric Conversion Factors	**Multiply by:**	
			Linear feet to meters	3.28	
			Square feet to square meters	10.764	
			Cubic yards to cubic meters	1.308	

Item	Per (unit)	Crew Ratio	Average Productivity	High, Reduce Factor by:	Low, Increase Factor by:
1. Hand excavation, light soil	cyd	labor	2.3		20–30%
2. Hand excavation, medium soil	cyd	labor	2.7		25–35%
3. Hand excavation, heavy soil	cyd	labor	4.2		25–35%
4. Hand trim bottom of excavations, earth	sft	labor	0.007		25–35%
5. Hand trim bottom of excavations, shale	sft	labor	0.023		25–35%
6. Hand trim to spread footings, earth	sft	labor	0.018		
7. Hand trim to spread footings, shale	sft	labor	0.07		
8. Hand rock excavation	cyd	labor	5.6		20–25%
9. Place and compact backfill	cyd	labor	0.48		20–25%
10. Trim and compact backfill placed by machine	cyd	labor	0.18	20–30%	25–35%
11. Underfloor fill, stone	cyd	labor	0.65	15–25%	25–35%
12. Underfloor fill, granular	cyd	labor	0.58	20–30%	25–35%
13. Weeping tile and fittings	cyd	labor	0.09	25–30%	25–35%
14. Bed and surround to weeping tile	cyd	labor	0.65		25–35%
15. Concrete sewer pipe and fittings (avg 6-in. dia.)	lft	labor	0.16		
16. Bed and surround to sewer pipe	cyd	labor	0.56		20–30%
17. Sand cushion on underfloor fill	cyd	labor	2.12		

TABLE 12–2   Schedule of labor-hour factors: perimeter shoring and underpinning

		Metric Conversion Factors	**Multiply by:**
		Linear feet to meters	3.280
		Square feet to square meters	10.764
		Cubic yards to cubic meters	1.308

Item	Per (unit)	Crew Ratio	Average Productivity
1. Place steel walers, struts, etc.	ton	2:1	19.50
2. Wood lagging	sft	labor	0.20
3. Remove wood lagging	sft	labor	0.16
4. Sand fill behind lagging	cyd	labor	1.75
5. Concrete fill to H-piles	cyd	labor	3.65
6. Pockets for rakers, formwork	sft	2:1	0.28
7. Pockets for rakers, concrete	cyd	labor	0.41

TABLE 12–3 Schedule of labor-hour factors: demolition

	Metric Conversion Factors	Multiply by:
	Linear feet to meters	3.280
	Square feet to square meters	10.764
	Cubic yards to cubic meters	1.308

Item	Per (unit)	Crew Ratio	Average Productivity
1. Break up & remove interior masonry	cft	labor	0.17
2. Break up & remove exterior masonry	cft	labor	0.19
3. Strip existing roofing & flashings	sft	labor	0.04
4. Remove plaster ceilings	sft	labor	0.03
5. Remove acoustic ceilings	sft	labor	0.02
6. Break up & remove terrazzo	sft	labor	0.08
7. Break up & remove glazed wood partitions	sft	labor	0.06
8. Remove existing doors and frames	ea	labor	2.60
9. Remove existing windows	ea	labor	3.50
10. Remove counter & cupboard units	lft	labor	0.92
11. Break up & remove concrete	cft	labor	0.32
12. Load debris into trucks or containers	cyd	labor	0.86
13. Remove metal roof or floor decks	sft	labor	0.03
14. Remove resilient tile and base	sft	labor	0.03
15. Dust screens, fabricate & erect	sft	carpenter	0.07
16. Dust screens, relocate	sft	carpenter	0.06

TABLE 12–4 Machine excavation

Probable Output/ Hour (cyd)	Equipment Hours (Incl. Lost Time Factor)	Number of Trucks per Hour (Avg. Speed 15 mph)		
		1-Mile Haul	2-Mile Haul	3-Mile Haul
20–50	1.15	2	3	4
60–90	1.15	3	4	5
100–115	1.15	4	5	7
115–125	1.15	5	6	8
130–150	1.15	5	7	10

TABLE 12–5 Schedule of labor-hour factors: concrete placing and finishing

	Metric Conversion Factors	Multiply by:
	Linear feet to meters	3.28
	Square feet to square meters	10.764
	Cubic yards to cubic meters	1.308

Item	Per (unit)	Average Productivity	Adjust for Higher or Lower Productivity	
			High, Reduce Factor by:	Low, Increase Factor by:
1. Isolated (column) footings	cyd	0.48	15–20%	25–35%
2. Pile and caisson caps	cyd	0.53	15–20%	25–35%
3. Wall footings	cyd	0.55	10–15%	25–35%
4. Foundation walls and pilasters (perimeter)	cyd	0.75	15–25%	25–35%
5. Foundation walls (interior)	cyd	0.78	15–25%	25–35%

continued

TABLE 12–5 *continued*

			Metric Conversion Factors	Multiply by:
			Linear feet to meters	3.28
			Square feet to square meters	10.764
			Cubic yards to cubic meters	1.308

			Adjust for Higher or Lower Productivity	
Item	Per (unit)	Average Productivity	High, Reduce Factor by:	Low, Increase Factor by:
6. Retaining walls	cyd	0.80	15–25%	25–35%
7. Columns and piers	cyd	0.96	15–20%	25–35%
8. Pits (walls and slabs)	cyd	0.85	–	–
9. Slabs on grade	cyd	0.54	20–30%	25–40%
10. Raft slabs	cyd	0.36	20–25%	–
11. Skim (mud) slabs	cyd	0.80	–	–
12. Skim coat to underside of footings	cyd	0.95	–	–
13. Suspended slabs (slab & beam)	cyd	0.85	25–40%	15–30%
14. Suspended slabs (flat slab)	cyd	0.80	25–40%	20–35%
15. Suspended slabs (metal pan/joist)	cyd	0.83	25–35%	20–35%
16. Slabs on V-rib forms	cyd	0.65	–	–
17. Miscellaneous (small) suspended slabs	cyd	1.20	–	–
18. Fill to metal deck	cyd	0.83	–	–
19. Isolated beams	cyd	0.80	–	–
20. Upstand beams	cyd	1.40	–	–
21. Floor toppings (separate)	cyd	1.45	–	25–35%
22. Floor toppings (monolithic)	cyd	1.86	–	30–40%
23. Fireproofing structural columns	cyd	1.70	–	–
24. Stairs and landings	cyd	1.80	–	30–45%
25. Exterior walks	cyd	0.96	–	–
26. Equipment bases	cyd	2.80	–	30–50%
27. Interior curbs	cyd	1.65	10–15%	–
28. Exterior curbs	cyd	0.86	15–20%	–
29. Shear and core walls	cyd	0.62	15–25%	–
30. Lightweight roof fill	cyd	1.70	–	–
31. Clean, patch and rub exposed concrete surfaces (vertical)	sft	0.053	5–10%	10–15%
32. Clean, patch and rub exposed concrete surfaces (horizontal)	sft	0.042	5–10%	10–15%
33. Set anchor bolts (structural steel bases)	pieces	0.75	–	–
34 a. Grout column base plates (not exceeding 24 sin.)	pieces	0.95	–	–
b. Grout column base plates (exceeding 24 sin.)	pieces	1.50	–	–

Notes:

1. Better-than-average productivity in placing footings and foundation walls would be possible in conditions where the concrete could be chuted directly from the truck, and also with very large spread footings where almost the entire contents of the truck could be discharged into one, two, or at the most three footings.

2. Foundation walls that extend above grade would probably require the use of mobile cranes, and if the concrete is placed directly from the bucket into the forms, an improvement in average productivity could be anticipated.

3. Large-sized columns will provide better output than those with slender dimensions, particularly if placed with crane and bucket or pump.

4. Suspended slabs and beams will reflect the highest output per labor-hour when the labor crew is supported by concrete-placing equipment such as a crane or concrete pump. Multistory buildings with repetitive slabs, which provide large quantity "pours," will lend themselves to maximum output. The labor-hour factors for average productivity are applicable to wheeling and placing with hand-propelled buggies. Thin slabs usually mean lower output per hr, as do slabs where the wheeling distance is greater than 80 ft.

5. Placing floor topping is not usually an operation that yields any great output, particularly if the partitions extend down to the structural slab, and the concrete topping has to be placed between the partition walls.

TABLE 12–6 Schedule of labor-hour factors: formwork

	Metric Conversion Factors	Multiply by:
	Linear feet to meters	3.28
	Square feet to square meters	10.764
	Cubic yards to cubic meters	1.308

Item	Per (unit)	Crew Ratio	Average Productivity	Adjust for Higher or Lower Productivity	
				High, Reduce Factor by:	Low, Increase Factor by:
1. Spread (column) footings	sft	1:1	0.16	10–15%	15–25%
2. Pile and caisson caps	sft	1:1	0.18	10–15%	15–25%
3. Wall footings	sft	1:1	0.192	10–15%	15–25%
4. Foundation walls					
not over 12 ft high	sft	1:1	0.13	10–15%	15–25%
12 ft to 18 ft	sft	1:1	0.14	10–15%	15–25%
Over 18 ft	sft	1:1	0.145	10–15%	15–25%
5. Interior walls (hand placed)	sft	1:1	0.12	20–30%	20–25%
6. Shear walls (gang formed)	sft	3:1	0.086	25–30%	–
7. Pilasters	sft	1:1	0.165	–	–
8. Columns and piers:					
Rectangular	sft	1:1	0.16	15–20%	20–25%
Shaped	sft	1:1	0.185	–	–
9. Pit walls	sft	1:1	0.19	–	–
10. Suspended slabs (hand placed)	sft	1:1	0.115	10–15%	15–20%
Shoring height over 12 ft	sft	1:1	0.135	–	15–25%
Using crane	sft	3:1	0.085	15–25%	–
11. Miscellaneous suspended slabs	sft	1:1	0.145	–	–
12. Beams (interior)	sft	1:1	0.182	10–15%	20–25%
13. Beams (spandrel)	sft	1:1	0.19	10–15%	20–25%
14. Drop slabs (edges and soffits)	sft	1:1	0.21	10–15%	20–25%
15. Isolated beams	sft	1:1	0.20	–	–
16. Upstand beams	sft	1:1	0.195	–	–
17. Fireproofing steel columns	sft	1:1	0.187	–	–
18. Fireproofing steel beams	sft	1:1	0.23	–	–
19. Stairs and landings	sft	1:1	0.31	–	25–40%
20. Slab edges	sft	2:1	0.19	–	35–45%
21. Slab edges (suspended)	sft	2:1	0.27	–	35–45%
22. Bulkheads to construction joints	lft	2:1	0.23	–	25–35%
23. Keys	lft	3:1	0.115	–	25–30%
24. Keys (continuous to footings)	lft	3:1	0.07	–	–
25. Chamfer strips	lft	3:1	0.05	–	–
26. Boxings	sft	2:1	0.28	–	25–35%
27. Circular columns (fiber tubes)	lft	1:1	0.70	–	–
28. Equipment bases	sft	2:1	0.32	–	30–40%
29. Interior curbs	sft	2:1	0.29	–	30–40%
30. Exterior curbs	sft	2:1	0.22	–	30–40%
31. Set screeds	sft	3:1	0.001	–	–
32. Prefabricated gang forms	sft	2:1	0.014	–	–

continued

TABLE 12–6 *continued*

			Metric Conversion Factors	Multiply by:	
			Linear feet to meters	3.28	
			Square feet to square meters	10.764	
			Cubic yards to cubic meters	1.308	

				Adjust for Higher or Lower Productivity	
Item	Per (unit)	Crew Ratio	Average Productivity	High, Reduce Factor by:	Low, Increase Factor by:
Install Miscellaneous Items:					
33. Waterstops	lft	1:1	0.13	–	–
34. Anchor slots	lft	1:1	0.026	–	–
35. Expansion joints	lft	1:1	0.11	–	15–25%
36. Anchors for precast concrete	pieces	carpenter	0.42	–	–
37. Inserts for shelf angles	pieces	carpenter	0.46	–	–
Forms to Architectural Concrete:					
38. Board finish	sft	1:1	0.25	–	–
39. Smooth finish	sft	1:1	0.21	–	–
40. Grooved finish	sft	1:1	0.24	–	–

Notes:

1. Improved productivity will always be achieved with a large quantity of items that are repetitive in size and shape (column footings, columns, piers, etc.), particularly where the forms can be prefabricated and then reused a large number of times.

2. Long straight walls of consistent height and with a minimum of pilasters or other projections will also provide good productivity. Pre-fabricated wood panels or metal forms will also assist output, but the estimator must always check that the cost of renting or purchasing special panels, be they wood or metal, does not offset any decrease in labor costs. (Even so, these could still affect savings by shortening the schedule.)

3. Circular work; surfaces with offsets, recesses, haunches, and similar; walls with fluctuating changes in height—all such conditions will impair productivity.

4. Suspended slabs in multistory buildings, particularly where "flying" forms can be constructed and handled with a tower crane, will provide the optimum output per labor-hour. Hand-placed formwork to repetitive floor slabs will also achieve excellent productivity if a system of metal (usually aluminum) joists is used. The aluminum joists and trusses are very light to handle and, except for the plywood soffits, a minimum of lumber is required. However, as these form systems are often rented from a specialist company, estimators should ensure that they will be put to continuous work during the course of the project. Bad weather, strikes, sheer bad planning, all these could result in the sad situation of paying monthly rentals for items that are not put to consistent use. Companies specializing in these systems will usually provide assistance in estimating a contractor's requirements.

5. Forms to slab edges (particularly when "suspended") and bulkheads at construction joints are always costly items, and very often the productivity will be less than average. The same applies to small equipment bases and interior curbs, particularly if scattered around a structure in various locations.

TABLE 12–7 Formwork to walls: lumber and plywood quantities per square foot

Stud Size and Spacing	Waler Size and Spacing	Board Feet of Lumber (per sft)	Plywood ⅝-inch (sft)
2″ × 4″ 12″ on center	Double 2″ × 4″ 30″ on center	1.2–1.3	1.05–1.10
2″ × 4″ 14″ on center	Double 2″ × 4″ 30″ on center	1.15–1.25	1.05–1.10
2″ × 6″ 12″ on center	Double 2″ × 6″ 36″ on center	1.7–1.9	1.05–1.10
2″ × 6″ 10″ on center	Double 2″ × 6″ 30″ on center	2.0–2.3	1.05–1.10

Notes:

1. The selection of factors applies to walls not exceeding 12 ft in height. For walls from 12 ft to 20 ft in height, add 3 to 5%. For walls greater than 20 ft in height, add 5 to 10%.

2. Hourly rise of pour up to 5 ft at 68°.

3. Miscellaneous stakes and bracing not included; add 5%.

TABLE 12–8 Formwork: lumber and plywood quantities

	Lumber (bft per sft)	Plywood ⅝ or ¾-inch (sft)
Column footings	1.2–1.5	1.05–1.10
Wall footings	2.2–2.8	
Columns	1.3–1.6	1.05–1.10
Suspended slabs (hand placed)	2.1–2.6	1.05–1.10
Beams	2.5–3.5	1.05–1.10
Stairs and landings	4.5–5.0	1.10–1.15

Notes: The suspended slab factor is based on:
  4 × 4 in. joists at 12 in. on center.
  Three 2 × 10 in. beams at each shore head (two per frame)
  Sills, 2 × 12 in.
  Scaffold frames at 5 ft on center, with 5 ft cross braces

TABLE 12–9 Schedule of labor-hour factors: masonry

Metric Conversion Factors	Multiply by:
Linear feet to meters	3.28
Square feet to square meters	10.764
Cubic yards to cubic meters	1.308

Item	Per (unit)	Crew Ratio	Average Productivity	High, Reduce Factor by:	Low, Increase Factor by:
1. Facing brick					
a. Stretchers	1000 pieces	2:1	22.00	10–15%	15–20%
b. 6 course, headers	1000 pieces	2:1	22.80	10–15%	15–20%
c. Full English bond	1000 pieces	2:1	24.00	5–10%	15–20%
d. Flemish bond	1000 pieces	2:1	23.50	5–10%	15–20%
e. Common brick	1000 pieces	2:1	19.00	5–10%	15–20%

continued

TABLE 12–9 *continued*

		Metric Conversion Factors	Multiply by:
		Linear feet to meters	3.28
		Square feet to square meters	10.764
		Cubic yards to cubic meters	1.308

Item	Per (unit)	Crew Ratio	Average Productivity	Adjust for Higher or Lower Productivity	
				High, Reduce Factor by:	Low, Increase Factor by:
2. Concrete block					
a. 2 in. (5 cm)	piece	1:1	0.06	–	10–15%
b. 4 in. (10 cm)	piece	1:1	0.07	5–10%	10–15%
c. 6 in. (15 cm)	piece	1:1	0.075	5–10%	10–15%
d. 8 in. (20 cm)	piece	1:1	0.095	5–10%	10–15%
e. 10 in. and 12 in. (25 and 30 cm)	piece	1:1	0.125	–	10–15%
f. Extra for exposed block faces	piece	1:1	0.01	–	–
g. Extra for special units	piece	1:1	0.01	–	–
h. Extra for block lintels	foot	1:1	0.08	–	–
3. Glazed concrete block:					
a. 2 to 6 in.	piece	1:1	0.105	–	–
b. 8 to 12 in.	piece	1:1	0.15	–	–
c. Special units	piece	1:1	0.25	–	–
4. Structural clay tile:					
a. 2-in. furring	piece	1:1	0.035	5–10%	10–15%
b. 4-in. backup	piece	1:1	0.04	5–10%	10–15%
c. 6-in. backup	piece	1:1	0.045	5–10%	10–15%
d. 8-in. backup	piece	1:1	0.06	5–10%	10–15%
e. 10 to 12-in. backup	piece	1:1	0.075	–	10–15%
f. 4-in. partition	piece	1:1	0.038	5–10%	10–15%
g. 6-in. partition	piece	1:1	0.042	5–10%	10–15%
h. 8-in. partition	piece	1:1	0.058	5–10%	10–15%
i. 10 to 12-in. partition	piece	1:1	0.073	5–10%	10–15%
5. Structural glazed tile:					
a. 2 to 6 in.	piece	1:1	0.10	–	–
b. 8 to 12 in.	piece	1:1	0.15	–	–
c. Specials	piece	1:1	0.25	–	–
6. Dampcourses and flashings	lft	2:1	0.04	–	–
7. Clean down masonry	sft	labor	0.005	–	–
8. Rake out and point	sft	2:1	0.02	–	–
9. masonry reinforcement	sft	3:1	0.004	–	–
10. Expansion joint	sft	3:1	0.06	–	–
11. Cavity wall insulation	sft	2:1	0.035	–	–

Notes:

1. The labor-hour factors include the unloading and site handling of materials, mixing of mortar, and normal cutting of masonry units. The factors applicable to "average productivity" allow for masonry construction up to a height of 30 ft. *Note:* The labor-hours applicable to erection and dismantling of scaffolding are shown separately.

2. Large wall surfaces with a minimum of corners and openings will improve on the average productivity, while the reverse must be expected with walls that are chopped up with openings, projections, recesses, decorative features, and so on. Also, cavity wall construction should be considered as slightly slower than solid masonry.

3. Furring around columns and pilasters is low-productivity work.

4. Only average productivity should generally be considered for structural glazed tile and glazed block units. This work demands high-quality workmanship and is not usually a high-production operation. The exceptions would probably be large areas of furring to concrete or masonry walls unbroken by openings or projections, and requiring a minimum of "special" units.

TABLE 12–10 Schedule of labor-hour factors: rough carpentry

			Metric Conversion Factors	Multiply by:	
			Linear feet to meters	3.28	
			Square feet to square meters	10.764	
			Cubic yards to cubic meters	1.308	

| | | | | Adjust for Higher or Lower Productivity | |
Item	Per (unit)	Crew Ratio	Average Productivity	High, Reduce Factor by:	Low, Increase Factor by:
1. Blocking to roof	lft	carpenter	0.08	15–25%	–
2. Roof cants	lft	carpenter	0.055	15–25%	–
3. Blocking around metal windows	lft	carpenter	0.11	–	20–25%
4. Miscellaneous blocking	lft	carpenter	0.12	–	20–25%
5. Wall strapping	lft	carpenter	0.06	15–25%	15–20%
6. Nailings strips to structural steel	lft	carpenter	0.096	–	–
7. Grounds	lft	carpenter	0.11	–	–
8. Plywood to parapets, soffits, etc.	sft	carpenter	0.12	–	–
9. Tongue and groove roof/floor decks	bft	carpenter	0.025	–	–

TABLE 12–11 Schedule of labor-hour factors: finish carpentry (millwork)

			Metric Conversion Factors	Multiply by:
			Linear feet to meters	3.28
			Square feet to square meters	10.764
			Cubic yards to cubic meters	1.308

Item	Per (unit)	Crew Ratio	Average Productivity
1. Counter units (includes door, drawers and trim)	lft	carpenter	1.30
2. Kitchen counters/cupboards (floor mounted)	lft	carpenter	0.56
3. Kitchen overhead cupboard units	lft	carpenter	0.43
4. Open shelf units	lft	carpenter	0.40
5. Miscellaneous trim	lft	carpenter	0.08
6. Wall battens	lft	carpenter	0.09
7. Ceiling battens	lft	carpenter	0.10
8. Handrails	lft	carpenter	0.32
9. Base (including nosing)	lft	carpenter	0.09
10. Paneling			
a. Moderate quality	sft	carpenter	0.09
b. Top quality	sft	carpenter	0.15
11. Vanity units (plastic laminate tops)	lft	carpenter	0.60
12. Window stools	lft	carpenter	0.156

166

TABLE 12–12 Schedule of labor-hour factors: doors, frames, screens

		Metric Conversion Factors	Multiply by:	
		Linear feet to meters	3.28	
		Square feet to square meters	10.764	
		Cubic yards to cubic meters	1.308	

				Adjust for Higher or Lower Productivity	
Item	Per (unit)	Crew Ratio	Average Productivity	High, Reduce Factor by:	Low, Increase Factor by:
1. Metal doorframes installed in masonry	ea	3:1	2.30	10–15%	15–25%
2. Metal doorframes installed in concrete	ea	3:1	3.25	–	–
3. Handle only frames to be installed by contractor	ea	labor	0.20	–	–
4. Metal doors	ea	3:1	4.20	–	–
5. Wood doors: interior hollow core	ea	3:1	2.10	5–10%	15–25%
6. Wood doors: interior solid core	ea	3:1	3.50	5–10%	15–25%
7. Plastic laminate doors	ea	3:1	4.80	–	15–25%
8. Doors, exterior	ea	3:1	4.60	–	–
9. Lead lined doors	ea	3:1	16.20	–	–
10. Hollow metal doors	sft	3:1	0.11	–	–
11. Borrowed lights	ea	3:1	2.15	–	–
12. Soundproof doors	ea	3:1	5.80	–	–
13. Sliding closet doors	pair	3:1	4.00	–	–
14. Bifolding doors	unit	3:1	1.80	–	–
15. Wood door frames	unit	3:1	2.50	–	–
Miscellaneous Door Hardware:					
16. Kickplates	ea	carpenter	0.25	–	–
17. Door closer	ea	carpenter	0.75	–	–
18. Door stops or holders	ea	carpenter	0.20	–	–

comments following each trade schedule define the conditions whereby production would be either improved or retarded.

The suggested crew ratios are shown to establish the appropriate composite rate for each item. If different crew compositions are contemplated, not only will the composite rate be revised but consideration should also be given to the labor-hour factor. As a general rule of thumb, if the principal trade proportion increases, the labor-hour factor could be reduced to allow for greater output. However, this would usually be a very nominal adjustment of less than 2 percent.

Crew ratios are not shown for trade divisions such as excavation, concrete placing, or work performed solely by laborers. In certain areas union agreements require a premium on the basic rate for concrete and other operations. Also, some trade sections are based on using the full-hourly rate for a carpenter, and allowance for the supportive work by a helper is included in the labor-hour factor. The adjustment to a composite rate was not considered to be significant for these items. The labor-hour factors include for unloading and handling of materials, and also allowances for lost or nonproductive time

Notes on Pricing: Earthwork

The unit prices for machine excavation are based on the table of factors in Table 12.4 as applied to the following equipment rental rates:

1½-cyd excavator	$57 per hr (fuel and operator included)
¾-cyd excavator	$52 per hr (fuel and operator included)
½-cyd excavator	$47 per hr (fuel and operator included)
Dozer	$50 per hr (fuel and operator included)
Trucks (tandem 9-cyd—bank measure)	$30 per hr (fuel and operator included)

Float charges = $160 for a maximum of 4 hr

The item for mass excavation to the building (Figure 12–1) is computed as follows:

Using a 1½-cyd shovel and assuming an average productivity of 50 cyd/hr:

Shovel $57 × 1.15 = $65.00
Trucks $30 × 3   =   90.00
$155.00 ÷ 50 cyd = $3.10 per cyd

Multiplying this unit by the total estimated quantity:

4,003 cyd × $3.10 = $12,409.00
Add float charges   320.00
$12,729.00 ÷ 4003 cyd = $3.18 per cyd

The following computation applies to the three items of excavation for footings and mechanical services. It is assumed the same 1½-cyd shovel will be used, but the hourly productivity is now assessed as 25 cyd:

Shovel $57 × 1.15 = $65.00
Trucks $30 × 2   =   60.00
$125.00 ÷ 25 cyd = $5 per cyd

The estimated unit rate for placing the backfill with a dozer is computed as follows:

Total rental period = 2 wk = 80 hr
@ $50 per hr = $4,000 ÷ 2,442 cyd (estimated)
= $1.64 per cyd

Note that a quantity of excavated material has to be retained for backfilling to perimeter foundation walls. The quantities and unit price for excavation included the

GENERAL ESTIMATE

Priced By: B.E.W.		Project:	Research Center		Division:	2200		Summary Sheet		
Checked By: J.M.		Architect:			Description:	Earthwork		Date: 6/8/1999		
								Sheet 1 of 1		

| DESCRIPTION / PRICE REFERENCE (QUANTITY ADJUSTMENT) | QUANTITY | | MATERIAL COST | | Labor Unit Price | LABOR SUB TOTAL | EQUIPMENT COST | | ITEM TOTAL COST |
	TOTAL	UNIT	Material Unit Price	MATL. SUB TOTAL			Equip. Unit Price	EQPT. SUB TOTAL	
Strip Topsoil (av. 6") & Stockpile on site	350	cyd	3.00	1050					1050
Bulk Excavation to Building (2 mile haul)	4104	cyd	3.18	13051					13051
Trench Excavation to Foundation	764	cyd	5.00	3820					3820
Excav. for Interior Column Footings	160	cyd	5.00	800					800
Excav. for Interior Trenches (Mechanical Trade)	554	cyd	5.00	2770					2770
Hand Trim to Surface (After Machine Excav.)	12479	sft			0.13	1641			1641
Hand Trim to Trench Bottoms	2346	sft			0.34	789			789
Hand Trim to Interior Col. Footings	80	sft			0.34	27			27
Backfill Perimeter Foundation Walls (Excav Mat.)	993	cyd	3.00	2979	3.43	3411			6390
Backfill Perimeter Foundation Walls (Imp. Granular)	604	cyd	7.00	4228	3.43	2075			6303
Backfill Interior Column Footings	186	cyd	7.00	1302	3.43	639			1941
Backfill Mechanical Trenches	665	cyd	7.00	4655	9.13	6075			10730
Stone Fill to Underside of Concrete Slab	280	cyd	12.50	3500	12.35	3458			6958
Weeping Tile - 6" diameter (Perforated Plastic)	209	lft	1.50	314	1.71	357			671
Weeping Tile - Extra for Special Fittings	10	ea	10.00	100					100
Pea Gravel Surround to Weeping Tile	154	cyd	13.00	2002	7.30	1643			3645
Equipment Rentals - Bulldozer (Placing Backfill)	2442	cyd	1.64	4005					4005
- Compaction Equipment	2	mos	350.00	700					700
				45276		20114			65390

FIGURE 12–1 Estimate pricing sheet—earthwork.

hauling away of this material, and it has been assumed that this unit price would also cover the cost of hauling it to and from a stockpile. The material unit rate against this item is for the cost of digging and hauling the material from the stockpile.

LABOR COSTS. In this example all the items are based on the labor-hour factors reflecting average productivity. Medium soil conditions are anticipated. The items for backfill are based on the material being pushed into place by the bulldozer. Trimming and compaction are performed by hand, with the exception of the pipe trenches, where the backfill is entirely hand-placed and compacted.

Notes on Pricing: Concrete

1. The ready-mix concrete prices are presumed to be the most competitive received from a number of suppliers. The premium charges for winter heat are applied to the quantities of items scheduled to be performed during the winter months. The item "miscellaneous charges" is a contingency amount to cover incidental charges for underloads and the like.

2. Labor costs: All items are priced on the basis of average productivity as noted on the labor-hour schedules with the exception of the following:

   Column footings: The total quantity for this item being very small, (Figure 12–2) the average factor has been increased by 35 percent.

   $$0.48 \times 1.35 = 0.65 \text{ labor-hour per cyd}$$

   $$0.65 \times \$19/\text{hr (labor)} = \$12.35 \text{ per cyd}$$

   Wall footings: Another low production operation; the average factor is increased by 35 percent.

   $$0.55 \times 1.35 = 0.74 \text{ labor-hour per cyd}$$

   $$0.74 \times \$19/\text{hr} = \$14.06, \text{ say } \$14.10 \text{ per cyd}$$

   Piers or pedestals: The average factor again is increased by 35 percent.

   $$0.96 \times 1.35 = 1.3 \text{ labor-hours per cyd}$$

   $$1.3 \times \$19/\text{hr} = \$24.70, \text{ say } \$25.00 \text{ per cyd}$$

   Suspended slab and beams: With the use of a mobile crane to place the concrete, and allowing for a minimum amount of wheel barrowing to those locations that could not be reached directly by the crane, it is considered that the average factor could be improved by approximately 15 percent.

   $$0.75 \text{ less } 15\% = 0.64 \text{ labor-hour per cyd}$$

   $$0.64 \times \$19/\text{hr} = \$12.16 \text{ per cyd}$$

   Stairs and landings: Always a costly operation, and in this case the small quantity would result in very low production. The average factor is escalated by 40 percent.

Summary Sheet

| Priced By: B.E.W. | | Project: | Research Center | Division: | | Date: | 6/8/1999 |
| Checked By: J.M. | | Architect: | | Description: | Concrete | Sheet 1 of 1 | 3300 |

DESCRIPTION / QUANTITY ADJUSTMENT — PRICE REFERENCE	QUANTITY		MATERIAL COST		Labor Unit Price	LABOR SUB TOTAL	EQUIPMENT COST		ITEM TOTAL COST
	TOTAL	UNIT	Material Unit Price	MATL. SUB TOTAL			Equip. Unit Price	EQPT. SUB TOTAL	
Ready-Mix Materials:									
1. 3000 P.S.I. (25 Mpa) - 3/4" Stone (5% waste)	41	cyd	48.00	1968					1968
2. 4000 P.S.I. (30 Mpa) - 3/4" Stone (2% waste)	1148	cyd	51.50	59122					59122
3. Lightweight Concrete	32	cyd	59.00	1888					1888
Premium Charges: Air Entrainment	1189	cyd	1.15	1367					1367
Winter Heat	300	cyd	3.00	900					900
Misc. Charges	Item			300					300
Strength									
Mix Placing To:									
1 Isolated Column Footings	4	cyd			12.35	49			49
1 Wall Footings	25	cyd			14.10	353			353
2 Foundation Walls and Pilasters	153	cyd			14.25	2180			2180
1 Piers (Pedestals) Below Grade	1	cyd			25.00	25			25
2 Columns	18	cyd			18.27	329			329
2 Suspended Slab (Flat Plate)	62	cyd			15.20	942			942
2 Suspended Slab (Include Beams)	687	cyd			12.16	8354			8354
3 Fill to Metal Deck (L/Wt. Concrete)	30	cyd			32.15	965			965
2 Slab on Grade	204	cyd			10.23	2087			2087
2 Stairs and Landings	2	cyd			48.00	96			96
1 Equipment Pads (18 ea.)	2	cyd			77.14	154			154
1 Fill to Metalstair Pans (32 ea.)	39	cft.			5.13	200			200
1 Sump Pits (Include Base and Walls)	5	cyd			16.08	80			80
Rub-Exposed Concrete Surfaces - Walls & Columns	2847	sft	0.03	85	1.02	2913			2998
Rub-Exposed Concrete Surfaces - Soffits	2352	sft	0.03	71	0.80	1891			1962
Asphalt Impregnated Expansion Joint									
6" wide X 1/2" thick	610	lft	0.36	220	0.80	485			705
Grout Column Base Plate	1	ea	12.00	12	25.00	25			37
Misc. Runways, Scaffolds & Ladders	Item			500		2000			2500
Concrete Placing Equipment:									
Mobile Crane (25 tons)	200	hrs	65.00	13000					13000
Buggies (2 X 6 mos.)	12	mos	85.00	1020					1020
Vibrators (2 X 6 mos.)	12	mos	175.00	2100					2100
				82553		23128			105681

FIGURE 12-2 Estimate pricing sheet—concrete.

171

GENERAL ESTIMATE

Summary Sheet

Priced By: B.E.W.	Project: *Research Center*	Division: 3300	Date: 6/8/1999
Checked By: J.M.	Architect:	Description: *Conc. Floor Finishing*	Sheet 1 of 1

DESCRIPTION / QUANTITY ADJUSTMENT — PRICE REFERENCE	QUANTITY TOTAL	UNIT	MATERIAL COST — Material Unit Price	MATL. SUB TOTAL	Labor Unit Price	LABOR SUB TOTAL	Equip. Unit Price	EQUIPMENT COST — EQPT. SUB TOTAL	ITEM TOTAL COST
Unit Prices by "J.A.J. Concrete Floors, Inc."									
Machine Trowel (Plain)	24200	sft	0.18	4356					4356
Machine Trowel (Hardened)	2352	sft	0.52	1223					1223
Wood Float at Roof	10000	sft	0.12	1200					1200
Membrane Curing	36522	sft	0.04	1461					1461
Finish to Equipment Bases (Hand Trowel)	79	sft	0.45	36					36
Finish to Sump Pit Base	81	sft	0.45	37					37
Finish to Stairs and Landings	122	sft	0.80	98					98
Finish to Cement Fill to Metal Stair Pans	229	sft	0.85	195					195
				8606					8606

FIGURE 12–3 Estimate pricing sheet—concrete finishing.

$$1.8 \times 1.40 \ = \ 2.52 \text{ labor-hours per cyd}$$

$$2.52 \times \$19/hr \ = \ \$47.88, \text{ say } \$48.00 \text{ per cyd}$$

Equipment pads: There are only 18 of these pads located in various parts of the average building. A factor of 4.06 labor-hours per cubic yard is used (an increase of 45 percent over the average labor-hour factor).

Fill to metal stair pans: This item does not appear on the labor-hour factor schedule, and is one of those items that can be more realistically priced by the cubic foot:

$$0.27 \text{ labor-hour per cft} \times \$19/hr = \$5.13 \text{ per cft}$$

Or price by the number of treads.

Notes on Pricing: Formwork

The following are some of the factors that contribute to formwork material costs:

Size and spacing of studs, bracing, and the like

Grade and thickness of the plywood sheathing

Cost and spacing of form ties

Shores and/or scaffold frames (usually a rent item)

Form oil

Rate of pour per hour

As stated in the schedule of items and measurements for formwork, the items for formwork hardware and accessories and form oil are recommended to be treated separately, as they are not subject to reuse adjustment factors.

The quantity of plywood sheathing required per square foot of formwork will be the formwork contact area plus a percentage to cover cutting and wastage. The lumber quantities of studs and walers, etc. are usually calculated with the use of prepared tables of factors showing the number of board feet of lumber required per square feet of formwork. Estimators can prepare their own tables or use ready-made tables available in text or reference books on estimating; however, these ready-made tables should be checked to establish knowledge and understanding of the data used in their preparation.

Table 12.7 shows a table of factors for wall forms based on various stud and waler sizes and spacing. It will be noticed that miscellaneous lumber for stakes and bracing is excluded from this table, but a percentage factor is suggested.

The factors do not include an allowance for reuse, which is usually achieved by dividing the established unit price by the number of times that the material will be used. This is quite sufficient for most items, particularly if the quantities involved are not excessive. However, for more contentious items a more constructive approach would be to assess the minimum quantity of plywood and lumber to be purchased for a specific operation.

In the example of a priced estimate for formwork (Figure 12–4), the item for materials to the foundation walls was calculated as follows: The total contact area

GENERAL ESTIMATE — Summary Sheet

Priced By: B.E.W.	Project: Research Center	Division:	Description: Formwork	3100		Date: 6/8/1999
Checked By: J.M.	Architect:					Sheet 1 of 1

DESCRIPTION / QUANTITY ADJUSTMENT PRICE REFERENCE	QUANTITY		MATERIAL COST		LABOR COST		EQUIPMENT COST		ITEM TOTAL COST
	TOTAL	UNIT	Material Unit Price	MATL. SUB TOTAL	Labor Unit Price	LABOR SUB TOTAL	Equip. Unit Price	EQPT. SUB TOTAL	
Isolated Column Footings	112	sft	1.25	140	3.59	402			542
Wall Footings	818	sft	0.46	376	4.29	3509			3885
Foundation Walls (Not exceeding 12' 0" high)	8084	sft	0.52	4204	3.77	30516			34720
Pilasters (Projections and Face)	202	sft	0.52	105	3.59	725			830
Piers (Below Grade)	110	sft	1.35	149	4.24	467			616
Columns	1936	sft	0.48	929	3.59	6946			7875
Beams - Spandrel Include Slab-Edges	6691	sft	0.70	4684	4.24	28388			33072
- Interior	3607	sft	0.70	2525	4.06	14628			17153
Soffit of Suspended Slab (Flat Plate)	2500	sft	0.70	1750	4.71	11765			13515
Soffit of Suspended Slab (Beam/Slab Construction)	19411	sft	0.70	13588	4.71	91346			104934
Stairs and Landings	165	sft	2.40	396	6.94	1145			1541
Equipment Pads (18 ea.)	103	sft	1.40	144	7.25	747			891
Sump Pits (Include Walls and Base)	306	sft	1.20	367	4.21	1289			1656
Key at Wall Footings (2" X 4")	581	lft	0.15	87	1.64	952			1039
Construction Joints (Vertical) - Bulkheads	86	lft	0.85	73	5.24	451			524
- Key (2" X 4")	86	lft	0.15	13	2.65	228			241
- Waterstop	86	lft	1.10	95	2.89	248			343
Construction Joints (Horizontal) - Bulkheads	388	lft	0.85	330	5.24	2034			2364
- Key (2" X 4")	388	lft	0.15	58	2.65	1029			1087
Slab Edges (Not exceeding 12" wide)	312	lft	0.85	265	4.37	1363			1628
Masonry Shelf - 4" X 6"	150	lft	0.90	135	6.24	936			1071
Shelf Angle Inserts (at Spandrel Beams)	206	ea	10.00	2060	10.92	2249			4309
Set Anchors for Precast Conc. Panels	200	ea			9.83	1965			1965
(supplied by Z.J. subcontractor)	A	A	A	A	A	A		A	
Anchor Slots	1983	lft	0.35	694	0.62	1237			1931
Set Screeds	36552	sft	0.01	366	0.02	855			1221
Formwork Hardware and Accessories	Item			4000					4000
Form Oil	Item			300					300
Misc. Small Tools and Equipment	Item			400					400
				38233		205419			243652

FIGURE 12–4 Estimate pricing sheet—rough carpentry (formwork).

quantity is 8,084 sft. It is assumed that a purchased quantity of materials sufficient to form 120 lft of walls would be sufficient. This indicates a quantity of approximately 2,900 sft of contact area (for each use).

Cost of form plywood = $0.85 per sft

Cost of lumber = $400 per thousand bft ($0.40 per bft)

The forms will be constructed with 2″ × 4″ studs at 12″ centers and double 2″ × 4″ walers at 30″ centers, which according to the table indicates a factor of 1.2 bft per sft.

$$\text{Plywood} \quad = \frac{2{,}900 \text{ sft} \times \$0.85 \times 1.05 \text{ (5\% for waste)}}{8{,}084 \text{ sft (Total quantity)}}$$

$$= \$0.32$$

$$\text{Lumber} \quad = \frac{2{,}900 \text{ sft} \times 1.2 \times \$0.40}{8{,}084 \text{ sft}}$$

$$= \$0.17$$

$$\$0.17 + \$0.32 = \$0.49$$

Add 5 percent for miscellaneous braces, and so on, and the total cost per sft is $0.514, say $0.52.

Table 12.8 shows a table of factors for other items of formwork. These factors have been used in the pricing examples, and for most items, because of the small quantities, only one reuse of material has been considered and, in some instances, no reuse at all.

The price for materials to the suspended slabs was computed as follows:

Purchase quantity: Plywood and lumber for one complete floor, equal to approximately 7,500 sft. The total gross area of all suspended slab soffits is 2,500 sft + 19,411 sft = 21,911 sft.

$$\text{Plywood:} \quad \frac{7{,}500 \text{ sft} \times 1.05 \times \$0.85}{21{,}911 \text{ sft}} = \$0.305$$

$$\text{Lumber:} \quad \frac{7{,}500 \text{ sft} \times 2.1 \times \$0.40}{21{,}911 \text{ sft}} = \$0.29$$

$$\$0.305 + \$0.29 = \$0.595, \text{ say } \$0.60 \text{ per sft}$$

To this unit price must be added the cost of scaffolding. It is calculated that 220 scaffold frames will be required to form one floor. The rental for each frame is $4.00 per month. Allowing a cycle of 1½ weeks per each half of the main building slabs yields 1.5 wk × 6 = 9 wk, or say, a 2-mo rental period. This calculates out as:

$$\frac{220 \text{ ea} \times \$4.00 \text{ per mo} \times 2 \text{ mo}}{21{,}911 \text{ sft}} = \$0.08 \text{ per sft}$$

The total unit price = $0.60 per sft (Cost of plywood and lumber)

<u>0.08 per sft (Cost of rental of scaffolding)</u>

$0.68 per sft (Total)

Add for reshoring   <u>$0.02 per sft</u>

Cost per sft $0.70

FORMWORK LABOR COSTS. Average productivity has been considered for all items except as follows. An allowance of 2 percent has been added to the composite rates for the working foreman's time (approximately $0.29 for each rate).

Wall forms: labor-hour factor is reduced by 10 percent as these walls have generally repetitive heights (except at stepped footings): 0.13 less 10% = 0.117 per sft.

Piers below grade: this quantity is very small and the factor is increased by 20 percent.

Suspended slabs: consideration was given to a 10 percent reduction in the average labor-hour factor = 0.104 labor-hours per sft. This factor computed by the composite rate of $22.29 × 10% = $2.32 per sft. However, this is a major item in the estimate and needs to be checked out more practically:

Assume a crew of 6 carpenters and 5 laborers, including a working foreman:

Foreman $26.50 × 1 = $16.50

Carpenters $25.00 × 5 =   125.00

Laborers $19.00 × 5 =   <u>95.00</u>

Total hourly cost of crew   = $236.50

If one-half of a typical floor slab (3,750 sft) could be formed and stripped in five days, which equals 40 hr, the estimated rate would be:

$$\frac{\$236.50 \times 40 \text{ hr}}{3,750 \text{ sft}} = \$2.52 \text{ per sft}$$

This indicates that the rate of $2.32 per sft is probably too optimistic and would be difficult to achieve, and therefore the rate of $2.52 is used in the estimate. In practice, some discussion with a superintendent or carpenter foreman would provide further considerations on this operation, with a resultant increase or decrease in the estimated unit.

All major and contentious items should be subjected to alternating methods of establishing estimated costs, with the estimator using the best possible judgment after reviewing all the options and alternatives.

Notes on Pricing: Masonry

1. All the items in this section (see Figure 12–5) have been priced on the basis of average productivity with the exception of the following:

GENERAL ESTIMATE — Summary Sheet

Priced By: B.E.W.		Project: Research Center		Division: 4000	Date: 6/8/1999
Checked By: J.M.		Architect:		Description: Masonry	Sheet 1 of 1

DESCRIPTION / PRICE REFERENCE (QUANTITY ADJUSTMENT)	QUANTITY TOTAL	UNIT	Material Unit Price	MATL. SUB TOTAL	Labor Unit Price	LABOR SUB TOTAL	Equip. Unit Price	EQPT. SUB TOTAL	ITEM TOTAL COST
Face Brick to Exterior Walls - 6th course headers; modular size, red, rug, 3/8" mortar joints	3900	ea	1.90	7410	4.60	17957			25367
Extra Over - Labor to Brick Sills	425	lft			1.33	563			563
Conc. Block, Lightweight - 8" backup to Brick & P.C. Panels	5924	ea	0.6	3554	1.86	10993			14547
Conc. Block, Lightweight - 6" Interior Partitions	10355	ea	0.54	5592	1.55	16013			21605
Conc. Block, Lightweight - 4" Interior Partitions	6162	ea	0.48	2958	1.44	8893			11851
Conc. Block Extra Over - Specials: Lintel Blocks	190	ea	0.12	23	0.21	39			62
Conc. Block Extra Over - Specials: Bullnose	70	ea	0.12	8	0.21	14			22
Conc. Block Extra Over - Labor only to Exposed Faces	280	ea			0.19	54			54
3000 P.S.I. Conc. & two (2) #4 reinf. Bars to block lintels	253	lft	1.55	392	1.62	410			802
Stone Coping at Parapet (Fasten) w/ Anchors - Measured Sep.	550	lft	11.00	6050	4.27	2349			8399
Anchors to Stone Coping	282	ea	0.75	212	5.52	1557			1769
Dampcourse (2 oz. Copper laminated paper) - 18" wide	605	lft	0.42	254	0.86	523			777
Flashings at Window Heads	1075	lft	0.42	452	0.94	1014			1466
Cavity Wall Insulation (1" Polystrene Type 4)	5492	sft	0.53	2911	0.75	4143			7054
Clean Down Face Brick	3936	sft	0.03	118	0.10	403			521
Clean Down Exposed Surfaces of Conc. Block	248	sft	0.03	7	0.15	37			44
Mortar (Type "N" - Masonry Cement)	56	cyd	44.55	2508		2508			2508
Cavity Wall Ties - Z Bars 3/16" Steel Wire	2300	ea	0.20	460		460			460
Dovetail Anchors (Hot Dipped Gald. 16. Ga. 1" X 3 1/2" X 3/8")	1400	ea	0.12	168		168			168
Scaffold Frames - Erect and Dismantle	326	ea			6.26	2040			2040
Masonry Equipment: Mortar Mixer	3	mos	250.00	750					750
Fork Lift	3	mos	900.00	2700					2700
Brick Buggies	3	mos	85.00	255					255
Masonry Saw and Blades	Item			1000					1000
Scaffolds (Frames, Braces, etc.)	320	mos	5.00	1600					1600
Scaffold Plank	Item			300					300
Misc. Small Tools & Equipment	Item			200					200
				39882		67001			106883

FIGURE 12-5 Estimate pricing sheet—masonry.

Face brick: Except for the window openings, the wall surfaces are straightforward and a little better than average productivity would be possible. Therefore, the average labor-hour factor is reduced by 10 percent.

$$22.80 - 10\% \ (2.28) = 20.52 \text{ labor-hours per 1,000 pieces}$$

The crew ratio is 2:1, which provides a composite labor-hour rate of $20.67, which is adjusted by 2 percent to allow for a working foreman:

$$\$20.67 \times 1.02 \ = \ \$21.08 \times 20.52 \text{ labor-hours per 1000 pieces}$$
$$= \ \$432.56 \text{ per 1,000 pieces}$$

2. The "extra over" item for brick sills is calculated as 10 percent of the basic rate of $432.56 per 1,000 pieces, or $0.43 per piece, multiplied by three pieces per lft equals $1.29.
3. The composite rates for concrete block are for a 1:1 ratio = $20.25 per hr, plus 2 percent for the foreman = $20.66. The factor for the backup block to face brick and precast concrete has been decreased by 5 percent = 0.09 labor-hour per block.
4. A 10 percent increase over the basic unit price has been allowed for the additional labor to exposed concrete block faces.
5. The cost of the concrete and reinforcing bars in concrete block lintels is stated as a linear foot item based on previous costs. The premium cost of the special lintel block is shown separately under "specials."
6. The cost of the mortar material is computed as follows:

Masonry cement	31.33 lb per cft at $0.027/lb	=	$0.85 per cft
Sand	80.00 lb per cft at $0.01/lb	=	$0.80 per cft
	Total mix	=	$1.65 per cft
	$1.65 per cft $\times$ 27 cft/cyd	=	$44.55 per cyd

NOTES ON PRICING: ROUGH AND FINISH CARPENTRY

In the examples given in Figure 12–6 and 12–7, only the factors for average production have been selected, with the exception of the following:

Curbs at skylights: These would be short pieces, with very little total quantity. There is no specific item for these curbs on the labor-hour schedule, so 15 percent is added to the average factor for roof blocking: $0.08 \times 1.15 = \$.092$.

GENERAL ESTIMATE | Summary Sheet

| Priced By: B.E.W. | Project: Research Center | Division: 6100 | Date: 6/8/1999 |
| Checked By: J.M. | Architect: | Description: Rough Carpentry | Sheet 1 of 1 |

| DESCRIPTION / QUANTITY ADJUSTMENT PRICE REFERENCE | QUANTITY | | MATERIAL COST | | Labor Unit Price | LABOR SUB TOTAL | Equip. Unit Price | EQUIPMENT COST | ITEM TOTAL COST |
	TOTAL	UNIT	Material Unit Price	MATL. SUB TOTAL				EQPT. SUB TOTAL	
The following in No. 2 Spruce (Construction Grade) unless stated otherwise									
A-4 Roof Carpentry: 4" x 4" Cant Strips	630	Lft.	0.50	315	1.38	872			1187
2' x 4" Blocking	630	Lft.	0.24	151	2.00	1260			1411
2' x 4" Curbs at Skylights	74	Lft.	0.24	18	2.33	173			191
6/1001									
Blocking at Window Stools - 2" x 4"	1087	Lft.	0.24	261	3.00	3261			3522
" Vanity Units - 1" x 2"	50	Lft.	0.08	4	3.00	150			154
A-6 1" x @" Wall Strapping to Recive Paneling	378	Lft.	0.08	30	1.50	567			597
8/1001									
Misc. Blocking - 2" x 4" at counter Units	66	Lft.	0.24	16	3.00	198			214
" - 2" x 6" at Misc. Fixtures	40	Lft.	0.43	17	3.00	120			137
Rough Hardware		L.S.		50					50
				862		6600			7462

FIGURE 12–6 Estimate pricing sheet—rough carpentry (roof and blocking).

| Priced By: B.E.W. | GENERAL ESTIMATE | | Project: Research Center | Description: Miscellaneous | | Summary Sheet | | Date: | 6/8/1999 |
| Checked By: J.M. | | | Architect: | Contractor's Work | | | | Sheet 1 of | 1 |

| DESCRIPTION / PRICE REFERENCE / QUANTITY ADJUSTMENT | QUANTITY | | MATERIAL COST | | Labor Unit Price | LABOR SUB TOTAL | EQUIPMENT COST | | ITEM TOTAL COST |
	TOTAL	UNIT	Material Unit Price	MATL. SUB TOTAL			Equip. Unit Price	EQPT. SUB TOTAL	
06200 - Finish Carpentry									
Detail									
6/1001 Window Stool	1035	lft	) supplied by		3.92	4054			4054
8/1001 Washroom Vanity (Fixed to Brackets - Supplied by Others)	48	lft	) millwork		15.00	720			720
Wood Paneling (Fixed to Wood Strapping)	1056	sft	) subcontracor		2.25	2376			2376
Counter Units - Av. 2'6" wide X 3'0" high	37	lft	) - firm price		33.33	1233			1233
Cedar Battens at Ceilings - 1 1/2" X 1"	600	lft	) quotation		2.50	1500			1500
Laminated Wood Handrails to Metal Stairs	210	lft			8.00	1680			1680
Rough Hardware	Item			100					100
				100		11563			11663
08100 - Metal Doors and Frames									
Metal Door Frames - Av. 3'0" X 7'0" Set in Block Partitions	45	ea			53.48	2407			2407
Metal Door Frames - Av. 3'0" X 7'0" to Exterior Wall	2	ea			61.59	123			123
Metal Doors - Av. 3'0" X 7'0"	2	ea			97.24	194			194
Misc. Rough Hardware, Braces, etc.	Item			100					100
				100		2724			2824
08200 - Wood and Plastic Doors									
Exterior Wood Doors - Oak 3'6" X 7'3"	2	ea			106.97	214			214
Plastic Laminated Doors at Interior Partitions	43	ea			113.45	4878			4878
						5092			5092

FIGURE 12–7 Estimate pricing sheet—miscellaneous notes.

13 ESTIMATING SITE OVERHEAD COSTS

13.1 DEFINITIONS

Site overhead costs are also termed indirect costs by some general contractors because they refer to items of work that, although necessary to the construction, are not identifiable with the work of specific trades. They also represent the cost (a significant cost, anywhere from 6 to 15 percent) of items that do not become functional parts of the completed building and visible to the building users, as do doors, windows, floors, ceilings, and so on. However, without these indirect items of work, the building would not, and in fact could not, be constructed. Although termed "indirect," these costs are chargeable to the project.

Specifications give various labels to this classification of work: General Conditions, Temporary Facilities, Contractor's Work, and so on. Masterformat Divisions 0 Bidding and Contract Requirements and 1 General Requirements state most of the applicable items. They differ from direct trade items, inasmuch as they are intangibles and not detailed on the drawings, with the possible exception of perimeter fencing and covered ways, and occasionally site offices. Certain items will be clearly specified and detailed, but generally the requirement is stated in terms of a desired performance or result. For example, the contractors are told the building must be maintained at a minimum temperature of 50°F (10°C) in cold weather. There may be some specified restraints regarding the type of heating equipment to be used; otherwise, it is left to the contractors to evaluate and decide on the methods and systems to satisfy the specified requirements.

Although few of these items will form part of the finished building, this does not mean that they will not be visible during construction. Site offices, temporary fences, cranes, hoists, pumps, wheelbarrows, rubbish containers, temporary piping—all these are very evident to a building owner when visiting the site.

Because only a few of these items appear on the drawings, the methods of estimating these costs will be different from the direct trades. With the exception again of wood walkways and fences, any takeoff work will be confined to things that, although not actually shown on the drawings, the drawings can still be useful for establishing their scope and measurements. For example, most specifications include a requirement for temporary doors and windows. These temporary items will not actually be detailed on the drawings (or very rarely so), but the permanent doors and windows will be shown and can be measured and counted.

Temporary access roads are sometimes shown on the drawings, but usually the drawings will only be used to plot and measure the extent of necessary access routes. Other items in this category would be temporary barricades around floor openings or the perimeter of suspended floor slabs, temporary stairs and ladders, areas for final cleanup, and rubbish chutes.

Obviously, some sort of planning and decision-making processes have to function before many of these items can be measured. The matter of who should make such decisions varies from company to company. Some construction firms consider it to be a normal function of an estimating department. Others consider it to be a managerial responsibility; many, though, consider the best results are achieved when this part of the estimate requires the involvement of both estimators and construction managers, working together as a team. Whoever is going to shoulder the responsibility of running the project should have some input into the estimate of these indirect cost items. A criticism sometimes expressed against this arrangement is that it can provide the opportunity for estimated costs to be escalated up to a comfortable level, where a supervisor would subsequently have little difficulty in improving on them and looking rather smug about it at the completion of the project. This, of course, is in a sense a Catch-22: if the estimated costs are too high, there will probably be no project to be smug about.

The combination of estimating skills and managerial or supervisory input will usually bring the most benefits. A good supervisor can provide sound practical suggestions based on experience with similar projects. Existing cost records are invaluable for this division of the estimate, but estimators should always aggressively seek out the background story to such reported costs. To be informed that on a certain project the cost of temporary heating totaled $25,000 does not tell the estimators very much unless they are also provided with more detailed information regarding the methods and equipment employed for this operation. Contacting the superintendent for this particular project will usually pay dividends to the estimator in obtaining this kind of background information.

13.2   SCHEDULE

Before proceeding with the estimate of job overhead, a project schedule should be prepared. For the purpose of the bid, this schedule will usually be a simple, time-honored bar chart. Certain complex projects might be better serviced at the bidding stage with a more sophisticated diagrammatic (critical-path method) type of schedule; however, there is usually insufficient time available to prepare this type of schedule in any great detail.

Many items pertaining to job-site overheads are time related, and the preparation of this schedule is essential for the purpose of assessing the anticipated total time duration. To arrive at this requires the calculation of start and completion dates for each major division of work, which in the aggregate will provide the total duration period. This schedule will also be useful in pinpointing the extent of the work being performed during the winter months, particularly excavation, concrete, and masonry. Also, the duration period for certain equipment (hoists, cranes, compactors, concrete placing equipment, etc.) can be assessed with the use of this schedule.

This schedule should not be prepared until quantities for key trades such as excavation and concrete (if applicable) are completed. The extent of these quantities will assist in assessing the time duration for these operations.

Figure 13–1 is an example of a schedule prepared for bidding purposes. It indicates the start and completion times of the major trades, and also shows which trades will be working during the winter months. If the bid is successful, then a more refined and detailed schedule is prepared for the project.

13.3 SITE VISIT

A familiar clause in many bid forms is the one that states that "the contractor is deemed to have visited the site and made a thorough examination of all existing conditions." Regardless of the existence or nonexistence of such a clause, it is doubtful if any experienced estimator would ever prepare a bid without visiting the site of the proposed construction.

Many estimators make more than one prebid site visit, and this is a good idea. An early (and probably brief) visit shortly after the receipt of the drawings will assist an estimator to "get a feel" for the project. At a later date, when more knowledge has been assimilated about the project's complexities, and prior to the preparation of the site overhead or indirect costs, a second visit will be necessary for a more in-depth investigation to establish firsthand information relative, although not limited, to the following items:

1. Existing structures (or portions thereof) requiring demolition.
2. Proximity of existing buildings, presenting possible requirements for underpinning and/or perimeter sheeting and shoring.
3. Availability of utilities: water, electric power, gas lines, sewer, telephone service, and so on.
4. Availability and extent of space for storage, site offices, trailers, parking, hoists, and similar equipment.
5. Obstructions to be removed: overhead wires and lines (intended use of a mobile crane or similar equipment would call for temporary removal and subsequent reinstallation), poles, fences, transformers, and so on.
6. Trees and brush to be removed.
7. Existing work requiring protection during construction and requirements for dust screens for interior renovation work.
8. Site access, temporary roads, traffic congestion problems.

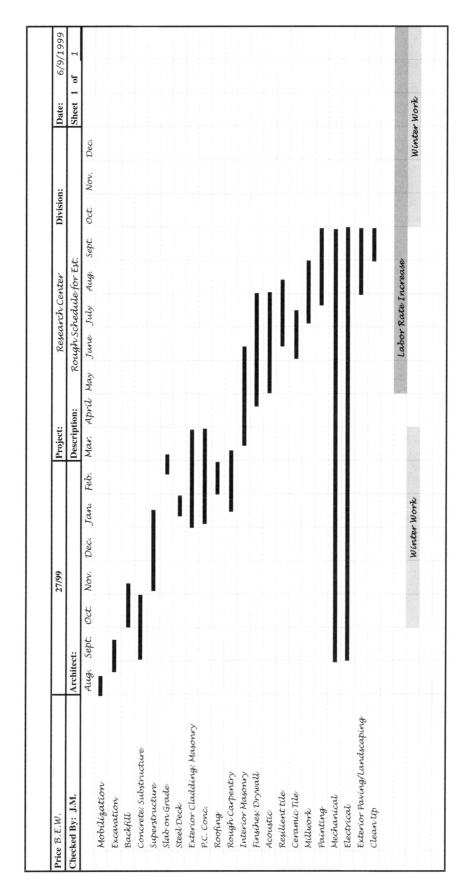

FIGURE 13–1 Schedule prepared for bidding purposes.

9. Soil and groundwater conditions.

10. Other pertinent information according to the nature and complexity of the project.

The use of a camera is highly recommended. It should preferably be a Polaroid-type camera to avoid an unnecessary return visit because the prints were not good and failed to provide a satisfactory picture of the site conditions. Views should be taken from a number of angles and a sketch provided to indicate the location of these views.

A site visit for a project in an out-of-town location, particularly in remote or country areas, will require additional information, including such items as:

1. Existing labor rates, union agreements, availability of existing trades.

2. Board and lodging facilities.

3. Travel factors: distances, public transportation facilities.

4. Well digging, access road construction, pole lines for power transmission.

5. Local building bylaws, building and other permits.

It is recommended that estimators prepare a standard company form for use on these site visits, which could be conveniently attached to a clipboard. This form would be in effect a check or "reminder" list of all items common to most projects, with space (on additional paper if necessary) for any additional information to be reported. Figure 13–2 shows an example of a standard prebid site form used for visits.

13.4   CATEGORIZING SITE OVERHEAD ITEMS

The various indirect items should be grouped and classified in certain categories. This will enable the estimator (also a construction manager or project supervisor) to consider together a number of items whose individual functions aggregate to a specific functional category.

EXAMPLE: "Hoisting." By combining all the items pertaining to cranes, material and personnel hoists, derricks, temporary elevators, conveyors, and the like, in one group, the estimator can concentrate on this category as a whole before considering another category.

The following pages show some suggested categories and the items applicable to each category. Some construction companies will probably have standard lists of items either longer or shorter than those shown here. It does not matter what sort of format an estimator decides to use, whether broken down into a larger number of items or reduced to a few specific classifications, as long as all the work required by the specifications is accounted for and a proper understanding prevails of what and why certain items have to be included in this part of the estimate.

The following are the principal categories of site overhead:

1. Project supervision.

2. Offices and administrative requirements.

3. Site access, protection, and security.

4. Temporary utilities.

```
┌─────────────────────────────────────────────────────────────────────────┐
│                          Pre-Bid Visit Report                             │
│                                                                           │
│                                                                           │
│   Project: Thompson High School              Date: Aug. 10, 1998          │
│   Location: Castro, California               Estimate No.: 15/81          │
│                                                                           │
│                                                                           │
│   1. Existing and Adjacent Work  (Demolition, underpinning, perimeter shoring) │
│                                                                           │
│            Remove existing garage  (wood framed)                          │
│            Remove existing chain link fence  (approx. 65' 0")             │
│                                                                           │
│                                                                           │
│   2. Access and Site Restraints                                           │
│                                                                           │
│        (a) Temporary road   Paved road at north, gravel at east - good access │
│                                                                           │
│        (b) Space for storage, offices, etc.   O.K                         │
│                                                                           │
│        (c) Disposal of excavated materials  Haul off site (5 miles)       │
│                                                                           │
│        (d) Other information                                              │
│                                                                           │
│                                                                           │
│   3. Existing Trees                                                       │
│                                                                           │
│        (a) Removal   Three @ 24' 0"; two @ 18" 0' - misc. bushes          │
│                                                                           │
│        (b) Protection  Five maple trees at north end of site              │
│                                                                           │
│                                                                           │
│   4. Soil and Water Conditions                                            │
│                                                                           │
│            Refer soil report                                              │
│                                                                           │
│                                                                           │
│   5. Utilities                                                            │
│                                                                           │
│        (a) Electric power    Available         (d) Gas    Being installed │
│                                                                           │
│        (b) Water     _____                (e) Telephone  Available   │
│                                                                           │
│        (c) Sewers    _____                                           │
│                                                                           │
│                                                                           │
│   6. Other Information                                                     │
│                                                                           │
│            Close to hospital - maybe noise restrictions? Good clean site  │
│   Report Prepared By:  J. L. J .                                          │
└─────────────────────────────────────────────────────────────────────────┘
```

FIGURE 13–2   A standard pre-bid site visit form.

5. Construction facilities and services.
6. Hoisting: materials and personnel.
7. Small tools and equipment.
8. Permits, insurance, and bonds.

13.5 CATEGORY 1: PROJECT SUPERVISION

This applies to personnel working directly and exclusively on a particular project. Personnel to be considered would include:

Item	Comment
Project managers and superintendents	On large projects these would include general superintendents, assistant superintendents, mechanical and electrical superintendents, and so on
Engineers	Project, field, office engineers, etc.
Estimators, quantity surveyors, and cost engineers	
Accountants and timekeepers	
Safety supervisors	This could be a mandatory requirement in the specification
Instrument men	
Secretarial and clerical	
Purchasing and expediting	

Each member of the project staff will be listed separately, stating the estimated time (usually in months) of duration and the salary. Fringe benefits and labor burdens should also be included, usually by the addition of an applicable percentage factor to the total sum of the salaries.

13.6 CATEGORY 2: OFFICES AND ADMINISTRATIVE REQUIREMENTS

Temporary Offices and Buildings

These would include on-site offices, storage sheds, temporary wash houses, lunchroom or canteen facilities, and other buildings as required by the specifications. A frequent specification clause is one that asks for the provision of a separate office facility for the sole use of the architects or engineers or their site representatives. A minimum floor area is often stated for this item. On large projects a separate facility for the storage of finish hardware materials may also warrant consideration.

If rented or purchased office trailers are to be used, they should be stated separately. When the construction of a building is sufficiently advanced, and providing the specification endorses the arrangement, general contractors often take a section of a floor and utilize this space for site office purposes. All costs should be included for the provision of temporary partitions, doors, shelving, cupboards, and similar items.

Large projects of long duration, and particularly those located in the downtown areas of cities, will often require rented office space in buildings adjacent to the site. This would be in addition to the on-site offices and trailers for field superintendents and engineers. Costs would include rent (or even purchase, of a small house, for example) and all necessary renovations and partitioning.

Costs must always be included for such items as:

1. Heating, ventilating, air conditioning, sanitation and lighting.
2. Painting of temporary buildings, allowing also for any necessary repainting during construction.
3. The dismantling and removal of temporary buildings at completion of the project.
4. Office furniture: desks, tables, chairs, drawing racks, storage cabinets, conference tables, and other similar items.

The specifications will probably state some minimum requirements for the architects' site office; sometimes this will be a complete inventory of items coupled with the request that all furniture and equipment is to be new (often office furniture catalog numbers will be quoted.). For the contractor's office the normal procedure is to move existing furniture from another (completed) project or place of storage to the new project, and purchase or rent additional items as required.

Estimators should also check the specifications regarding temporary buildings for the use of subcontractors. For major subtrades (mechanical and electrical, for example) it is usually specified that these contractors include the cost of all temporary buildings in their quotations; sometimes, however, this is specified to be a cost carried by the general contractor; more ominously, some specifications remain silent on the matter. To avoid possible conflicts about this matter at a later date, it is best to solicit prebid clarification from the architect on this item.

Supplies and Equipment

Include for the cost of items such as:

Computers

Software for: word processing, spreadsheets, contract control, scheduling, estimating

Fax machines

Network in trailer

Stationery and miscellaneous office supplies

Writing and printing materials

Typewriters, calculators, adding machines, photocopying equipment

Postal equipment

Drafting supplies

Bookkeeping, accounting, timekeeping supplies

A monthly cost should be established to cover these items. Previous cost information will be useful. Certain of the more specialized items (photocopiers, postal equipment, special drafting equipment, for example) should probably be identified as separate costs. An experienced office manager would be able to advise the estimator on all these items and costs.

Janitorial Services

This service may be stated in the specification as a mandatory weekly requirement for the architect's office, and the contractor will either hire a specialist company or perform the work with direct labor. This function is sometimes included in the rental charges for temporary offices in existing buildings.

The estimate should include a lump-sum total or weekly cost as quoted by a janitorial service company. If the work is to be performed with direct labor, an estimated number of labor-hours will be given.

13.7 CATEGORY 3: SITE ACCESS, PROTECTION, AND SECURITY

Temporary Roads

This will vary according to the type and location of the project. Some projects will require special roads for construction purposes to be brought into the site from existing main access roads, and the drawings and specifications will provide detailed information regarding construction of such roads. However, for most projects the specifications will only stipulate the requirement for this work; the estimate of cost will be based on standard construction practices applicable to the locality or region. This estimate will usually be confined to the rental of equipment to rough grade, spread, and compact purchased granular materials, and possibly the labor costs of any necessary hand trimming.

Some specifications allow the early placement of the stone or gravel subbases for the permanent access routes to be used for temporary road purposes, with the final asphalt coating to be applied at the completion of the project. As this permanent paving work will usually be a subcontract item, the paving trade contractors will have to be consulted about this arrangement; the estimate should also include an allowance for "making good" to this subbase before the paving work is completed.

Apart from major access roads into the site, the estimate should also allow for temporary roadwork around the structure and into storage areas and hoist locations. Available cost information from other projects might be useful in establishing unit prices (per linear or square foot), which could be updated to reflect current material and labor costs. It is important on projects of long duration to allow for some maintenance work to these temporary roads. Also check if the specifications make reference to any special requirements for dust control.

Fences, Wood Barricades, and Covered Walkways

The specifications will often contain definitive instructions about these items. They are usually noted on the site plot plans, enabling the total length to be measured with reasonable accuracy. A typical specification item for a perimeter hoarding might read:

Provide wood barricades at property line constructed with 4 × 4 in. studs at 2 ft centers, ½-in. plywood good 1/side. Allow for gates. Paint barricade two coats, color to be approved by the architect. Maintain and repair during construction; dismantle and remove from site at completion. It is recommended that a unit price per linear foot (or meter) be established by taking off the materials in detail for a specific length of the hoarding (say 10 feet) and then applying this unit price to the total length measured on the drawings. However, some specifications may refer the estimator to a "suitable wood barricade to be constructed in accordance with local municipal regulations" or similar phraseology; in this case, other authoritative literature will need to be examined.

This applies particularly to covered walkways. Although, like the wood barricade, this item may be specified in detail, very often the estimator will be referred to local regulations not only for the construction but also for information as to the conditions that make the provision of a covered way mandatory. When standard details of wood barricades and covered ways exist, the materials could be taken off for a specific length and a factor established indicating the number of board feet of lumber per linear foot of hoarding or covered way. This would simplify the task of estimating the material costs for these structures; there would be no necessity to build up prices from scratch for every estimate. Cost records would be the best source of information regarding the installation, maintenance, dismantling, and removal of these structures.

Sometimes a snow fence is specified around the perimeter of the site or a portion thereof; it should also be priced by the linear foot. The cost will include both the fence material and the metal posts, which are usually sold separately. Also, as in the case of wood barricades and covered ways, the item must include for subsequent dismantling and removal.

An item that can be overlooked is lighting in the covered ways. Some estimators may consider that this cost is applicable to the item for "temporary wiring and lighting"; the most important thing is to ensure it is included somewhere in the estimate.

Other items that relate to access would be:

1. Stairs and ladders to projects with deep excavations. These are usually wood-constructed structures designed and built to meet local or regional safety requirements. This item should be measured and priced on the total board feet of lumber required.

2. Temporary stairs and ladders in the structure required before the installation of the permanent stairs.

3. Temporary (wood) treads to metal stairs. This could be an enumerated item.

Protection

This requirement will vary according to different conditions and specifications. It usually refers to the protection during construction of adjacent structures, roads, walks, curbs, landscaping, and so on. The estimator is usually faced with the choice of being realistic and allowing a single sum of money to cover this item, or being optimistic that any damage occurring during the course of construction will not be the fault or to the cost of the contractor. The following are two specific items that should be identified and priced individually:

1. Protection of existing trees on the property. This will usually entail a physical count at the site. Close boarding or snow fencing is usually specified and can be an onerous item, particularly where the specification warns about a penalty sum for every tree damaged by construction.

2. Protection of finished floors. This should be taken off in square feet and priced according to the material specified (usually plywood).

Watchman and/or Security Services

A typical specification clause will state that a watchman's services will be required at all times outside regular working hours. It is usually included in the estimate as an hourly cost. The number of hours can be calculated by establishing the total number of hours for the period when the watchman will be required and deducting from this the number of regular working hours.

EXAMPLE: A watchman is required for a 12-mo period. The total number of hours for that period is $365 \times 24 = 8760$ hr. The number of regular working hours for the same period (based on an 8-hr day = 40 hr per wk) would be $52 \times 40 = 2080$ hr. Therefore, the watchman would be required for $8760 - 2080 = 6680$ hr.

If a specification requires the employment of a professional security agency, a quotation should be obtained from the applicable companies. This will usually be on a weekly or monthly basis. If the project is within a large industrial plant complex, the specification might state that the permanent plant security staff would be responsible for the construction site area.

Temporary Parking Areas

This could be stated as a separate item or included with the item for temporary access roads. This is another item where the updating of a basic unit price per square foot will be useful. Some projects may permit the use of permanent parking spaces for a limited number of cars; if the contractor's requirements are for more than that number, the additional parking spaces will be subject to a stated monthly cost, which should be included in the estimate.

13.8 CATEGORY 4: TEMPORARY UTILITIES

General

Some of the items in this category can run to fairly excessive costs, particularly on large projects. Temporary heat, light, and power can run into large sums of money. They are difficult to estimate and, if not properly planned and controlled at the project level, can soon exceed the budgeted costs.

For most of these items, historical data should be the basis for a realistic estimate of related costs. Previous cost records, the advice of project supervisors, debate and discussion, and comparative cost studies relative to the choice of methods and equipment, all these things will assist the estimator to produce intelligent cost planning.

Water

This item would normally include the following work:

1. Provision of temporary water lines, including excavation and backfill. This could be priced as a cost per running foot of water line, using either an

updated unit cost from a previous project or soliciting a price from a plumbing subcontractor.

2. Connections to an existing water main.

3. Payment of local authorities' fees for water consumption, or metered costs if so specified. (Note: The specification might signify the building owner's intention of supplying water to the contractor without charge.)

4. Specifications usually obligate the general contractor to provide hoses for the use of subcontractors.

5. Well drilling may be necessary on projects in isolated or rural areas.

This item could be shown in the estimate by a single sum of money or it could be split into two items: (a) the total cost of providing the service lines, branches, connections, and the like; and (b) the water supply, shown as a cost per month.

Temporary Electrical Work

This should be considered in terms of three subdivisions:

Power

Electrical service

Distribution and lighting

These can be included in the estimate under one item of cost, or shown separately. Some estimators might prefer to show the first separately, but to combine the second and third into one item.

The most costly item would probably be power, although this could vary from project to project. Hoists, climbing cranes, temporary elevators, and similar equipment all affect the demand for electrical power. If the specification states that the owner will supply the temporary power to the contractor, then only the costs of lighting and electrical service will have to be considered. Estimators should always confirm that such a clause also means that it will be supplied free of charge to the contractor. Allow for metering costs. Temporary electrical power should be stated in the estimate as a cost per month. Check the specification carefully regarding such time as when the owner will take over and pay for operation.

Temporary electrical work can range from connections to existing services to the more costly construction of pole lines into the site, particularly in rural or isolated areas. An electrical subcontractor should be consulted on this work. Allow for extension cords, outlets, transformers, panels, overhead cables, and so on. The cost of this work on a previous project of a similar size and function would provide a good base that could be updated and developed accordingly. The total estimated cost should be established as one lump-sum amount.

Distribution and lighting refers to such items as wiring, panels, lights, lamps, transformers, and so on, everything to distribute the power brought into the site by the electrical services. This has to be a single amount item, and again a similar project's cost records will be helpful. In all temporary electrical work, make proper allowance for local charges where applicable.

Temporary Heat

This should be subdivided into two divisions:

1. Heating for specific construction purposes (concrete, masonry, defrosting frozen ground, etc.).
2. Heating within an enclosed structure.

The first category applies to the heating necessary for the cold-weather placing of concrete or masonry work. The following items should be considered:

1. Purchase or rental of heaters, stating type (gas, oil, or propane) and capacity.
2. Estimated fuel requirements, stating estimated gallons, liters, pounds, and kilograms.
3. Labor for handling the equipment and fuel estimated on an hourly cost basis.

Some construction companies may consider that the estimated heating costs pertaining to concrete placing or masonry work should more correctly be included as part of the estimates for those trades, and there is merit in this consideration. They still remain indirect items, whether tacked onto specific trades or not, and for the purpose of this book have been included with general site overhead items. Also, it is very doubtful if many subcontractors for masonry or concrete work would include such items. There would be a risk of them being accidentally overlooked in the analysis of subtrade bids.

Heating an enclosed building will be accomplished with either portable heaters (using oil, gas, or propane) or by using the permanent heating system. The second method can only be used if the specification condones it. A typical specification clause for this item would read:

> The permanent heating system may be used for temporary heating purposes, subject to the Architect's approval. . .

Where a project is an addition to an existing building, or is an additional building within a complex of existing buildings (say a large hospital or university), the specification may state that steam will be available from an existing boiler room. It should also state if the steam is supplied free of charge or at cost to the contractor. If the last condition exists, the estimator will have to contact the maintenance engineer at the building to obtain a unit cost per pound (kilogram) of steam. The cost of a meter will also have to be included. Other items to be considered when using the permanent heating system would include:

1. Attendance on equipment (check local union regulations, which may demand the use of skilled operators for this work). This item should be given in total estimated labor-hours.
2. Refurbishing and cleaning at completion (lump-sum item).
3. Temporary unit heaters and piping (rental or purchase).
4. Fuel consumption (or steam as already mentioned).

If the permanent system is not used, the estimate will have to be based on portable heating units, including for the same items as outlined for heating to concrete or masonry work.

On very large projects, estimators should check with a reliable mechanical contractor regarding this heating, particularly if the permanent system can be used. This contractor will be able to offer expert advice and might even be prepared to submit a quotation for this work. However, this quotation would be conditional upon this contractor also being the successful bidder for the permanent mechanical work in the project, which is not unreasonable.

The cost of temporary heating (both for enclosed structures and specific trade operations) can be very excessive, depending upon the number of winter months in the project duration, and also upon the geographical location. In northern provinces or states these will be very contentious items.

Sanitary Facilities

Specifications require the provision of temporary toilets, usually of the portable chemical type. These are generally a rental item, and the estimator should assess the number required (usually based on 1 unit per 20 employees) and the anticipated duration. The rental rate usually includes the servicing.

Specifications also usually allow for the use of permanent plumbing services when these are installed and to which contractors may connect temporary water closets and wash basins. A sum of money to cover the supply and installation costs of water closets, toilet bowls, and sinks (often "second quality") will be established for this item. Some sort of enclosure may be considered if the permanent cubicles are not installed. Also, cleaning and maintenance of plumbing services should be taken into account.

Temporary Telephone Service

There is usually a specification requiring the general contractor to provide temporary telephone service for the duration of the project. On small projects this service might be stipulated as being for the use of the contractor, the subcontractor, and the architect. (This usually means the architect's site representative, i.e., clerk of works.) On large projects the requirement is for the on-site architect (or representative) to have a separate telephone, and this is very often specified in the section dealing with the architect's site office.

The estimator should use up-to-date charges obtained from the local telephone company office for:

Installation costs (per telephone)

Number of extensions and push buttons

Number of lines required

Networking

As contractors, owners, and designers increase the number of computers on a project, the need for networking these computers together is starting to become more important. The idea of sharing a printer, faxing directly from your computer, the use of e-mail, and Web site collaboration is increasing the need for a networked project environment. This should be priced using an information technology person and not left to the estimator alone.

An allowance should be made for the additional cost of long distance calls initiated by the contractor. Normally, the specifications decree that long distance calls by subcontractors, architects, or other people outside the contractor's organization will be charged to the parties originating the calls.

Faxes

On today's projects this is one of the devices used frequently when conditions of urgency or crisis warrant the dispatching of a document to expedite materials or equipment, or other documents in the form of ultimatums to subcontractors or suppliers who have fallen behind schedule. The phone charges are generally estimated along with other phone costs, but paper and the machine itself should be accounted for separately.

Major projects in the multimillion-dollar range, where completely equipped offices will be provided for a duration of two, three, or more years, require multiple lines for faxes, modems, and phones. The local telephone company should be contacted for applicable costs for installation, monthly rates, servicing, and so on.

Public Address, Paging Systems, Radios

Large multistory buildings, or projects with various buildings under construction spread over a large site, usually mean key supervisory personnel need a fast means of communicating with the main project office, and vice versa. This will rarely be a specification requirement; it is something on which a contractor would make an in-house decision in the interests of all-round efficiency. Intercom systems, two-way radios, and pocket pagers all serve useful functions, and any reluctance to include such an additional item of cost in the bid should be balanced against the costs involved in the nonproductive time of people looking for people. (Charlie searching the site with an urgent message for Joe and finally locating Joe in Charlie's office.) Cellular phones are given to most project managers, and we are seeing the same for superintendents on projects today. If the project is to carry these costs, then they must be accounted for and budgeted for in the estimate.

13.9 ▪ CATEGORY 5: CONSTRUCTION FACILITIES AND SERVICES

Layout and Surveys

A typical specification clause requires the contractor to be responsible for all layout, lines, levels, and grades, with the possible exception of the lot lines, which are often established by the owner.

This item should include the costs of stakes, batter boards, lines, and so on. The purchase or rental of surveying instruments is another applicable cost to be considered and either included with this item or identified separately. The labor cost will be shown as the estimated number of labor-hours pertaining to carpenters, helpers, and rod holders. An instrument operator would either be shown as a separate item or included with the item for the salaried or supervisory and technical personnel.

If the specification requires the services of a professional land surveyor to check and verify the layout and provide a necessary certificate, the fee for this service should be obtained from a land surveyor's office.

Trucking

This item could refer to either the hourly costs of company-owned trucks or the rental of vehicles from a truck-hire company. Some construction companies do not own any trucks, or only own one or two, and make use of hired trucks to meet additional demands.

The trucking allowance in an estimate of site overheads is to cover the costs applicable to the pickup and delivery of miscellaneous materials and the transfer of tools and equipment between projects within a specific area or between the site and a company equipment storage yard. A contractor doing formwork with direct labor will incur considerable trucking costs for the pickup and delivery of form lumber, scaffold frames and shores, metal form panels, joists and trusses, and similar items.

The cost of company-owned trucks should be computed as an hourly, weekly, or monthly rental cost, including fuel, lubrication, and repairs. The truck driver's time and rate should be given as a separate item. If a truck-hiring facility is used, the driver's time might be included in the rental rate.

Cleanup During Construction

Most specifications call for the site to be maintained free from excessive accumulation of debris and rubbish, items that most construction sites can provide without any apparent effort. The estimate should include costs of rubbish chutes, built either with lumber or metal. Chutes can also be rented.

The costs of garbage containers are obtained from companies specializing in this service. These containers vary from 14 to 40 cubic yard capacities, and the charge (per container) will vary with the size. Estimators should check that the charges include the removal of a loaded container to the dump.

If the specifications make the general contractor responsible for providing these containers for all trades, at the contractor's cost, then the estimator should allow for loading the contractor's own debris into the containers; the subcontractors will be responsible to load their own rubbish. In many instances the contractor will do this work and back-charge the subcontractor with the cost. (Back-charges for cleanup are the cause of a perennial war between general contractors' and subcontractors' supervisors, which can only be tempered with good organization and straightforward handling, although, in a dispute, each side will claim sole ownership of both these virtues.)

Final Cleanup

This cost is usually estimated on the basis of separate unit prices for material and labor to be applied to the total gross floor area of the project. Although applied to a floor area, this unit should cover all items of final cleaning to all floors, walls, ceilings, and partitions in the finished project.

Some contractors include the cost of cleaning the glass areas with this item, while others prefer to measure and price it separately. It is usually estimated as a unit cost per square foot of glass area (i.e., the unit cost provides for cleaning two sides of the glass).

Sometimes architects request that these final-cleaning operations must be carried out by approved specialist cleaning companies, in which case quotations should be solicited from these companies.

Modern high-rise structures with large areas of glass and aluminum require a professional cleaning company with the staff and equipment to perform such work. Such a company will usually quote as a cost per square foot of gross wall area. Estimators should question these companies carefully about the computation of this area, as it will be the basis of payment.

Construction Safety Requirements

Safety regulations demand that guardrails be provided at slab perimeters, around openings in floors and roofs, and at other locations that are 10 feet or more in height from the ground. The perimeter of the floor slabs and slab openings should be measured in linear feet (meters) and separate unit prices established for material and labor costs. These rails usually have a minimum height of 3 feet, and can be built with 2 × 4 inch lumber, or purposely made metal and wire mesh perimeter barricades are often acceptable. If lumber is to be used, estimators should allow approximately 1.8 board feet of lumber per linear foot of perimeter. Installation (and final removal) costs should be allowed as approximately 8 to 10 carpenter hours per 100 linear feet of railing. (Note: This does not allow for any temporary removal and reinstallation of sections to allow necessary access for material handling or other operations.)

An allowance should be included to cover the estimated material and labor costs of other miscellaneous barricades, platforms, runways, ramps, and similar structures whose scope and extent is difficult to determine on the drawings.

Snow and Ice Removal

This could apply both to access roads and to the structure under construction. Snow and ice removal to the structure should be estimated as a labor-hour cost. For the larger areas of roads and parking lots, the rental costs of bulldozers, graders, and similar equipment should be assessed, plus any applicable hand labor costs.

The cost of snow and ice removal will naturally vary according to the geographical location of the project, from zero costs in Los Angeles to the other extreme in Alaska. Previous data will be valuable as a guide. Estimators can only resort to a "crystal ball" to predict the number of heavy snow or ice storms that might occur in a winter season (again depending on location), and then allow for so many hours of clearance work per occurrence. For example, an average of five storms per winter month, assuming four months, would yield (5 × 4) 20 incidents. Snow-removal equipment might average 4 hours each time; therefore, at least 80 hours of equipment rental should be allowed. The number of labor-hours for manual shoveling and ice-breaking could run to 8 hours per occasion (8 × 20), or 160 hours. Chipping ice from parts of the structure could be a costly labor item under certain conditions.

Broken Glass

It happens on all projects. On small jobs it may not be a significant item, and if the culprit responsible for the breakage was a subcontractor, then (theoretically) there will be no costs accruing to the general contractor. On major projects it can be a very contentious item. The cost should include the cleaning up and removal of the broken glass and also the material and labor costs of glass replacement.

Temporary Enclosures

This item is specified for protection against the environment and also vandalism or crime. Temporary doors and windows are usually priced separately and estimated on the basis of total square feet of openings to be enclosed, or the items could be enumerated. Temporary doors will be necessary on all projects, but the need for temporary windows can be eliminated (or reduced to a minimum) if the permanent windows can be scheduled for installation before the arrival of inclement weather.

Attention should be paid to any large items of equipment—boilers, chillers, storage tanks, refrigeration equipment, switch gears, and other large size items—that may require portions of exterior walls being left out to provide access into the building. These temporary openings will also require enclosures during cold weather.

Enclosures for maintaining heat during the construction of the structure are usually made with tarpaulins or polyethylene, often attached to a framework of lumber. The net area in square feet of the area to be enclosed should be measured, and either priced at a unit cost per square foot or at a unit cost per tarpaulin. Make all necessary adjustments to the measured surfaces for overlapping.

In some areas complete enclosures will be necessary for the placing of concrete or masonry. Where possible, these should be prefabricated in pieces light enough to be moved by hand, or they can be moved by crane if necessary. These are best estimated as a cost per each section, with an allowance for repairs. The labor cost will be per number of times installed and removed. (Sometimes these might be built on skids and could be pulled horizontally for a tunnel or duct.)

Duct screens are usually specified where demolition or renovation work is to take place in an existing building. Sometimes they will be required at an opening in walls where the new structure "ties in" to the existing. These can be simple enclosures of wood framework and tarpaulins or polyethylene, or soundly constructed partitions faced at one or both sides with either plywood or gypsum board. Insulation may also be specified. It is recommended that estimators build up a price based on the specification for a particular length, 10 linear feet, to establish a unit cost per running foot. The full extent of dust screen requirements can then be measured in linear feet. If the screens can be relocated several times during the course of the work, then it is recommended that two items be measured:

1. The maximum length of screens to be fabricated. The labor unit will provide for the first in place, including the cost of dismantling.
2. The subsequent relocation costs, including dismantling at the balance of the necessary locations.

Progress Photographs

A common specification requirement is for the contractor to arrange for progress photographs to be taken, usually at monthly intervals. The number of different viewpoints will be stated and also the number of prints required. (Usually these photographs are stated to be in black and white, but sometimes there will be a requirement for a special colored set at the completion of the project.) Photographic agencies that specialize in taking progress pictures of construction projects should be contacted for the monthly cost of photographs and prints.

Additionally, contractors will want to take their own set of progress/documentation photographs of the work. Pricing a camera, film, and film processing should occur. Many contractors are also videotaping parts of the work, while others are using digital cameras. Recently, contractors are being asked to provide live Web cameras on projects so that the owner and designer can follow progress from home office settings. These video cameras can cost $3000 to $4000 and should be included in the contractor's budget.

Scheduling Costs

This refers to a specific requirement for computerized preparation and updating of a schedule (usually CPM), and would include a consultant's fees (where applicable), drafting, computer, and printing charges. A total cost should be built up and included in the estimate as a single-sum item. In some contracts, the contractor is required to use a specific piece of software and also provide the owner or construction manager their own copy of the software. Depending on the software required, this item could run from a low end of $400 to a high of $2500.

13.10 CATEGORY 6: HOISTING, MATERIALS AND PERSONNEL

The word "hoisting" can be something of a misnomer. A crane can be used for both raising and lowering, and a project starting at a depth of 30 to 40 feet below street level will have certain materials or equipment that have to be lowered to the required location. However, it is normal to refer to cranes, elevators, hoists, and the like, as "hoisting" equipment.

The shape and height of a building influence the requirements for hoisting. A building of only one to three stories spread over a large area would influence a contractor's choice toward a mobile crane, or a material hoist at a central location, or two hoists, or a hoist plus a crane, and so on. High-rise structures constitute an automatic demand for climbing cranes; they will probably also require material and personnel hoists, usually after the structural framework is completed and the climbing cranes dismantled and removed.

Many companies own their own hoists, towers, and cranes, but (and this applies to all equipment discussed in this book) these items should still be considered as rented or purchased for the project. Proposals from equipment rental companies will usually assist the estimator to establish an all-inclusive estimate of costs by highlighting all those items of work or equipment to be provided by the contractor.

Mobile Cranes

Mobile cranes can be rented by the hour, week, or month. If small-sized cranes are required only at certain intervals, estimators should consider hourly rental. Established crane rental companies should be contacted for applicable rates. These rates will vary according to the weight and capacity of the crane. Quotations should be checked carefully regarding:

Minimum rental period (usually 4 hours)

Transportation time (usually 1 to 1½ hours each way)

An operator being included

Costs of premium time for operator

Boom trucks usually have different rental rates from mobile cranes. If the mobile crane is to be used solely for the purpose of placing concrete, lifting and moving formwork, and hoisting reinforcing steel, these costs should more properly be included with the estimate for that division of work; this practice is followed by some construction companies. In this book, all equipment is being considered with the site overhead estimates, but sufficiently identified as to function to allow it to be transferred to another division if required. This would be essential if a proper comparison had to be made against a quotation for this work from a subcontractor that included all hoisting costs.

Estimators should study the drawings carefully (also the site) regarding access for the crane. For example, it may only be possible to properly service two sides of a structure. This will mean horizontal transportation across the floor with pumps to place concrete or other materials to the inaccessible locations. Also will overhead wires and the like have to be relocated?

Tower Cranes

These fall into three categories: (a) climbing, (b) stationary, and (c) traveling. In high-rise buildings the climbing crane is the type universally selected for the construction of a reinforced concrete structural frame. Positioned in the center of the structure, or as close to the center as possible, it can provide maximum coverage to the building area. Smaller buildings, where the reach is not excessive, can sometimes be serviced by a stationary crane, or a traveling crane may be a feasible solution in some instances.

On the assumption that the climbing crane is the feasible selection, the estimator must check the drawings to see whether an elevator shaft can be utilized (if reasonably close to the desired location), or if openings need to be provided in each successive floor slab. This will mean allowances for bulkhead forms, possible additional reinforcing steel (for structural reasons), and a premium cost of placing the concrete when the crane is removed.

The selection of the size and capacity of the crane will be based on the manufacturer's data regarding lifting capacity at the maximum reach radius. For example, say a crane is to be used for the hoisting of precast 3-ton concrete panels, with the minimum distance from the crane position to the point of joisting 170 feet. The crane selected will be the one that can lift that weight with the trolley and hook extended that distance. To maximize the use of this equipment, the selected crane must have the capacity to hoist concrete, prefabricated "gang" forms, flying shores, and the like at the maximum radius location.

A number of circular cutouts can be made with stiff paper or cardboard scaled in size to the maximum radius of each size of crane and with the lifting capacities graduated on the surface. These can be laid on the drawing (the scale will of course have to be identical) with the center at the intended crane position, and it will be a simple matter to check the capacity at the longest reach.

Climbing cranes are either purchased or rented (or even acquired by a rental-purchase arrangement). Some manufacturers or equipment rental companies also provide additional services such as erection, dismantling, and raising; or the general contractor will do these. There are also companies which specialize in crane erection and dismantling, servicing, repairs, inspection, and so on.

When the size and capacity of the crane have been determined, the items to be considered in the estimate will include:

Rental (or purchase price)

Erection and dismantling

Raising

Maintenance, servicing, repairs

Electrical work (hookup, transformers, cable, etc.)

Concrete bucket

Freight (if excluded from rental or purchase costs)

Miscellaneous items: wire rope, guying, and inspection

Operator's hours, including premium and shift time

Outer tower charges, where applicable

Items that will most certainly have to be provided by the general contractor would include:

1. Concrete foundation pad. A recommended size will be given on the manufacturer's data sheets (although this may have qualifications regarding soil conditions). A detailed estimate could be prepared of all applicable items, but to save time it is recommended that only the cubic volume of the concrete be measured and priced at a single unit price inclusive of the supply, placing, and finishing of concrete, formwork, reinforcing steel, and anchor bolts. This unit price could be updated for each bid.

2. Additional reinforcing steel might be necessary at any special openings made in the concrete slabs; also, shoring may be necessary here.

Many projects will provide conditions where concrete is required at some locations that extend beyond the reach of the crane, but where the concrete quantities are insufficient to justify a second climbing crane. Estimators should allow for some miscellaneous rental time of mobile cranes to service these locations.

Material Hoists and Towers

These will be used for the hoisting of all materials, including concrete, if a crane is not considered practicable. On large high-rise projects, the cranes will usually be dismantled when the structural work is complete, and the balance of the hoisting accomplished with material hoists. These towers will be either single or double well. They are usually located so as to give easy access by trucks hauling the material into the site.

Items to be allowed in the estimate will include:

1. The cost of the tower (single or double well), including repairs
2. The cost of the hoist (state number of drums), including repairs
3. Erection and dismantling costs of the tower (per linear foot)
4. Installation and removal of the hoist
5. Landings and gates: one per floor
6. Freight (if excluded from manufacturer's charges)
7. Wire rope, signals, and so on
8. Electrical hookup
9. Cost of the operators: labor-hours, including premium time

Note: if the tower is to be used for hoisting concrete, special handling equipment should be allowed for, such as a bucket, hopper, and loading chute. Also, a Chicago boom will be an additional item that might be required. An enclosure for the heat may also be necessary during inclement weather.

Personnel Hoists

These will be necessary on high-rise buildings where many workers (both general and subcontractors' employees) will be engaged at different levels. The items noted for the material hoist will apply to this equipment, except of course for the special items (e.g., Chicago boom, concrete handling equipment).

Forklift

This is rather a modest piece of hoisting equipment after considering tower cranes and material hoists, but it serves many useful functions. It is limited to the reachable heights, approximately 25 feet, and is very much in evidence in masonry work. This is usually an hourly rental item.

Temporary Elevators

This applies to the use of permanent elevators for temporary construction purposes, if permitted in the specifications. The estimator should allow for protection to the cab (tarpaulins or polyethylene), temporary shaft partition, and the hourly cost of skilled operators.

13.11 CATEGORY 7: SMALL TOOLS AND EQUIPMENT

Most construction companies have a standard (typed or printed) list of items to be included in this category, and they can vary from reasonably condensed lists to sheets of paper cataloging just about every tool or piece of equipment imaginable. The following is a modest schedule of the items to be considered, either as purchases or rentals:

Small tools: This refers to hand tools, which some companies express in two categories: expendable and nonexpendable. Usually, a sum of money, based on past cost records, is placed against this item. Expendable tools are generally expensed on the one project, while nonexpendable tools may have a longer life.

    Expendable tools:
    Shovels
    Hammers
    Brooms
    Ladders
    Cords

    Nonexpendable tools:
    Concrete equipment: concrete buckets
                                buggies (hand- or motor-powered)
                                vibrators
                                machine trowels
                                elephant trunks
                                grinders

    Electric power tools: Skil saws
                                  Radial saws
                                  Electric drills

Compressors and air tools

Hose and cable (water hoses, extension cables, etc.)

Scaffold frames and planks

Compaction equipment (tampers, vibratory plates, etc.)

Electric generators

Pumping equipment

    Separate allowances should be made against these items (where applicable) for repairs, fuel, and lubrication. As already stated, some companies might lean toward including these items with the appropriate trade estimates, such as concrete, excavation, and so on.

13.12   CATEGORY 8: PERMITS, INSURANCE, AND BONDS

The estimate should include for all permits required by authorities having jurisdiction. Some specifications state that the building permit will be paid for by the owner, in which case the cost will be excluded from the bid. It is a good idea for estimators to prepare a schedule of all permits and rates pertinent to different localities within a region and update this schedule periodically. It will serve as a good checklist and also save a lot of unnecessary telephoning for each bid.

Insurance

The most common types needed are fire (builder's risk), public liability and public damage (PL and PD), and automobile and vehicle. The specification should be checked as to which are carried by the contractor and which the owner pays for. Most contractors deal with a selected insurance company that will provide the rates to be used in a bid to cover these requirements.

Bonds

Specifications often require the contractor to provide in the bid the cost of a 50 or 100 percent performance bond. A construction company usually has a bonding or surety company which will supply the cost of these bonds. They are quoted at a cost per thousand dollars per annum.

EXAMPLE: The bond cost is $5.00 per $1,000.00. The estimated value is $2,000,000.00, with duration of one year. The premium amount will be 2,000 × 5 = $10,000.

Some general contractors consider it prudent to include in their bids the premium costs of bonding major subtrades. This is rarely a specification requirement, because this bond is only a protection for the contractor against the financial failure of a subcontractor. The performance bond from the contractor already protects the building owner. In effect, the general contractor is asking and paying for the same protection from a subcontractor that the owner is receiving from the general contractor by virtue of the performance bond. Of course, as this amount is included in the bid, the owners do in fact pay this cost, and some owners get disgruntled at what they consider to be double bonding. Indirectly, the owner is receiving some additional protection because the bankruptcy of a major subcontractor can delay the project and nearly everyone gets hurt, and particularly so if there was no bond on the subcontractor.

13.13 REVIEW

It is difficult to define the limitations of items and work that qualify for inclusion in the category of site overhead or indirect costs. Specifications differ regarding the allocation of items to this division or to some other trade division. Various general contractors tend to hold conflicting views as to the extent and limitations of standard company checklists of related items; too often such lists can grow uncontrollably, and very often additional items are created as a result of some isolated incident that happened on one particular project. "Better put that on the list," someone will growl. "Might happen again." Other contractors may consider such out-of-the-way incidents as part of the "risk" syndrome to which all contractors are exposed, believing it more important to consider ways to prevent such recurrences rather than putting additional sums of money in a bid that is intended to be competitive.

Estimators should prepare notes from the specifications, writing down all the items properly identified. The standard checklists should then be consulted for all other items that are included in the specifications by inference, or that would be dictated by standard practice. Because there is no specified reference to the services of a watchman, this does not mean a watchman is not required. A clause holding the contractor responsible for "the protection and security of the site at all times" is contractually sufficient to bind a contractor to provide the services of a watchman or equivalent. Equally, if a contractor decides to provide a watchman service for valid reasons of company security, he can do so (and include the cost in the bid) even though there may be no contractual requirement for this service. There will be other similar items that although not asked for by the owner will still be necessary for the contractor's operations.

14 CLOSING THE BID

14.1 GENERAL

The day when the bid must be finished and submitted to the owner is always an ominous one for estimators. At a certain hour on this day, the brakes are applied and the whole bid process grinds to a halt. Whatever has been forgotten or omitted, or was not properly checked, or could (or should) have been done differently—with the striking of the hour it is too late for regrets or second thoughts. A well-known verse from Edward Fitzgerald's translation of the "Rubaiyat of Omar Khayyam" is a grim reminder:

> The Moving Finger writes; and having writ,
> Moves on: nor all thy Piety nor Wit
> Shall lure it back to cancel half a Line,
> Nor all thy Tears wash out a word of it.

Most estimators would sympathize with the urge to "lure it back to cancel half a line." Bid-day tensions can bring a series of problems, and even the bid that has been well planned and superbly organized can come apart at the seams in the final closing hours. The atmosphere in a general contractor's office on the final day usually appears to be one of turmoil and confusion. The closest comparisons might be the backstage of a theater on opening night of a new show or the hectic bidding at the stock market before closing. Telephones ring, calculators rattle, blood pressures ascend, heartbeats accelerate, and things that seemed certainties two days ago now whisper alarming doubts.

Did I take off the concrete fireproofing in the penthouse?

Did I allow a compaction factor?

We should have figured eight space heaters, not six.

Venerable estimators will entertain their grandchildren with enthralling tales about some of their most memorable bid-closing experiences, and featured in these stories will usually be the one about the bid "When Everything Went Wrong." The favorite will probably be "When Everything Went Wrong but We Got the Job Anyway." (Whether any money was made on that job never comes into the story.)

It is difficult to avoid a bid-closing day without some snags or problems cropping up; particularly in those trade areas where it is the rule rather than the exception for 80 percent of the quotes to be telephoned into the contractor's office within the short span of about 3 hours. Good organization and forethought can assist in reducing problems, or at least eliminating those that only became problems because they were left until the last day.

Apart from the obvious advantages of having all quantity takeoffs and pricing completed beforehand, there are a number of items that experienced estimators usually write into a checklist and try to do two days ahead or at least early in the morning of bid day. Many of these are simple routine matters that can be accomplished easily and quickly in advance, and it is usually because they seem so mundane that they get pushed temporarily to one side. The next section provides a checklist of some such items to be considered.

14.2   BID-CLOSING CHECKLIST

1. Has the bid form been signed (by an officer of the company with signing authority) and witnessed or sealed?

2. Has the bid bond (if applicable) been processed and signed and is it ready at hand? (Not stuck away in someone's drawer.) Has the certified check been arranged for? This can be a problem if the amount is to be a specified percentage of the bid total, the actual amount of which is not known until near the final hour. However, at the earliest opportunity a reasonable assessment should be made (leaning toward the "high" side as a precaution) and the check processed.

3. Is the bid envelope ready? The "Instructions to Bidders" will most probably provide instructions regarding the name and address to be typed on the envelope and also the format of the envelope. Some bid-calling authorities provide special preaddressed envelopes for the bid. (Someone should know where this was filed when it arrived with the other documents.)

4. Some bids require a statutory declaration to be included with the bid documents. Has this been processed? Where is it?

5. Has someone ascertained whether telephones are available at the place where the bid is to be delivered? Most bids are completed by telephone communication between the estimating office and the person delivering the bid, and it is strongly recommended that a prebid reconnaissance be made to locate the proximity of the public telephones. If the nearest public telephone is a mile or so down the road, then contact should be made with nearby gas stations or restaurants, or there may be adjacent private offices

where some sort of a "deal" could be made for a half-hour use of a telephone. Failing that, send a hefty-size courier and have him (or her) "gate-crash" someone's office for a telephone. If a cellphone is going to be used, a check needs to be made for the quality of reception.

6. If the normal mail delivery to a contractor's office is late in the day, arrangements should be made with the nearest post office for a mail pickup on bid day. This particular day's delivery will probably include quotations from subcontractors and suppliers, which the estimator needs to see as early as possible.

7. Have the Agreements to Bond (if pertinent) been received from the surety company?

8. Are there any miscellaneous "bugs in the works"?
   - A plentiful supply of telephone quotation receipt pads? Are they accessible, not on the top shelf of a dimly lit storeroom?
   - Paper in the adding-calculating machine?
   - Staples in the stapling machine?
   - Paper clips?
   - Sharpened pencils?

Nearly all these items can be attended to before the actual bid day, and irritating as it may sound, that's the time to think about them.

14.3 THE BID FORM

The checklist included a reminder about the signing of the bid form. There are a number of items pertaining to bid forms that could be completed ahead of time, or if that is not possible, at least some preliminary planning will be beneficial.

Bid forms vary in size and the information required. Some bid-calling authorities appear to have been indoctrinated into the belief that a bid is not bona fide unless the weight of the paper is equal to the weight of the intended structure. Others are quite satisfied with a single sheet that tells the owner in simple terms the sum of money for which the contractor will construct the building in accordance with the bid documents, which is really the "bottom line" in which the owner is most interested.

The following are some items included in the average bid proposal form:

1. Addenda: There is usually a requirement to confirm the numbers and dates of all addenda issued during the bidding period. This can be attended to at least the day before the bid, unless one is dealing with an architect notorious for issuing bulletins up to an hour before bid closing.

2. Unit prices: Most bid forms include a schedule of unit prices to be used for changes to the contract, either as additions or deletions. These are usually confined to excavation, backfill, and concrete work; however, some bid-calling authorities request unit prices for nearly all trades. Estimators should note which unit prices pertain to general contractor's work and which to work by subcontractors. As subcontractors rarely see the general contractor's bid form, they will probably not be aware of what unit prices are required. It will be advisable to contact them in advance and alert them

to this requirement. Unit prices for general contractor's work can be established any time after the pricing of the pertinent trades is completed. This subject is further discussed in Section 14.10.

3. Alternate prices: Bid forms often require information regarding cost adjustments for alternative materials and methods, and these will refer to either specified alternate prices or alternates volunteered by the general contractor. For the specified alternates, the estimator is advised to prepare estimate sheets ahead of time noting all the pertinent items to be adjusted. For general contractor's trades, these could be priced and dispensed with very early, but the greater percentage of these alternates will most likely require input information from the subtrades. If appropriate analysis sheets are prepared in advance, all that needs to be done is insert the monetary amounts when they are known, and do the math to verify the adjustment amount.

Figure 14–1 shows an example of an estimate sheet prepared in advance to determine the cost difference for an exterior wall to be finished in face brick in lieu of a base bid requirement for precast concrete. The face brick quantities have been measured and priced, with all labor burdens added; the only item not yet included is the quotation from the precast concrete contractor, which will clarify whether this alternate will increase or decrease the contract sum.

Some alternate prices concern items of work that are included in the main bid but that the owner may decide to abandon if the bid amount is excessively higher than the owner's budget, and for which it is important to know the estimated cost immediately. These can vary from simple items like the anticipated deletion of a sauna, for example, or they can be very complex like a complete floor of a hospital or a wing to a school.

Many owners and architects encourage contractors to provide on the bid form any proposed alternate methods, materials, or systems based on previous experience on similar projects. Sometimes these unsolicited alternates originate as suggestions by subcontractors to be passed on by the general contractor.

4. Separate prices: These usually refer to items of work that are excluded from the main bid but that the owner is contemplating adding into the contract depending on the estimated cost. Like alternate prices, these could be very modest requirements or very costly ones. (The contractor should pay attention to this well in advance to ascertain the effect their inclusion might have on the scheduled duration of the project.) Sometimes the title "separate price" will be given to items already discussed in "alternate prices," which have reference to items that the owner may wish to deduct from the contract.

5. Itemized prices: These normally refer to items included in the main bid, but of which the owner wishes to know the cost. It is important for contractors to check with the architects if there is any doubt about the true intent of this request for information. It is usually required as information relating to taxation or cost-sharing matters.

6. Names of subcontractors: Most bid forms require the general contractor to list the names of subcontractors whose quotes were included in the bid. Some bid-calling authorities restrict these lists to the major subtrades; others thirst for all the information available, sometimes not only the name of

| Priced By: B.E.W. | | Project: | Research Center | Division: | | | Date: | | 6/9/1999 |
| Checked By: J.M. | | Architect: | | Description: | | | Sheet 1 of 1 | | |

DESCRIPTION	QUANTITY ADJUSTMENT PRICE REFERENCE	QUANTITY		MATERIAL COST		Labor Unit Price	LABOR SUB TOTAL	Equip. Unit Price	EQUIPMENT COST	ITEM TOTAL COST
		TOTAL	UNIT	Material Unit Price	MATL. SUB TOTAL				EQPT. SUB TOTAL	
Alternate No. 1 = Precast Conc wall panels										
in lieu of facing brick										
a) Delete:										
Facing brick		3900	ea	1.90	7410	4.60	17957			25367
Mortar		11.60	cyd	44.55	518					518
Clean down brick		3936	sft	0.03	118	0.10	394			512
Dovetail anchors		1400	ea	0.12	168					168
					8214		18350			26564
	Add: Labor charges 36%						6606			6606
										33171
b) Add:										
Qoutation - P.C. Concrete Subcontracor									Difference: $	
(Note: No adjustment for masonry equipment.										
Items - steel required for back up materials)										

FIGURE 14–1 Estimate sheet with alternates.

the masonry subcontractor but also who is going to supply and mix the mortar. The usual directive regarding work that the contractor does not intend to subcontract is to write the words "by own forces" in the appropriate space on the bid form.

7. Cost breakdown of bid: At times, this is to be submitted with the bid. There are already enough things to keep estimators busy while trying to arrive at the final bid total, and this requirement adds a further irritant factor to the process. Attendance to this request usually means something else has to be neglected, and that could include the recording and processing of all the late subtrade quotes (usually the most aggressively competitive prices), all of which are to the owner's advantage if reflected in the bid total. If such a breakdown is requested for submission at the time of the bid, the architects should be approached for permission to have it submitted at least 24 hours later. The normal procedure is for these kinds of breakdowns to be submitted after, or at the time of, the contract award, when they are required for payment purposes.

8. Completion dates: Bid documents usually require contractors to make some statement regarding the anticipated duration and completion date of the project. Once the schedule has been agreed upon and finalized, this information can be entered on the bid form.

Some bid forms will include all the types of items just reviewed. Others will be satisfied with half of them or less, while some bid-calling authorities will require twice as many items. These portend more bid-closing headaches for estimators, because most of them cannot usually be processed beforehand. However, advance knowledge and clear understanding of such requirements are still more desirable than becoming aware of them only on the last day. At least some methods and strategy can be planned to handle these items as efficiently as possible at the appropriate time.

14.4 TELEPHONE BIDS

With the exception of a few subcontractors who will submit their quotations in letter form, and also those areas where a large percentage of the subtrade contractors bid the general contractors through the offices of a bid depository, most of the subtrade bids are telephoned in on the closing day.

Figure 14–2 shows an example of a typical form used by a general contractor to record bids received by telephone. Although these verbally transmitted quotes do not possess the legality of written quotes, estimators should attempt to have them recorded in such a manner that, except for the lack of a signature, they represent a formal communication.

The printed information requirements are useful to remind estimators about the pertinent items to be checked when the subcontractor calls. This will save calling back and asking questions like: "Did you include sales taxes?" or "What addenda have you included?" It is important also to ask the name of the bid caller; this saves time if a return call is necessary to query an item. (Contact can be quickly re-established with, "Can I speak to Bill Green, please," rather than, "I was just talking to someone in your office about such and such a job . . .")

The need to write legibly is obvious. Everyone's handwriting is different, and where there might be problems printing should be suggested (tactfully). Of course,

Snyder Construction Co.		
Telephone Quotation		

Project	_Research Center_	Date	_February 9, 1999_
Company	_Sycamore and Madrone, Inc._	Estimate No.	_27/82_
Address	_1322 Franklin Ave. Nowhere, CA_	Telephone	_555-2222_
Trade Division	_09250 - Gypsum Wallboard_	Addenda	_1 to 4_

Scope of Work	Amount
a) Work Included	
All as per drawings and specifications	$106,400
b) Work Excluded	
Acoustic ceilings (specified Section 09500)	
c) Alternate or Separate Prices	

Taxes	Included	Excluded	
Federal	XX		Quotation Given By _J. Green_
State	XX		Received By _J.L.J._
Others			

FIGURE 14–2   Sample telephone quotation—wallboard.

even the neatest handwriting can suffer when quotes are telephoned in during the pressures of the final 15 minutes. At this time estimators recording telephone bids should concentrate on getting three things down clearly and accurately:

1. The name of the company calling.
2. The trade division being quoted.
3. The price.

Badly transcribed figures can cause many more problems than words. The digits 4 and 7 are vexsome, and the European 7 is strongly recommended. A missing zero can be disastrous if not spotted in time ($40,000 written as $4,000, for example).

The format of the telephone bid form can also be used to guide long-winded or inarticulate bid callers into more precise and factual statements about their quotations. Interrogatory questions such as, "Are you quoting in accordance with the drawings and specifications?" will direct such bid callers onto the right track. The specification section numbers should also be checked and confirmed. For example, Masterformat states the following trade divisions: 09300 Tile and 09400 Terrazzo. A telephone communication might start along the lines of: "I want to give you a price on the ceramic tile in the washrooms, and I'm also including the quarry tile to the lobby and the terrazzo; and also those brass expansion strips shown on the drawings . . ."

The statement about the ceramic tile being located in the washrooms and the quarry tile in the lobby might be perfectly correct, but the estimator is not usually sitting at the telephone with a floor finish schedule facing him. During a telephone bid, time is running too short for all this to be checked out. The estimator wants the satisfaction of knowing that the subcontractor's quotation includes all ceramic tile, quarry tile, divider strips, everything that is called for in those specific trade divisions. Subcontractors should be encouraged to first state the numbers and titles of the division on which they are quoting, and then proceed with their lists of qualifications or exclusions. This would assist in avoiding any misunderstanding at the time and reduce the chances of future confrontations.

14.5   BID DEPOSITORY QUOTATIONS

The bid depository system of processing subtrade quotes to general contractors exists in many regions, towns, and cities. The rules and procedures tend to vary in each county, as well as the number and classification of trades participating in the system; however, most or all of the following basic principles seem to apply universally.

To quote from one bid depository's standard rules and regulations: "The Bid Depository provides for the reception of sealed Bids from Specialty Contractors whereby the sanctity of the Bidding is protected and those General Contractors receiving these bids obtain firm quotations in writing."

As already stated, the number of trades which participate in the bid depository system differs across the North American continent. In larger cities, for example, a greater percentage of trades make use of this service than in smaller cities; in many areas its use is currently confined to a few major trades such as mechanical, electrical, sprinklers, and, sometimes, structural steelwork.

Some fairly standard conditions regarding bid depositories are:

1. They are usually managed and supervised by local or regional construction association offices ("Builder's Exchange" is a time-honored appellation).
2. The time at which bids must be submitted to the designated depository offices is usually 24 or 48 hours prior to the general bid closing time.
3. The bids must be submitted on official bid depository forms (white, pink, yellow, etc.), and in official envelopes, addressed to the various general contractors known to be bidding the project.
4. The general contractors will pick up their bids at the prescribed time.

Most bid depositories have many more rules and procedures than the few basic ones just outlined, which illustrate the methods for the submission and receipt of the bids.

The most significant and seemingly advantageous aspects of bid depository quotes to estimators are:

1. They are received well ahead of the general bid closing. This provides reasonable time for proper analysis and also for checking out the proposed duration schedule with the low bidders to ascertain if it is realistic in regard to their trades. This would apply particularly to the delivery dates of major equipment items.

2. It is the accepted rule in most bid depository systems that the subcontractors' bids must include everything contained in the bid documents applicable to their trades, so all subcontractors are bidding on the same basis, "apples with apples."

The last two statements infer some bid closing alleviations for the estimators; to an extent it places the quotes in the same category as formal written quotes. However, sometimes and in certain localities a number of things can happen that detract from these advantages. For example, most bid depository systems allow for trade contractors to withdraw their bids up to three hours before the general bid closing. The usual reason for a withdrawal would be the discovery of an error in the bid or the suspicion of an error if the bid amount came in extremely low ("too much left on the table").

The withdrawal of a bid cancels out some of the advantages stated in list item 1. The general contractor may suddenly have to start talking to another company (usually the second bidder) regarding schedules and other matters, with possibly only three hours or less before the bid deadline (although most estimators would prefer three hours to three minutes, which might be the case with telephoned quotations).

Item 2 does not always hold absolutely true. In some cities or regions the subcontractors may use the weight of their trade associations and mutually agree to formally exclude certain work, which, although called for in the specification for their trade, they do not agree as being applicable to their operations. Their bids will have uniformity in respect to all other items, but the general contractor is still left with the problem of establishing or obtaining cost estimates for the excluded work. Excavation, backfill, concrete, and miscellaneous metal and steelwork are some of the items often in this category. However, the point must be conceded that if estimators are knowledgeable about these standard qualifications, they will automatically prepare prebid estimates of the cost of these items for inclusion in the bid, in the same way as they would with prebid proposals discussed in section 14.6.

14.6 PREBID SUBTRADE PROPOSALS

The general contractor will often receive "lead" letters from trade contractors in advance of the bid-closing day, outlining the terms and conditions of the quotes they intend to submit. This is a commendable practice; particularly where the subcontractors may be only interested in performing certain portions of the work included in the specifications for their trade divisions. Formwork subcontractors, as an example, may only be interested in quoting on the principal structural elements in a project where they can be assured of a continuity of work for their labor force. It would not be economical for them to make intermittent return trips to the site to perform miscellaneous work to equipment bases and curbs, exterior landscaping, and similar items. The same could probably hold true for excavation contractors, who are often only interested in the main items of earthwork in the structure, which can be performed in one period of time.

The proposal letters are beneficial to estimators. Prebid arrangements can be made to simplify the necessary analysis of the actual quotations when they are received. The following examples illustrate how this prebid information can be used in the formats set up to properly analyze the subtrade bids when they are received.

EXAMPLE 1: Figure 14–3 shows a letter sent to all general contractors from a precast concrete company outlining the work and items that will form the basis of the quotation they intend to telephone out to the contractors on the day of the bid.

Figure 14–4 shows a second prebid proposal from another precast concrete company. This one has been received verbally and is recorded on a telephone bid form. The basis of this quotation is different from the first example and another analysis sheet should be prepared.

With the information provided on these two prebid proposals, the estimator can prepare analysis formats for purposes of quick comparison between the quotes when they are received. The items that will be excluded from the quotes will be measured and priced, and only the actual quote amounts would then be required to obtain a true comparison between these two quotes, or any others that might be received.

The necessary quantities and prices shown in the following examples should in practice be written on formal estimate sheets (not on the backs of quotations or pieces of scratch paper).

(a) Aggrestone Precast Enterprises, Inc.

Installation of P.C. pavers: 6,861 sft at $0.90	=	$6,175.00
Installation of P.C. planters: 15 each at $35.00	=	525.00
Labor burdens (31% × $6,700)	=	2,077.00
Additional cost for mobile crane	=	5,000.00
		$13,777.00
Quotation		?
Projected total:		$?

(b) Mold Cast Products, Inc.

Installation of P.C. pavers: 6,861 sft at $0.90	=	$6,175.00
Labor burdens (31% × $6,175)	=	1,914.00
		$8,089.00
Quotation		?
Projected total:		$?

EXAMPLE 2: Prebid proposals are received by telephone from two formwork subcontractors, A and B.

J. A. J. Precast Incorporated
123 South Construction Street
Anywhere, CA

K. Fines Contractor
5432 Sawhorse Road
Nowhere, CA

February 9, 1999

Re: Research Building, Santa Monica

We are preparing a quotation for the precast concrete work as detailed in Division 03400 of the specifications. Please note our quotation will include the following items:

a) Supply and erection of the precast concrete wall panels.

b) Supply only of the precast concrete paving slabs and planters.

Our quotation is to be based on the general contractor providing all hoisting facilities. If the use of our mobile crane is required, there will be an additional charge of $5,000.00.

All taxes included. Quotation open for acceptance within 60 days.

Our price will be telephoned to you prior to the closing time.

Yours truly,

J. A. J. Precast Incorporated

FIGURE 14–3 Pre-bid "lead" letter from subcontractor.

```
┌─────────────────────────────────────────────────────────────────────┐
│ Snyder Construction Co.                                               │
│                                                                       │
│                    Telephone  Quotation                               │
│                                                                       │
├─────────────────────────────────────────────────────────────────────┤
│ Project      Research Center          Date        February 9, 1999    │
├───────────────────────────────────────────────────────────────────── │
│ Company      Mold Cast Products, Inc.  Estimate No. 27/82             │
├─────────────────────────────────────────────────────────────────────┤
│ Address       456 Whose Street  Anywhere, CA   Telephone   555-1111   │
├─────────────────────────────────────────────────────────────────────┤
│ Trade Divisio   03400 - P.C. Concrete    Addenda    1 to 4            │
└─────────────────────────────────────────────────────────────────────┘
```

Scope of Work Pre-bid Info	Amount
a) Work Included	
All as per drawings and specifications (Excl. as below)	
(Include supply and installation of P.C. planter)	
(Price to be phoned in)	
Note: Will provide own mobile crane	
Included in bid amount	
b) Work Excluded	
Installation of P.C. pavers	
c) Alternate or Separate Prices	

Taxes	Included	Excluded	
Federal	XX		Quotation Given By G. South
State	XX		Received By J.A.J.
Others			

FIGURE 14–4 "Lead" message from subcontractor received by phone.

The basis of contractor A's intended quote is that only the following items will be included:

■ Formwork to foundation and superstructure walls, columns, beams, suspended slabs and stairs

■ Formwork to all other items (including footings) is not included.

- Other exclusions: waterstops, expansion joints, setting of screeds, anchor bolts and other embedded items, bulkheads and keys
- Hoisting to be provided by the general contractor.

Contractor B's proposal is somewhat different:

- Formwork to all items excluding equipment bases and curbs, bulkheads, keys and setting of screeds.
- Installation only: waterstops, expansion joints, anchor bolts, embedded items (materials to be provided by general contractor).
- Separate price to be quoted for placing of concrete to all above items only, excluding the finishing of exposed concrete surfaces after forms are stripped.
- Additional cost of mobile crane for hoisting of own work only: $10,000.00.

The analysis sheets prepared for these quotes will include the estimated costs of the numerous items noted for exclusion from the quotes. The source of the quantities and costs for these items will be the general contractor's own estimates for concrete and formwork. The detailed analysis sheets for both quotations are demonstrated in Section 14.7 of this chapter.

These examples illustrate the "apples and oranges" syndrome of some quotes. Obviously, the basic quote amounts from each subcontractor will be meaningless until the analysis process reduces them all to common denominators. This will have to be done as speedily as possible after the quote amount is received.

The estimator now has advance knowledge of how some trade contractors intend to quote, but how about the other contractors who have not made known their intentions? Aggressive telephone canvassing is probably the only method by which an estimator might succeed in "flushing out" the prebid information. However, trade contractors cannot always make these decisions until they have gained sufficient knowledge about the project. Most of these contractors will cooperate with the general contractor by supplying the information as soon as it is known.

Estimators are also conditioned to the additional irritant of the subcontractor who suddenly decides to revise the conditions on the prebid proposal; sometimes these changes are not announced until the time when the price is telephoned in by the subcontractor (probably 20 minutes to zero hour).

Over a period of time estimators are able to recognize that certain trade contractors are consistent in their bid conditions and have certain standard exclusions or are members of trade organizations which impose these conditions. Thus when these contractors are known to be bidding, the format of the analysis can be visualized ahead of time; estimators should always brace themselves for some surprises, however.

14.7   SUBTRADE QUOTATION ANALYSIS

The following are some examples of the various items to be considered when analyzing subcontractors' quotes, particularly those where only part of the specified work will be included.

FORMWORK

Referring back to Section 14.6 (Example 2), which illustrated the prebid proposals from formwork subcontractors, if the analysis sheets had been prepared in advance, then as the quotes were received each analysis could be completed. Figure 14–5 illustrates the analysis, and the result indicates subcontractor B as having a low bid, but only when the separate price for concrete placing is taken into account.

However, although the analysis process revealed the bid from B as being more favorable than the one from A, the situation might exist where the general contractor's

---

Analysis of Formwork Quotations

Subcontractor A

Quotation:		$226,000
Add:	Value of exclusions	30,101
	*Labor charges (on exclusions)	7,192
	Contractor's estimate concrete labor	23,128
	Labor charges on last item	8,326
	Contractor's crane cost	13,000
		$307,748

* 36% of $19,978.00

Subcontractor B

Quotation:		$234,300
	Separate price concrete placing	17,000
	Separate price, mobile crane	10,000
Add:	Value of exclusions (concrete & forms)	16,802
	*Labor charges on exclusion	4,823
		$282,926

* 36% of $13,397.00

Contractor's Estimate (for comparison and adjustment)

Total cost, formwork		$243,652
Labor costs, concrete		23,128
Labor burdens (on concrete & forms):		82,277
36% of $228,547.00		
Mobile crane, rental		13,000
		$362,057
	Less:	282,926
		$79,131

FIGURE 14–5   Analysis sheet—formwork quotes.

own estimate for this work was lower than all the subbids received. If the amount of difference was small, the contractor might still favor subcontracting the work, particularly to a reliable company. This would reduce the contractor's risk factor on direct labor.

It will be noticed in the examples shown that only one subcontractor intended to provide a mobile crane. As the quote stated specifically, this cost applied only to hoisting operations for the concrete and formwork. Allowance should have been made on the analysis to cover the cost of the additional use of this crane for the unloading and handling of reinforcing steel. It should also be observed that the subcontractor would take no responsibility for the finishing of formed surfaces after the formwork had been stripped. This work could be very costly, especially if the architect demanded a high-class finish on the concrete and the contractor was faced with repair work rather than finishing because of faulty formwork.

PRECAST CONCRETE

Section 14.6 (Example 1) demonstrated the analysis sheets prepared in accordance with the prebid proposals received from two precast concrete subcontractors. The following shows the final projection of these analyzed quotations:

	(a)	(b)
Quote:	$86,400.00	$90,511.00
Exclusions:	13,777.00	8,089.00
	$100,177.00	$98,600.00

The quotation for (b) is the most favorable. It provides a lesser amount plus the advantage of a lower risk in the direct labor estimate.

MISCELLANEOUS TRADE ANALYSIS

The following are some trade examples picked at random where problems could arise if no analysis were made or the terms of the quotation were not fully read or understood.

1. Structural steel: The quotation might refer to the inclusion of "field painting as specified," which could be misinterpreted if the specification only referred to "field touch-up," with the actual field painting to be done by the painter.

2. Glass cleaning: The subcontractor for windows or curtain walls might state that all cleaning of glass is included in the quote. However, careful reading of the specification could reveal a requirement for this subcontractor to clean the glass at the completion of its work, while the general conditions would still require final glass cleaning at the end of the project.

14.8 | SALES TAX

Quotes should be checked carefully regarding the inclusion or exclusion of applicable sales taxes: state, federal, or others. This applies particularly to bids received by telephone. With time running short and other expediencies to be handled, a quick and clear understanding is vital about the status of these taxes in a quote. Considerable sums of money could be involved, which could be financially harmful if omitted from the total bid or could impair the competitiveness of that bid if included unnecessarily.

Very often subcontractors and suppliers are not absolutely certain about the sales tax applications to specific projects, and it is not uncommon for the quote amount to be given followed by the statement: "Amount of sales tax applicable is $15,000.00." In most instances this could be taken to mean that the amount of $15,000.00 will be added if sales taxes are to be included. It could, however, mean that the amount is already included in the quote, and was left to the contractor to make the adjustment if this amount could be omitted. Persons recording telephoned quotes should clarify and properly record this information before passing the quote on to another person to analyze.

A further complication can occur when a subcontractor quotes on the supply and installation of a specified item and merely states the official percentage to be added for sales tax. The problem here is that the sales taxes are usually only applicable to the cost of the material, and do not apply to the transportation or installation charges, and those amounts need to be known for the correct tax adjustment to be made:

EXAMPLE:

Total amount of quotation:	$175,000.00
Less: Installation	45,000.00
Less: Freight	1,000.00
Amount subject to sales tax	$129,000.00

As can be readily calculated, a 7 percent tax on $175,000.00 and the same percentage applied to $129,000.00 produces a difference of $3,920.00—not a large sum but still a contribution to a low bid.

Estimators should familiarize themselves with regional sales tax regulations. Certain materials might only have tax exemptions applied to the parts and not to the whole (e.g., concrete or concrete masonry units).

14.9   MAIN ESTIMATE SUMMARY

Figure 14–6 shows a (completed) format for a bid summary sheet including all the amounts and adjustments to arrive at a final bid total. All construction companies will differ (some slightly, some widely) on the format of a main estimate summary sheet necessary for determining the final bid total. The example shown provides for all the direct trade estimate amounts and the subtrade amounts to be entered in the applicable columns. These amounts should be totaled as shown, preferably not less than one hour before the bid closes. This allows time to make the necessary calculations regarding labor burdens, insurance, bonds, and permits and for a total sum to be established.

However, as subtrade bids might still be pouring in by telephone, only easing off probably in the last ten minutes, it will be necessary to allow for late price adjustments. These adjustments are shown in the appropriate column and represent the differences between the amounts already entered and the revised amounts, whether more or less. Often subcontractors will raise their prices if they discover an error (or consider the possibility of an error if informed that their bid is uncomfortably low). The total of these adjustments will either decrease or increase the final bid amount.

The percentage for head office overhead and profit (usually combined) will be added to the total at this stage. The percentage of desired profit will have been con-

Bid Summary Sheet

Estimate Number: 27/81   Project: *Research Center*   Date: *July 9, 1999*

Div. No.	Trade Section	Material	Labor	Sub Quotation	Total	Adjustment
02200	Earthwork	45276	20114		65390	
02480	Landscaping			9700	9700	
02500	Paving & Surfacing			15000	15,000	(1500)
03100	Formwork	38233	205419		243,652	(79131)
03200	Rein. Steel-Supply/Detail			10700	10,700	
	-placing mesh				Incl. Above	
	-wire mesh				Incl. Above	
03300	Cast in Place Concrete	82553	23128		105681	
	Concrete Floor finish			8606	8606	
03400	Precast Conc. Wall panels			90511	90511	
	Paving		6175	Inc. Above	6175	
04200	Unit Masonry	39882	67001		106883	
05300	Metal Decking			7800	7800	
05500	Metal Fabrication		4200	35000	$39,200	
06100	Rough Carpentry	862	6600		7,462	
06200	Finish Carpentry	100	11563	16000	27,663	
07100	Waterproofing			25000	25,000	(2000)
07500	Membrane Roofing			48600	48,600	
07900	Sealants			11000	$11,000	
08100	Metal Doors and Frames	100	2724	10300	13124	
08200	Wood & Plastic Doors		5092	7875	12967	
08500	Metal Windows			47000	47000	(3500)
08800	Glazing				Inc. above	
09250	Gypsum Wallboard			106400	106400	(8700)
09300	Tile			19750	19750	
09500	Acoustic Treatment			57400	$57,400	
09650	Resilient Flooring			38600	38,600	
09680	Carpeting			3600	3,600	
09900	Painting			17800	17800	
10000	Specialties	4500	6200	32000	42,700	
15000	Mechanical			350000	$350,000	(6000)
16000	Electrical			186500	186,500	
		211506	358216	1155142	$1,724,864	(100831)
	Site Overheads	53975	71652		125627	
		265481	429868	1155142	1850491	(100831)
			Labor burdens		154753	
			‖		2005244	
			Office Overhead/Profits		100262	
			‖		2105506	
	Bid: $2,004,675.00		Adjustments		(100831)	
			Bid Total		$2,004,675	

FIGURE 14–6   Completed bid summary sheet.

sidered earlier by senior management, but very often the final decision is not made until the adjusted summary total is known. The total labor content will have some influence on this margin. As stated in Chapter 11, this provides the biggest risk to a contractor. Also the caliber of some of the subcontractors who have provided the lowest quotes may be taken into consideration as other risk factors.

The example shown demonstrates the methods by which the adjustments resulting from the analysis of the formwork subcontractors' quotes previously discussed are recorded. The net adjustment includes an amount of $77,454 ($82,277 less $4,823) applicable to the labor burden charges already included in the summary total. Also, this reduction of the labor content alleviates the accompanying risk factor, and a modified percentage for margin can be considered.

14.10 UNIT PRICES

Item 2 in Section 14.3 dealt briefly with the requirement in most bid documents for unit prices to be used as contract adjustments. Estimators should be wary about units that very often cover certain operations generally rather than specifically, and consideration must be given to the price or rate to be applied against each unit. For example, a unit might be described very simply as "Supply, place, and finish 3,000 p.s.i. (pounds per square inch) concrete, per cubic yard." The estimator will have no problem with the material cost of the concrete, which can be extracted from the priced estimate; but what about the placing and finishing costs? They vary considerably with different items—footings, walls, slabs and so on. Which category is most likely to be subject to any revisions, requiring more or less quantities? One way of dealing with the problem is to decide on the category most likely to fluctuate and then qualify the unit price accordingly, that is, revise the item to read "Supply, place, and finish 3,000 p.s.i. concrete to foundation walls below grade."

Markup for overhead and profit should be added to the unit prices for additional work. The deleted items can be quoted at "cost," although some contractors adjust these rates to provide some percentage for overhead.

Unit prices for excavation and backfill should be checked to see if the quantities are to be based on bank measure or if the measurements are to be kept within defined lines. This will mean that all allowances for side slopes, compaction, and similar factors will have to be included in the unit rate. The same holds for rock overbreak.

14.11 BID DELIVERY

It is the rule rather than the exception that in most cities and regions the bid has to be kept "alive" until at most, the final quarter of an hour. This means that the estimators are kept "hopping" right up to the end taking quotes, adding up summary sheets, calculating adjustments, and so on. Because of this, usually some other person in the company (clerk, junior engineer, secretary) will be delegated to take the uncompleted bid form down to the official place of submission and telephone back to the main office for the final total, information, and bid total. (Item 5 in Section 14.2 already emphasized the need for prebid reconnaissance regarding telephones).

When the final bid amount is known, it should be given out to the bid deliverer as slowly and clearly as possible during those closing moments of tension, and have him or her repeat it back immediately. Most bid forms require that the bid amounts be stated in both figures and words. Always ask the courier to write down the figures first, and then to repeat the amount back slowly in words both before and after writing the words on the bid form. If two people have been assigned to deliver the bid, both should check and agree that the amounts expressed in figures agree with those in words. (A word of caution, the words will take precedence over the digits, and

15 COMPUTERIZED CONSTRUCTION ESTIMATING

15.1 INTRODUCTION

Estimating is a structured process. Its pricing is based on historical costs from past work and experiences, stored in often elusive places. In today's estimates from general contractors, the majority of costs come from subcontracting quotes, requiring both a notification process to identify subcontractors that may be interested in the work and a method of incorporating these quotes into the estimates and bids. Job site overhead costs (job site indirect costs) are often preprinted lists, with items being relatively the same from job to job. Call end-of-bid items, add-ons, or markups are generally based on a percentage of a total or part of the estimate subtotals.

Reviewing the previous paragraph, one quickly notes how many of these items can be done quicker or more efficiently using some form of computerized system. Additionally, with the widespread use of the fax machine by members of the construction community, communication between parties has continued to increase in speed.

If we were to ask about major changes and trends happening in construction project management today, one would answer that owners are looking more at GMP and design-build as the choice delivery systems, and that contractors, designers, and owners are using the computer to do more and more. These two trends are also affecting estimating today and will continue to change what we do as estimators in the future. More firms today are using some form of computerized help or computerized estimating versus doing the process completely by manual systems. Most firms use fax machines for receiving quotes from subcontractors and answering/asking questions.

15.2 THE TRANSITION FROM MANUAL SYSTEMS TO COMPUTERIZED SYSTEMS

Manual systems employ plans and specifications, calculators for extensions and totals, paper for recording entries, paper cost data bases (e.g., Means cost books), measuring devices (rolling wheels, tapes, and scales), and phone quote sheets to record subcontractor quotes. While most firms still use all of the tools available to the contractor still using manual systems, most of them also use spreadsheet software for summary of detail sheets and fax machines or PC/modems for subcontractor quotes. Many firms are also using spreadsheets for the adjustment process to finalize their prices. Firms are using digitizers to help the quantity takeoff, and in some cases the plans and specifications are being delivered electronically (CDs or downloaded directly). The transition from a manual to a computerized system can follow many different paths. A typical path is

- First comes the use of fax machines to receive faxes and to send subcontractor bid inquiries.
- Next, commercial firms add computer spreadsheets to do the summary sheets, while heavy firms are using spreadsheets to help complete their unit price bids.
- Thirdly, they create new spreadsheets to help with analysis of subcontractors' quotes and to adjust final numbers.
- Many firms then continue to expand their spreadsheets to do detail sheets and add spreadsheet databases to work with their existing spreadsheets.
- At this point many firms start to find that maintaining and changing their custom in-house spreadsheets is becoming too cumbersome and make the change to proprietary software. They want all the pieces to be integrated for easy use and standardized training.
- One of the last pieces commercial firms will put in place is the movement to digitizers to help in takeoffs. Heavy contractors have found that using digitizers for earthwork takeoff is a great help and have adopted the use of digitizers much earlier in their process.

15.3 TRENDS IN COMPUTERIZED ESTIMATING

We have suggested that the trend to computerized estimating is happening today in most firms both large and small. We also have analyzed the path firms are taking to fully change from the manual system to computerized systems, but the question of why this trend is happening needs further discussion before moving to an examination of a typical computer system. Trends like this suggest that the benefits must outweigh the downsides. Moving to computerized systems can have its downsides. Estimators, because of the nature and importance of their work, are not entry level people. They are experienced at their trade, managers in their own right, and quite often key employees in their firms. Experience comes with time and the opportunity to learn. While entry level employees may be able to quantify and take off materials, they lack the experience to price labor and make critical estimating decisions that are required to complete the estimate. The computer revolution has not swept along all members of the construction industry equally. Many older estimators still cling to their "black" books of unit prices, productivity rates, and notes to complete quality estimates. As a firm changes its systems and standards, the potential for costly errors could occur. Most firms cannot afford to lose potentially profitable work or tolerate estimating errors. Errors occur when systems are built in-house and not fully checked or when systems are continually changed or upgraded. Estimators must believe in the tools they use, as do the field people, to accomplish their work. As systems are put in place and quickly stabilized, younger (in fact, all flexible) estimators quickly adapt to these new systems. They see that, instead of increasing errors, the reality is that mathematical errors are eliminated almost immediately. An additional early benefit of the standardization and use of a computerized system is the ability it provides estimators to begin sharing their estimates with others for checking and reviewing. More than one estimator can participate in the understanding, building, and analysis of the estimate. Standardization somewhat forces organization, quality of work, and all the other items discussed in the beginning chapters of this book. Time saving is the second major reason why the trend is continuing. Estimators are finding that as they continue the transition from manual methods to computerized methods, they can accomplish some of the time-consuming tasks slightly faster, giving them more time to analyze the cost and methods they are proposing to use. Another time-saving factor of a computerized system lies in its ability to bring costs from electronic cost databases quickly, make the pricing extensions, and total the estimate. The use of digitizers in earthwork takeoffs has increased accuracy and decreased the time it takes to accomplish these tasks.

Computerized estimating can be broken into five major areas:

1. Use of spreadsheets
2. Use of dedicated estimating software
3. Support software
   - Word processing, Web browsers, etc.
4. Electronic mail
   - More and more information distributed by the Web and e-mail
   - Project information and pricing electronic in form
   - Bid announcements and bid delivery also electronic
   - Bid announcements to subcontractors
   - Receiving subcontractor quotes at bid time
5. Digitizing (electronic measurement)

15.4 ELECTRONIC DISTRIBUTION OF PLANS AND SPECIFICATIONS

A new trend today is the use of plans and specifications being distributed by CDs and electronic downloading. The Corps of Engineering is leading the way in this area for companies with the ability to download plans and specifications off a Web-based server. (See their Web site at http://www.sas.usace.army.mil/contract.htm) It is not intended that contractors will make changes to these plans and specifications, but will either use the computer to read these documents or will print them out for themselves. It is expected that most contractors will print the documents out and have a

FIGURE 15–1   Contract viewer tool bar.

"hard" copy (or multiple copies) to work on in much the traditional way of reviewing plans and taking off the quantities. The use of the CD today is a way of transferring printing costs to the user instead of the owner. In the future, as monitors continue to grow larger, easier on the eyes, and cheaper, one can envision all of the work being done on a workstation itself. Figure 15–1 shows the switchboard or tool bar used by the reader.

The tool bar for the reader will appear on your desktop, so that you can now open the plans and specifications. (Your computer needs to have the Adobe Acrobat Reader installed. If your computer does not have Acrobat Reader (for reading PDF files), you must first install that program. It is a freeware program from Adobe and can be obtained from a number of places. It can be downloaded from Adobe's Web site at http://www.adobe.com/.) A measuring device is also part of the plans reader, allowing the estimator to electronically measure and count on the CD itself. This works much like digitizer software with the major drawback being the same as theirs:

- Lack of large enough screen for viewing complete areas at the scale one wishes to use
- Screen quality often poor enough to cause eyestrain
- Lack of experience with this system causing errors to creep in

This form of plan distribution has not been embraced to the same extent in the private sector by the architectural community. Copyright and ownership of plans and specifications is of major concern along with the potential for unauthorized changes being made. Owners may start requesting this form of distribution of plans and specifications if they see a reduction of their printing costs and the speed of delivery of the project documents.

15.5   DIGITIZERS

Modern day digitizers have become a necessity for most companies that do earth-work. Earthwork takeoff, as described in Chapter 6 of this text, works through the process required to take off quantities from the civil plans using the grid method and the average end method. Both of these techniques have been computerized. The key to quantifying earthwork is the digitizer. In it simplest application, a takeoff person would trace the existing contours on the plans and then secondly trace the new con-tour. The computer would apply a grid on the traced contours, and make the needed calculations. One can also use a similar technique when dealing with road sections. In this case, the computer would use the average end method for its calculation instead of the grid method. Digitizers originally were sound based (sonic digitizers) or field based (board digitizers). Today most digitizers sold are field based. Field-based digitizers consist of a solid material underlaid by a tight grid of wires. Using a mouse or stylus device, the operator can mark on the board a location or multiple

FIGURE 15–2 Board
digitizer.

FIGURE 15–3 Rollup digitizer.

locations (as in tracing). The digitizer then mathematically calculates the distance between the points. In the case of tracing, the operator can assign a number to the line created, given that the points on the line are of small value (e.g., a contour line). Using the mouse or stylus and the digitizer, the operator can also perform counts, create graphic representations of what is being digitized, and use virtual calculators. These field-based digitizers can be either rigid boards or flexible rollup boards. Figures 15–2 and 15–3 show these two types of digitizers in use.

	A	B	C	D	E	F	G	H	I	J	K	L	M	N	O
2			Item	Takeoff		Labor	Labor	Material	Material	Subcontractor	Subcontractor	Subcontractor	Total	Total	
3		CSI	Description	Qty	Unit	$/Unit	Total	$/Unit	Total	Name	$/Unit	Total	$/Unit		
4							=G4*E4		=I4+E4		=M4/E4		=O4/E4	=H4+J4+M4	
5							=G5*E5		=I5+E5		=M5/E5		=O5/E5	=H5+J5+M5	
6							=G6*E6		=I6+E6		=M6/E6		=O6/E6	=H6+J6+M6	
7							=G7*E7		=I7+E7		=M7/E7		=O7/E7	=H7+J7+M7	
8							=G8*E8		=I8+E8		=M8/E8		=O8/E8	=H8+J8+M8	
9							=G9*E9		=I9+E9		=M9/E9		=O9/E9	=H9+J9+M9	
10							=G10*E10		=I10+E10		=M10/E10		=O10/E10	=H10+J10+M10	
11							=G11*E11		=I11+E11		=M11/E11		=O11/E11	=H11+J11+M11	
12							=G12*E12		=I12+E12		=M12/E12		=O12/E12	=H12+J12+M12	
13							=G13*E13		=I13+E13		=M13/E13		=O13/E13	=H13+J13+M13	
14							=G14*E14		=I14+E14		=M14/E14		=O14/E14	=H14+J14+M14	
15							=G15*E15		=I15+E15		=M15/E15		=O15/E15	=H15+J15+M15	
16							=G16*E16		=I16+E16		=M16/E16		=O16/E16	=H16+J16+M16	
17							=G17*E17		=I17+E17		=M17/E17		=O17/E17	=H17+J17+M17	
18							=G18*E18		=I18+E18		=M18/E18		=O18/E18	=H18+J18+M18	
19							=G19*E19		=I19+E19		=M19/E19		=O19/E19	=H19+J19+M19	
20							=G20*E20		=I20+E20		=M20/E20		=O20/E20	=H20+J20+M20	
21							=G21*E21		=I21+E21		=M21/E21		=O21/E21	=H21+J21+M21	
22							=G22*E22		=I22+E22		=M22/E22		=O22/E22	=H22+J22+M22	
23							=G23*E23		=I23+E23		=M23/E23		=O23/E23	=H23+J23+M23	
24							=G24*E24		=I24+E24		=M24/E24		=O24/E24	=H24+J24+M24	
25							=G25*E25		=I25+E25		=M25/E25		=O25/E25	=H25+J25+M25	
26							=G26*E26		=I26+E26		=M26/E26		=O26/E26	=H26+J26+M26	
27							=G27*E27		=I27+E27		=M27/E27		=O27/E27	=H27+J27+M27	
28							=G28*E28		=I28+E28		=M28/E28		=O28/E28	=H28+J28+M28	
29							=G29*E29		=I29+E29		=M29/E29		=O29/E29	=H29+J29+M29	
30							=G30*E30		=I30+E30		=M30/E30		=O30/E30	=H30+J30+M30	
31							=SUM(H4:H30)		=SUM(J4:J30)			=SUM(M4:M30)		=SUM(O4:O30)	

FIGURE 15–4 Electronic spreadsheet.

15.6 SPREADSHEET ESTIMATE FORMS

Many estimators have moved to using spreadsheets. These spreadsheets can be easily set up to look just like the paper form they replace. The electronic form can also easily be made to add, multiply, divide, and perform many other common mathematical functions. Estimators that are more mathematical use some of the higher spreadsheet functions by combining processes in a "macro." A macro is defined as "one instruction that represents a sequence of simpler instructions." Macros cannot only do simple mathematical functions, but also look up items from tables or databases. Macros can perform multiple functions or processes, making extensions, totaling, adding of unit prices, and other functions automatically. Figure 15–4 shows a simple pricing spreadsheet with its formulas displayed. A disk with these electronic forms has not been included with this text. We have found that for the student, making these forms is a very good exercise, and for the experienced estimator, most prefer to create their own (knowing that they work the way that they should, without errors).

15.7 DEDICATED ESTIMATING SOFTWARE

This text has included a disk (CD) containing a version of one of the most popular dedicated estimating software packages for the use of the reader. The disk is from Win Estimator, one of the long-term leaders in the area of dedicated estimating software. This software does include all of the advanced features but is limited to one hundred line items in the estimate. The authors intend that the software will help the estimator be more effective in a multitude of different areas and ways. It also can be used by an instructor and students in an estimating class. Win Estimator is driven by a number of databases, allowing the user to standardize a company's labor rates,

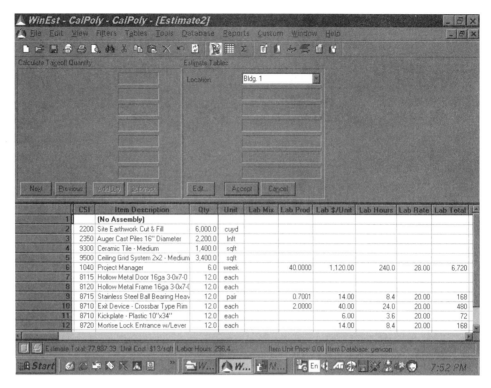

FIGURE 15–5 WinEst Item Takeoff window. (WinEst 5.0 version courtesy of WinEstimator.)

costs, cost accounts, end-of-bid items, and general conditions, to name but a few of its features. Win Estimator approaches computerized estimating by creating a look and feel that most estimators will recognize.

After a project is set up in Win Estimator and a cost database is chosen, the estimator arrives at a window which allows item takeoff, using either an estimate sheet or a total page. Figure 15–5 shows that takeoff window.

This window is used to navigate between three key areas while completing the estimate. The icon bar, like many windows products, is fully customizable by the estimator. This page (window), as its name reflects (the Estimate Sheet) also begins to take on the look and feel of most custom spreadsheets used for estimating. Figure 15–6 is an example of this window without any information yet added. In Figure 15–7 the reader will see how this window grows as information is added.

As soon as the takeoff item is completed using the takeoff menu and the quick takeoff window (Figure 15–5), the quantity is transferred to the spreadsheet (Figure 15–7). Pricing for the items that were just taken off is brought forward from the appropriate databases and the subtotal and total are completed. This discussion may make the use of Win Estimator appear to be a simple process. It is when all of the housekeeping items are completed ahead of time and information transferred from previous estimates are complete. The creation of standardized information to share in the estimating process is a very complicated, time intensive, and ongoing process, however. Certain of these preliminary items are best described in a discussion concerning the relationship between the databases and the

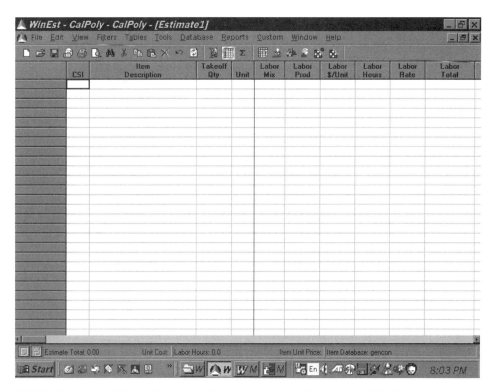

FIGURE 15–6 WinEst Estimate Sheet—without information. (WinEst 5.0 version courtesy of WinEstimator.)

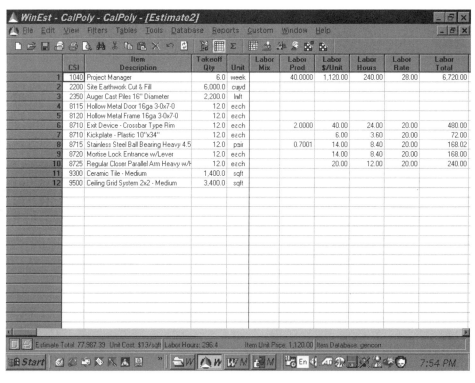

FIGURE 15–7 WinEst Estimate Sheet—with information. (WinEst 5.0 version courtesy of WinEstimator.)

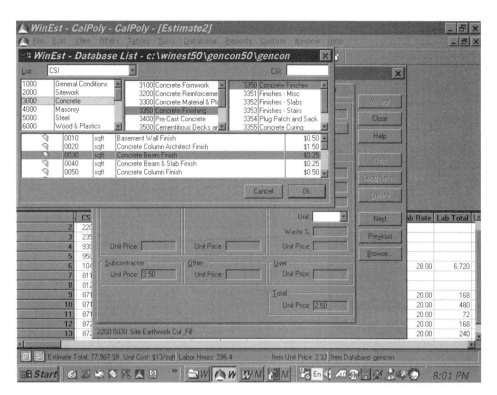

FIGURE 15–8 WinEst example of database structure. (WinEst 5.0 version courtesy of WinEstimator.)

estimate. A company's cost database should contain all items that the company normally self-performs. These items should have the company's historical costs for each item, including productivity and comments. This information cannot be generated anywhere but in one's own estimating department.

The best way to visualize most computerized estimating systems is to visualize the estimate itself. These stand-alone software products look much like the manual forms and pages that all estimators are used to. The difference is that the software allows the user to incorporate wording and numbers into the form and make mathematical calculations. In addition to the adding and totaling, the programs will incorporate pricing from cost resources books in the form of databases. A general concept is that once information is put into the estimate, it is dynamic and anything can be easily changed to fit the project one is working on. The truth is, though, databases are rather static and general for the company as a whole, and changes made require extra time and computation (to put together a set of standardized cost resources). So as cost or specific productivity is changed in the estimate, it may not be reflected in the databases. If these costs and productivity changes hold up and are reproducible in another project, the databases are then changed to reflect these new costs and labor productivity numbers. Figure 15–8 is an example of a database structure and typical different databases.

Note in Figure 15–9 showing the Totals Page, how the different information is summarized and subtotaled and the different markups are applied. The computer software allows the estimator to add, change, and allocate any markup item to any of the different subtotals.

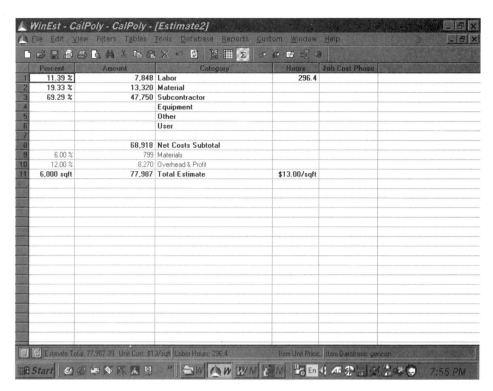

FIGURE 15–9   WinEst Totals Page. (WinEst 5.0 version courtesy of WinEstimator.)

15.8 REQUIREMENTS OF COMPUTERIZED SYSTEMS

Important features to look for in a dedicated computerized system are:

- The estimate should be "disk-based," that is, the information is written directly to the hard drive so the estimator does not have to worry about loss of information at critical times.
- The estimator must be able to view the information in different ways and at different summary levels.
- The end-of-bid items must be flexible enough to be able to perform their calculations based on different total, subtotals, numbers, nested numbers, or other methods of allocation.
- Help needs to be available from all locations within the program.
- The system must accept digitized quantities.
- It must have a calculator and a way of creating formulas for speed calculations.
- Estimate information must have the ability to transfer from one estimate to another.
- The estimator must be able to attach notes, locations, and other descriptions to the takeoff items. When checking quantities, the estimator must be able to find where on which drawing the work quantified was detailed.

- Takeoffs of unique items not typically found in a cost resource book (or database) must be titled and quantified easily.

- The entering of subquotes must be clear and easy to accomplish.

- The software must have the ability to transfer estimates to budgets, and later, to cost systems as the project work begins.

- The software must also have the ability to combine and summarize the estimated costs into activity costs for cost loading schedules.

- Lastly, the program must be easy to learn and intuitive, and must emulate the estimator's manual tools, and be able to quickly gain the estimator's confidence.

As estimators gain experience with a dedicated program, most will also start to look at some of the more advanced tools. The software tools that are considered more advanced are able to estimate, assemble, and conceptualize building costs. The ability to conceptualize complete buildings using tools that model or compare the proposed building with existing structures are just now becoming available.

15.9 CONCLUSION

The future of computerized estimating lies in object orientated design. As designers start to use more tools that allow them to actually incorporate objects into their drawings (e.g., a door that is not just a group of lines on a floor plan but an object with height, thickness, and specification), computerized estimating programs will be able to capture that information for the estimate and use it to price the right product, total the number without manually counting each item, and perform a number of other time saving functions. Conceptual estimates are another area in which the future looks bright for computerized estimating. Estimators will be able to compare completed buildings with proposed buildings with more accuracy concerning budget projections. This technology will allow owners to be able to give designers much more accurate ideas of what exactly is wanted in their new buildings.

Computerized estimating will not eliminate estimators, but will save them time in which to evaluate the information they have produced. This will generate better estimates for construction firms vying for work, making them more competitive in the construction market, and giving owners better budgets and control for future projects.

CONSTRUCTION SPECIFICATIONS INSTITUTE FORMAT

MASTERFORMAT LITE INDEX

- **Introductory Information**
- **Bidding Requirements**
- **Contracting Requirements**
- **Facilities and Spaces**
- **Systems and Assemblies**
- **Construction Products and Activities**
  - Division 1—General Requirements
  - Division 2—Site Construction
  - Division 3—Concrete
  - Division 4—Masonry
  - Division 5—Metals
  - Division 6—Wood and Plastics
  - Division 7—Thermal and Moisture Protection
  - Division 8—Doors and Windows
  - Division 9—Finishes
  - Division 10—Specialties
  - Division 11—Equipment
  - Division 12—Furnishing

- Division 13—Special Construction
- Division 14—Conveying Systems
- Division 15—Mechanical
- Division 16—Electrical
- Copyright Notice

INTRODUCTORY INFORMATION

00001 Project Title Page
00005 Certifications Page
00007 Seals Page
00010 Table of Contents
00015 List of Drawings
00020 List of Schedules

BIDDING REQUIREMENTS

00100 Bid Solicitation
00200 Instructions to Bidders
00300 Information Available to Bidders
00400 Bid Forms and Supplements
00490 Bidding Addenda

CONTRACTING REQUIREMENTS

00500 Agreement
00600 Bonds and Certificates
00700 General Conditions
00800 Supplementary Conditions
00900 Modifications

FACILITIES AND SPACES

Note: *MasterFormat* currently does not include a list of facilities and spaces.

SYSTEMS AND ASSEMBLIES

Note: *MasterFormat* currently does not include a list of Systems and Assemblies. Use *UniFormat* for element numbers, titles, and descriptions, associated with systems and assemblies.

CONSTRUCTION PRODUCTS AND ACTIVITIES

DIVISION 1—GENERAL REQUIREMENTS

01100 Summary

01200 Price and Payment Procedures

01300 Administrative Requirements

01400 Quality Requirements

01500 Temporary Facilities and Controls

01600 Product Requirements

01700 Execution Requirements

01800 Facility Operation

01900 Facility Decommissioning

DIVISION 2—SITE CONSTRUCTION

02050 Basic Site Materials and Methods

02100 Site Remediation

02200 Site Preparation

02300 Earthwork

02400 Tunneling, Boring, and Jacking

02450 Foundation and Load-bearing Elements

02500 Utility Services

02600 Drainage and Containment

02700 Bases, Ballasts, Pavements, and Appurtenances

02800 Site Improvements and Amenities

02900 Planting

02950 Site Restoration and Rehabilitation

DIVISION 3—CONCRETE

03050 Basic Concrete Materials and Methods

03100 Concrete Forms and Accessories

03200 Concrete Reinforcement

03300 Cast-in-Place Concrete

03400 Precast Concrete

03500 Cementitious Decks and Underlayment

03600 Grouts

03700 Mass Concrete

03900 Concrete Restoration and Cleaning

DIVISION 4—MASONRY

04050 Basic Masonry Materials and Methods

04200 Masonry Units

04400 Stone

04500 Refractories

04600 Corrosion-Resistant Masonry

04700 Simulated Masonry

04800 Masonry Assemblies

04900 Masonry Restoration and Cleaning

DIVISION 5—METALS

05050 Basic Metal Materials and Methods

05100 Structural Metal Framing

05200 Metal Joists

05300 Metal Deck

05400 Cold-Formed Metal Framing

05500 Metal Fabrications

05600 Hydraulic Fabrications

05650 Railroad Track and Accessories

05700 Ornamental Metal

05800 Expansion Control

05900 Metal Restoration and Cleaning

DIVISION 6—WOOD AND PLASTICS

06050 Basic Wood and Plastic Materials and Methods

06100 Rough Carpentry

06200 Finish Carpentry

06400 Architectural Woodwork

06500 Structural Plastics

06600 Plastic Fabrications

06900 Wood and Plastic Restoration and Cleaning

DIVISION 7—THERMAL AND MOISTURE PROTECTION

07050 Basic Thermal and Moisture Protection Materials and Methods

07100 Dampproofing and Waterproofing

07200 Thermal Protection

07300 Shingles, Roof Tiles, and Roof Coverings

07400 Roofing and Siding Panels

07500 Membrane Roofing

07600 Flashing and Sheet Metal

07700 Roof Specialties and Accessories

07800 Fire and Smoke Protection

07900 Joint Sealers

DIVISION 8—DOORS AND WINDOWS

08050 Basic Door and Window Materials and Methods

08100 Metal Doors and Frames

08200 Wood and Plastic Doors

08300 Specialty Doors

08400 Entrances and Storefronts

08500 Windows

08600 Skylights

08700 Hardware

08800 Glazing

08900 Glazed Curtain Wall

DIVISION 9—FINISHES

09050 Basic Finish Materials and Methods

09100 Metal Support Assemblies

09200 Plaster and Gypsum Board

09300 Tile

09400 Terrazzo

09500 Ceilings

09600 Flooring

09700 Wall Finishes

09800 Acoustical Treatment

09900 Paints and Coatings

DIVISION 10—SPECIALTIES

10100 Visual Display Boards

10150 Compartments and Cubicles

10200 Louvers and Vents

10240 Grilles and Screens

10250 Service Walls

10260 Wall and Corner Guards

10270 Access Flooring

10290 Pest Control

10300 Fireplaces and Stoves

10340 Manufactured Exterior Specialties

10350 Flagpoles

10400 Identification Devices

10450 Pedestrian Control Devices

10500 Lockers

10520 Fire Protection Specialties

10530 Protective Covers

10550 Postal Specialties

10600 Partitions

10670 Storage Shelving

10700 Exterior Protection

10750 Telephone Specialties

10800 Toilet, Bath, and Laundry Accessories

10880 Scales

10900 Wardrobe and Closet Specialties

DIVISION 11—EQUIPMENT

11010 Maintenance Equipment

11020 Security and Vault Equipment

11030 Teller and Service Equipment

11040 Ecclesiastical Equipment

11050 Library Equipment

11060 Theater and Stage Equipment

11070 Instrumental Equipment

11080 Registration Equipment

11090 Checkroom Equipment

11100 Mercantile Equipment

11110 Commercial Laundry and Dry Cleaning Equipment

11120 Vending Equipment

11130 Audio-Visual Equipment

11140 Vehicle Service Equipment

11150 Parking Control Equipment

11160 Loading Dock Equipment

11170 Solid Waste Handling Equipment

11190 Detention Equipment

11200 Water Supply and Treatment Equipment

11280 Hydraulic Gates and Valves

11300 Fluid Waste Treatment and Disposal Equipment

11400 Food Service Equipment

11450 Residential Equipment

11460 Unit Kitchens

11470 Darkroom Equipment

11480 Athletic, Recreational, and Therapeutic Equipment

11500 Industrial and Process Equipment

11600 Laboratory Equipment

11650 Planetarium Equipment

11660 Observatory Equipment

11680 Office Equipment

11700 Medical Equipment

11780 Mortuary Equipment

11850 Navigation Equipment

11870 Agricultural Equipment

11900 Exhibit Equipment

DIVISION 12—FURNISHINGS

12050 Fabrics

12100 Art

12300 Manufactured Casework

12400 Furnishings and Accessories

12500 Furniture

12600 Multiple Seating

12700 Systems Furniture

12800 Interior Plants and Planters

12900 Furnishings Repair and Restoration

DIVISION 13—SPECIAL CONSTRUCTION

13010 Air-Supported Structures

13020 Building Modules

13030 Special Purpose Rooms

13080 Sound, Vibration, and Seismic Control

13090 Radiation Protection

13100 Lightning Protection

13110 Cathodic Protection

13120 Pre-Engineered Structures

13150 Swimming Pools

13160 Aquariums

13165 Aquatic Park Facilities

13170 Tubs and Pools

13175 Ice Rinks

13185 Kennels and Animal Shelters

13190 Site-Constructed Incinerators

13200 Storage Tanks

13220 Filter Underdrains and Media

13230 Digester Covers and Appurtenances

13240 Oxygenation Systems

13260 Sludge Conditioning Systems

13280 Hazardous Material Remediation

13400 Measurement and Control Instrumentation

13500 Recording Instrumentation

13550 Transportation Control Instrumentation

13600 Solar and Wind Energy Equipment

13700 Security Access and Surveillance

13800 Building Automation and Control

13850 Detection and Alarm

13900 Fire Suppression

DIVISION 14—CONVEYING SYSTEMS

14100 Dumbwaiters

14200 Elevators

14300 Escalators and Moving Walks

14400 Lifts

14500 Material Handling

14600 Hoists and Cranes

14700 Turntables

14800 Scaffolding

14900 Transportation

DIVISION 15—MECHANICAL

15050 Basic Mechanical Materials and Methods

15100 Building Services Piping

15200 Process Piping

15300 Fire Protection Piping

15400 Plumbing Fixtures and Equipment

15500 Heat-Generation Equipment

15600 Refrigeration Equipment

15700 Heating, Ventilating, and Air Conditioning Equipment

15800 Air Distribution

15900 HVAC Instrumentation and Controls

15950 Testing, Adjusting, and Balancing

DIVISION 16—ELECTRICAL

16050 Basic Electrical Materials and Methods

16100 Wiring Methods

16200 Electrical Power

16300 Transmission and Distribution

16400 Low-Voltage Distribution

16500 Lighting

16700 Communications

16800 Sound and Video

COPYRIGHT NOTICE

B

FORMULAS

B.1 AREAS OF PLANE FIGURES

NOMENCLATURE

a, b, c, d — Lengths of Sides
A — Area
d, d_1, d_2 — Diameters
e, f — Lengths of Diagonals
h — Vertical Height or Altitude
l, l_1, l_2 — Length of Arc
L — Lateral Length or Slant Height
n — Number of Sides
θ — Number of Degrees of Arc
p — Perimeter
r, r_1, r_2, R — Radii

RIGHT TRIANGLE

$p = a + b + c$
$c^2 = a^2 + b^2$
$b = \sqrt{c^2 - a^2}$
$A = \dfrac{ab}{2}$

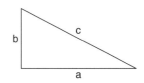

EQUILATERAL TRIANGLE

$p = 3a$

$h = \dfrac{a}{2}\sqrt{3} = .866\,a$

$A = a^2\dfrac{\sqrt{3}}{4} = .433\,a^2$

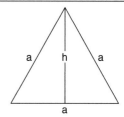

GENERAL TRIANGLE

Let $s = \dfrac{a + b + c}{2}$

$p = a + b + c$

$h = \dfrac{2}{a}\sqrt{s(s - a)(s - b)(s - c)}$[b]

$A = \dfrac{ah}{2}$

$A = \sqrt{s(s - a)(s - b)(s - c)}$

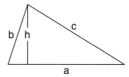

SQUARE

$p = 4a$

$A = a^2 = .5e^2$

$e = a\sqrt{2} = 1.414\,a$

RECTANGLE

$p = 2(a + b)$

$e = \sqrt{a^2 + b^2}$

$b = \sqrt{e^2 - a^2}$

$A = ab$

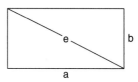

GENERAL PARALLELOGRAM OR RHOMBOID; AND RHOMBUS

Rhomboid—opposite sides parallel

$p = 2(a + b)$

$e^2 + f^2 = 2(a^2 + b^2)$

$A = ah$

Rhombus—opposite sides parallel and all sides equal

$a = b$

$p = 4a = 4b$

$e^2 + f^2 = 4a^2$

$A = ah = \dfrac{ef}{2}$

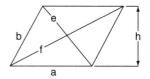

TRAPEZOID

$p = a + b + c + d$

$A = \dfrac{(a + b)}{2}h$

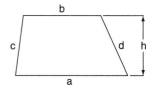

TRAPEZIUM

$p = a + b + c + d$

A = Sum of Areas of two major triangles

$$A = \frac{(h_1 + h_2)g + fh_1 + jh_2}{2}$$

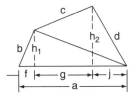

REGULAR POLYGON

Let n = number of sides

$p = na$

$a = 2\sqrt{R^2 - r^2}$

$$A = \frac{nar}{2} = \frac{na}{2}\sqrt{R^2 - \frac{a^2}{4}}$$

$= n \times$ Area of each triangle

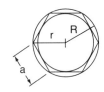

CIRCLE

$p = 2\pi r = \pi d = 3.1416d$

$$A = \pi r^2 = \frac{\pi d^2}{4} = .7854d^2$$

$$= \frac{p^2}{4\pi} = .07958\, p^2$$

HOLLOW CIRCLE OR ANNULUS

$$A = \frac{\pi}{4}(d_2{}^2 - d_1{}^2) = .7854\,(d_2{}^2 - d_1{}^2)$$

$$= \pi\,(r_2{}^2 - r_1{}^2)$$

$$= \pi\,\frac{d_1 + d_2}{2}\,(r_2 - r_1)$$

$$= \pi\,(r_1 + r_2)\,(r_2 - r_1)$$

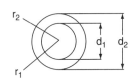

B.2 VOLUMES OF SOLID FIGURES

(V = volume)

CUBE

$V = a^3$ (in cubic units)

RECTANGULAR SOLIDS

$V = L \times W \times h$

PRISMS

$$V\,(1) = \frac{B \times A}{2} \times h$$

$$V\,(2) = \frac{s \times R}{2} \times 6 \times h$$

$$V = \text{Area of end} \times h$$

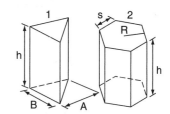

CYLINDER

$$V = \pi R^2 \times h$$

CONE

$$V = \frac{\pi R^2 \times h}{3}$$

PYRAMIDS

$$V\,(1) = L \times W \times \frac{h}{3}$$

$$V\,(2) = \frac{B \times A}{2} \times \frac{h}{3}$$

$$V = \text{Area of Base} \times \frac{h}{3}$$

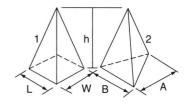

SPHERE

$$V = \frac{1}{6}\,\pi D^3$$

CIRCULAR RING (TORUS)

$$V = 2\pi^2 \times Rs^2$$
$$V = \text{Area of section} \times 2\,\pi\,R$$

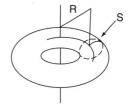

C

THE METRIC SYSTEM

The neatest thing about the metric system is that all units are based on decimal mathematics. A kilometer is 1000 meters and kilogram is 1000 grams (you'll understand later why there are no commas). Say goodbye to eight pints to the gallon and 5,280 feet to the mile. There are no mils, inches, feet, yards, fathoms, rods, chains, furlongs, or miles.

BASIC DEFINITIONS

Meter (m): The basic measure of distance in the metric system, a little longer than a yard.

Kilometer (km): The basic measure of longer distances, a little longer than a half-mile.

Millimeter (mm): For measuring the little stuff (a dime is about a millimeter thick). There's a centimeter, too (about a third of an inch), but some construction designers, such as Caltrans (Department of Transportation in California), won't measure in centimeters.

Liter (L): The metric system's basic measure of liquid, a little larger than a quart.

Gram (g): For weighing the little stuff. A paper clip weighs about a gram.

Kilogram (kg): One thousand grams, weighing a little more than two pounds. The tonne or metric ton, about the weight of a fast sports car (1000 kilograms), is used for larger weights.

Time (s): The second, the basic measure of time, remains the same as in the US system.

Ampere (A): The basic measure of electric current, same as in the US system.

Candela (cd): The basic measure of luminosity.

Temperature (K): The basic measure of temperature. Celsius temperature (°C) is used more commonly than kelvin (K), but both have the same temperature gradients. Celsius temperature is just 273.15 degrees warmer than kelvin, which begins at absolute zero. Water freezes at 273.15 K and at 0°C. To move between Celsius and kelvin, add or subtract 273.15.

The **radian (rad)** and **steradian (sr)** denote plane and solid angles. They are used in lighting work and in various engineering calculations. In surveying, the units degree (°), minute (′) and second (″) continue in use.

METRIC CONVERSION FACTORS

METRIC TO ENGLISH

Length
1 millimeter (mm) = 0.039 inch
1 meter (m) = 3.28 feet
1 kilometer (km) = 0.621 mile
1 mile = 1.621 km

Area
1 square meter (m2) = 10.764 square feet
1 hectare (ha) = 2.471 acres

Volume
1 cubic meter (m3) = 1.308 cubic yards
1 liter (L) = 0.219 gallon

Mass
1 kilogram (kg) = 2.204 pounds
1 tonne (t) = 1.102 ton

ENGLISH TO METRIC

Length
1 inch = 25.4 mm
1 foot = 0.304 m
1 yard = 0.9144 m

Area

1 square foot = 0.093 m2

1 acre = 0.405 ha (10000 m2)

Volume

1 cubic yard = 0.765 m3

1 gallon = 3.785 L

Mass

1 pound = 0.454 kg

1 ton (2,000 lbs.) = 0.907 t

Note: Above factors are rounded off to a maximum of three decimal places.

MULTIPLICATION FACTORS

Multiple	Prefix	Symbol
$1\ 000\ 000\ 000 = 10^9$	giga	G
$1\ 000\ 000 = 10^6$	mega	M
$1\ 000 = 10^3$	kilo	k
$100 = 10^2$	*hecto	h
$10 = 10^1$	*deka	da
$0.1 = 10^{-1}$	*deci	d
$0.01 = 10^{-2}$	*centi	c
$0.001 = 10^{-3}$	milli	m
$0.000\ 001 = 10^{-6}$	micro	μ
$0.000\ 000\ 001 = 10^{-9}$	nano	n

*avoid where possible

RECOMMENDED PRONUNCIATIONS

Prefix	Pronunciations
giga	jig' a (i as in jig, a as in a-bout)
mega	as in mega-phone
kilo	kill' oh
hecto	heck' toe
deka	deck' a (a as in a-bout)
deci	as in deci-mal
centi	as in centi-pede
milli	as in mili-tary
micro	as in micro-phone
nano	nan' oh (an as in ant)

CONVERSION AND ROUNDING

General

- Conversion from US to SI may be either exact ("soft"), or a suitable approximation ("hard").
- In a soft conversion, the US unit is converted to an exact metric equivalent.
- In a hard conversion, the US unit is converted to a new rounded, rationalized metric number convenient to work with.
- In all conversions, use SI equivalents similar in magnitude to the original. If a 1/16 inch scale was suitable for the original measurement, a 1 mm metric scale is suitable for the conversion.

Conversions

Always establish intended precision as a guide to how many digits to retain after conversion. The number 1.1875 may be a very accurate decimalization of a number that could have been expressed as 1.19. The value 2 may mean "about 2," or it may be a very accurate value of 2, expressed as "2.0000."

The converted dimension should be rounded to a minimum number of significant digits so the unit of the last place is equal to or smaller than its conversion.

EXAMPLE. Precision of a 6 inch stirring rod is estimated at about 1/2 in ($\pm$ 1/4 in) or, converted, 12.7 mm. The converted dimension, 152.4 mm, should be rounded to the nearest 10 mm and shown as 150 mm.

Converted values should be rounded to the minimum number of significant digits in order to maintain the required accuracy.

EXAMPLE. A length of 125 ft converts exactly to 38.1 m. But if the 125 ft length was obtained by rounding to the nearest 5 ft, the conversion should be given as 38 m; if it had been obtained by rounding to the nearest 25 ft, the result should be rounded to 40 m.

A stated limit such as "not more than" must be handled so the limit is not violated. "At least 3 inches wide" requires a width of at least 76.2 mm, or at least 77 mm.

When converting, multiply a value by a more accurate factor than required, then round appropriately afterward. Rounding before multiplying will reduce accuracy.

EXAMPLE. When converting 3 feet 2 9/16 inches to meters ($9/16'' = 0.5625''$):

$$(3 \times 0.3048) + (2.5625 \times 0.0254) = 0.979\ 487\ 5 \text{ m, rounds to } 0.979 \text{ m}$$

Significant Digits

When converting integral values of units, consider the implied or required precision of the integral value to be converted.

EXAMPLE. The value "4 in." may represent 4, 4.0, 4.00, 4.000 or 4.0000 in. Any digit necessary to define the specific value or quantity is significant.

EXAMPLE. Measured to the nearest 1 m, a recorded distance of 157 m would have three significant digits. Measured to the nearest 0.1 m, a distance of 157.4 m would have four significant digits.

Zeros may indicate either a specific value or an order of magnitude. As an example, the population of the United States in 1970, rounded to thousands, was 203 185 000. The six left-hand digits are significant, each measuring a value. The three right hand zeros indicate that the number has been rounded to the nearest thousand.

Identifying significant digits is only possible by knowing the circumstances by which they were originally arrived at. For example, if the number 1000 is rounded from 965, only one zero is significant. If it is rounded from 999.7, all three zeros are significant.

When adding or subtracting, the answer must contain no significant digits to the right of the least precise number.

EXAMPLE. Round the numbers one significant digit to the right of the least precise number and take the sum as follows:

163 000 000	163 000 000
217 885 000	217 900 000
96 432 768	96 400 000
477 317 768	477 300 000

(Round the total to 477 000 000 as called for by the rule)

When multiplying or dividing, the product or quotient must contain no more significant digits than the fewest significant digits used in the multiplication or division.

EXAMPLE

$113.2 \times 1.43 = 161.876$ (round to 162 because 1.43 has three significant digits)

$113.2 \sim 1.43 = 79.160\ 8$ (round to 79.2 for same reason)

Rounding Values

When the first digit discarded is less than 5, the last digit retained is not changed.

EXAMPLE. 3.463 25, rounded to four digits would be 3.463; if rounded to three digits, 3.46.

When the first digit discarded is greater than 5 or is a 5 followed by at least one digit other than 0, add 1 to the last digit retained.

EXAMPLE. 8.376 52, rounded to four digits would be 8.377; if rounded to three digits 8.38.

When the first digit discarded is exactly 5 followed only by zeros, the last digit retained should be rounded upward if it is odd. No adjustment is made if it is an even number.

EXAMPLE. 4.365, rounded to three digits becomes 4.36. The number 4.355 would round to the same value, 4.36, if rounded to three digits.

Most of this appendix was taken directly from "Getting Into Metrics," Metric Primer, Fourth Edition, ©January 1998. Provided by The State of California, Department of Transportation.

INDEX